C0-AVS-780

Group Intervention

GROUP INTERVENTION

How to Begin and Maintain Groups in Medical and Psychiatric Settings

Elaine Cooper Lonergan

JASON ARONSON INC.
Northvale, New Jersey
London

Copyright © 1989, 1985, 1982 by Jason Aronson, Inc.

New Printing 1989

All rights reserved. Printed in the United States of America. No part of this book may be used or reproduced in any manner whatsoever without written permission from Jason Aronson Inc. except in the case of brief quotations in reviews for inclusion in a magazine, newspaper, or broadcast.

ISBN: 0-87668-887-3

Library of Congress Catalog Number: 84-46149

Manufactured in the United States of America. Jason Aronson Inc. offers books and cassettes. For information and catalog write to Jason Aronson Inc., 230 Livingston Street, Northvale, NJ 07647.

To
my husband, Ted
and
my friend, Lurline

"Man *is* an island—in an archipelago."

Arnold Abrams, 1963

Contents

Acknowledgments

Lurline Aslanian, Susanne A. Kohut, Helen Grand, Henry Grand, Geraldine Alpert and Edmund T. Lonergan reviewed the original manuscript for this book in its entirety. Their contributions not only improved the quality of the book but gave me the encouragement I needed to complete the book. Others who offered constructive criticism of the manuscript were: Henriette Glatzer, Beatrice Saunders, Anne Boland, Jack Aslanian, Joan Erdheim, and Tom McGourty.

I take this opportunity to acknowledge my teachers over the years; thanks to them I have not stopped learning. Some of the teachers who have stood out for me as exceptional are: Irving Marks, Morgan Yamanaka, Armaity Desai, Helen Grand, the late Edrita Fried, Alexander Wolf, Isaac Youcha, and Susanne Kohut.

The following group leaders contributed clinical material that was utilized in this book. They are dedicated and competent social workers, nurses, doctors, and physical therapists.

Social Workers: M.S.W.s include Frank Attanasia, Rita Berger, Sara Bookbinder, Alice Brown, Lee Buchman, Carol Chetrick, William Cook, Carol Coven, Maureen Dorsey, Nancy Halper, Barbara Horn, Mary Innes, Wayne Kadis, Ellen Kutcher, Lorna LeSueur, Margaret Longto, Gaetana Manuele, Patricia Mendell, Geraldine Natwin, Kathleen Nugent, Barbara Olvany, Sara Ponte, Ann Sparks, Elaine Stachew, Sr. Mary Sugrue. B.S.W.s include Geraldine Curtin, Judi Kortina, Joyce Laudon, Diane Litwin, Maureen Manley, Jeannette Quinn. Students include Milton Haynes, Anne Kaul, Kay McKenna, Patricia Morrissey, Susan Rothschild, Lorraine Wesley.
Nurses: Clinical specialists include Larry Dormer, Deborah Foster, Kathleen McQuade, Sr. Marita Rose O'Brien, Sr. M. Patrice, Wendy Schneider. Head nurses include Mary Ann Buckley, Linda Haselman, Diane Mancuso, Barbara Roberts. Nurses include Sr. Maureen Bernius, Marcy Dorcy, Diane Martins, Margaret Monahan, Barbara Woods.
Doctors: James Pollowitz, Emile Powe.
Physical Therapists: Ingrid Krooval, Ann Schroeder.

This book is based in large part on my experience as Group Work Coordinator for St. Vincent's Hospital and Medical Center of New York, Department of Social Work. I am indebted to administrative and supervisory staff for their support while I was developing a group program in the general hospital. The following people were especially helpful:

Department of Social Work: Anne Boland, Hazel M. Halloran, Elizabeth Healy, Susanne Kohut, Herbert Rosenberg, Margaret O'Reilly.
Department of Nursing: Johanna Basile, Mary Ann Durinski, Margaret Hanrahan.
Department of Medicine: Philip Brickner, the late William J. Grace, James Mazzara, Alfred Vitali.
Administration: John T. Fales.

These lists may seem long but they are a small reflection of the cooperative effort that was involved in the writing of this book.

Introduction

There are three women in the group today—all on involuntary holds, as they were suicidal when admitted to the hospital. This morning, each person in the group still shows signs of great emotional distress. Lori is covering her face but between her fingers one can see it screwed up. She asserts that her mother should have let her die from the overdose of drugs; she doesn't deserve to live. Janet sits guiltridden. She has just learned that her ex-husband has AIDS. He will certainly die; it should have been she that got it. Sophie was raped. When she told her husband, who she always felt was too good for her, he walked out on her and the children.

Janet and Sophie cannot stop crying. Lori is choking on swallowed tears. Nevertheless, she trys to comfort the other two. Seeing their pain is unbearable to her. She wants them to feel better and stop crying. In her effort to comfort, she begins to monopolize the discussion.

I am the consultant, sitting in the room, outside the circle formed by the patients and their two leaders, apart from the group, watching, observing. I guess that the group leaders, along with me and the patients, are overwhelmed by the pervasive despair. I identify with these women. How do I know that under similar circumstances I might not be in their place? It is painful to think about.

It is my turn to join the patients and share with them my view of the process. I quickly try to remember the principles I teach: the importance of self-esteem, how contact helps self-esteem, how there must be something good about every person. I refresh myself on pre-group technique: connecting members, boosting self-esteem, reinforcing narcissistic defenses. I decide that these women can use a bit of grandiosity; they need to leave the group feeling better about themselves. They need more potent narcissistic defenses.[1]

Hospital staff members are sitting behind a one-way mirror observing me and the group. They see me get up and join the group of patients. As I sit down, I see a glimmer of hope on three pained faces. I take a moment to look

---

[1] For a discussion of narcissism and narcissistic defenses, see pp. 147–160.

at each person and then I say, "I'd like each of you to tell me something you like about yourself." The group leaders look at me in astonishment. I learn later than an observer behind the mirror mumbled, "I bet they'll say 'nothing.'" Other observers nodded in agreement.

I look at the members with absolute, positive expectation, as though it would never occur to me that they would not answer. I turn to Sophie first because she has stopped crying and looks the most ready to talk. She says, "When I go shopping, I always buy the best items. Others buy junk, but not me." "So you have good taste?" I ask. "Yes." "And you like that about yourself?" "Yes." "Good!"

I face Janet, who is trying to stop sobbing so that she can answer me. While she is choking and swallowing tears, she gets out the words, "You may find this hard to believe, but I have a good sense of humor." I smile at her. She doesn't smile back, but she stops crying and looks directly at me.

I turn to Lori, purposely leaving her for last because she is crying the hardest, and her face is covered by her hands. Two fingers part so that I can see her eyes. She says, "Me, too. I have a sense of humor, too. I realize it isn't obvious today." I smile broadly, "And you like that about yourself?" "Yeah." "That's terrific! You all did great! A sense of humor can certainly help people get through hard times."

This vignette provides a recent example of how well distressed people often respond to self-esteem boosting technique. My continuing work in the field reinforces my conviction in the theory and technique presented in this book. One of the comments that pleased me most when the book first appeared was from a social worker: "You can tell this book was written by someone who was *there*—actually working with the patients—and not just thinking about them or observing. Her suggestions are practical; they work."

In writing the book I made a point to include many clinical examples. At the time, I was supervising about twenty groups and keeping detailed process notes on each meeting. Thus, when it came time to write the book, I could use the best and most telling examples. I tried to hear what the patients were telling us in the groups—not only what they said but also how they responded to specific intervention. *Group Intervention* remains the only book that presents the theory and technique of leading medical groups.

SELF PSYCHOLOGY

When I was originally sorting out the clinical material presented in this book, self psychology as a branch of psychoanalysis was just coming to the fore.

Self psychology focuses on helping people make psychic structural change through the establishment of self-object transferences. These transferences are combined with gratification and optimal frustration missed in childhood. This book is *not* about helping patients make personality changes. It *is* a book about facilitating coping and adaptation.

It seemed to me that these new ideas were the best way of understanding *why* and *how* the Pre-Group worked. The theory stressed the importance of a positive, authentic, and empathetic approach, which I felt was *especially* important for the medical patient and the severely disturbed patient who suffered from damaged or wounded self-esteem. In fact, Kohut's theory focused on self-esteem and the facilitation of healing. Now there was a sound theoretical basis for a supportive approach: appreciating defenses and devaluing hostility and aggression except as an expression of reckoning with narcissistic injury. Wilson, a group therapist, states: "Previously I felt like the adversary of the defense; now I feel like the ally of the patient" (p. 10).

More recently, Josephs and Juman (1985) report a similar enthusiasm for the application of self psychology to the treatment of chronic schizophrenia:

> The emphasis on providing self-esteem enhancing experiences is consistent with schizophrenic patients' needs for validating responses from mirroring self-objects as a means of eventually internalizing positive self regard. The avoidance of negative transferences and the emphasis on the therapist's empathetic interest in patients makes the therapist available as an archaic self-object with whom belated development can resume. The functions of group cohesiveness from a Self Psychology model are that group members can serve as mirroring self-objects for each other and that the group as a whole can represent an idealized self-object of which individual members can feel a part. (p. 23)

As self psychology has developed, the understanding of narcissistic defenses has increased and become clearer. Along with the importance of idealization and grandiosity is mirroring, twinship, partnering, merger, and alter-ego. Kohut (1981) sums these up: "Being reflected by the self-objects (mirroring), being able to merge with their calmness and power (idealization), sensing a silent presence to their essential alikeness (twinship), the baby is strong, healthy, vigorous" (p. 29).

Again, these concepts seem especially applicable for understanding why the techniques presented in this book work so well. With "mirroring" from the therapist and other patients, the group member gets positive feedback on his true strengths. The example with which I started this introduction illustrates a leader trying to mobilize this process. Kohut sees this feedback as necessary for psychic growth and development. Many of the severely disturbed patients didn't get enough of this kind of positive reflection and their growth was, therefore, stunted. A group that provides mirroring is providing a basic human need; those with wounded or damaged self-esteem are starved for it.

Bacal (1985) writes that the infant's first narcissistic need is for idealization, then twinship or alter-ego or partnering, where one links with a buddy and feels equal. Third is the need for mirroring. The need for twinship or partnering (which Bacal suggests is a derivative of the more primitive merging transference) may explain why so many patients who join groups report tremendous relief at the "welcome to the human race" experience. The power of "universality," one of Yalom's curative factors, is seen repeatedly in groups. People come to the group feeling isolated and disconnected from the mainstream of humanity. They then experience being an equal, valued, and accepted member. Their self-esteem starts to soar; another narcissistic defense has been mobilized.

Group therapists have now begun to apply self psychology theory to the general practice of group therapy. They make the following points to explain why group therapy is curative:

1. Various group relationships make it possible for the member to have different self-object transferences simultaneously. These may even conflict and be played out with several people or parts of the group (Bacal, 1985).
2. The fact that members can shift self-objects in the group lessens vulnerability and increases patients' control over the process (Harwood, 1983).
3. Group therapy offers an arena where optimal frustration necessary for psychic growth occurs. The group, by design, is a nonprotective experience, and breaks in empathy often occur (Weinstein, 1987).
4. Self-esteem is dependent on how one is viewed by peers. Group therapy is a place to learn peer management skills (Grunebaum and Solomon, 1987).
5. The potential empathy of a group is broader than that of a therapist alone (Horwitz, 1984).

A POSITIVE APPROACH

Others have noted the importance of having a positive approach to group intervention. Bales argued that for any group to be successful, positive reinforcements had to exceed negative ones. He perceived negative reactions to reduce motivation and satisfaction of the group member; he therefore deduced that for every negative reaction, a positive one was needed to counteract. "A group needs positive reactions in excess of negative ones in order to get its tasks successfully completed, hence, to get satisfaction from task performance itself" (McGrath, 1984, p. 151). McGrath, in his book on research of groups, writes that there is no hard data supporting the fact that groups with higher positive ratios have greater satisfaction or that members with higher positive feedback are more satisfied, but there is indirect evidence to support these notions:

1. Higher status members get higher positive/negative ratios and also have higher satisfaction. (This is evidence based on covariation, and not direct evidence of a relation between positive/negative ratio and satisfaction.)
2. Members who are rejected reduce communication (Dittes and Kelley, 1956) and communication to them is also reduced (Schachter, 1951).
3. Members who get support from others communicate more (Pepinsky et al., 1958).
4. Members in more active places in the communication net of the group also are more active and have more satisfaction (Leavitt, 1951; Shaw, 1959) (McGrath, p. 152).

While the evidence for the importance of positive reinforcement is persuasive, it would be absurd to think that someone could lead a group of severely disturbed members and be totally positive. A useful example is stopping the monopolizer on page 87. What I suggest is concordant with Bales' recommendation of placing a positive reinforcer before a negative. For example, "The topic you have brought up is very relevant for everyone here, so I am going to stop you now in order to hear what others have to say."

Feilbert-Willis, Kibel, and Wikstrom (1986) struggled with the balance of positive and negative reinforcement in the day hospital. They found that focusing on the negative, acting neutral, or overemphasizing the positive added to the group's negative feedback loop and confirmed patients' worst fears about themselves. It was only when the therapists acknowledged the negative but also supported the positive that the negative cycle was broken.

It is important for the therapist to be authentic and not ignore a negative when it is obviously present, or to underestimate the value of repeatedly pointing out a positive. Feilbert-Willis et al. (1986) refer to the "simpleness" of the technique, and I have said that I sometimes feel like a nursery school teacher (p. 159). We convey a certain embarrassment about our recommendations, knowing that people might relegate them more to the arena of common sense than to complex theory making. It is important to remember that "empathy" by definition is a response to something in another person that might be quite different from what we need ourselves; thus the appropriate technique might not be one from which we would benefit. Certainly empathy is hardest when the gap is large between the therapist's emotional needs and those of the patients.

PSYCHIATRIC GROUPS

As was the case nine years ago, the efficacy of group therapy in psychiatry continues to be accepted and demonstrated. Toseland (1986) searched for studies that compared outcomes of individual and group therapy. He found seventy-four studies; thirty-two met basic standards for good research. In twenty-four of the thirty-two there was no difference in outcome between group and individual therapy. In eight studies, or 25 percent, group therapy was more effective. In no study was individual therapy more effective. Twelve studies dealt with cost-effectiveness. In ten out of the twelve, group was more efficient (cost-effective). In one study, long-term group and short-term individual were more cost-effective than long-term individual or short-term group. Pyle and Mitchell (1985) compared outcome studies for bulimic patients and found that 93 percent improved with both individual and group therapy as compared to 46–71 percent with individual alone and 54 percent with group alone.

Group intervention is still most extensively practiced with the severely disturbed patient, particularly on inpatient services. A year after this book was originally published, Irvin Yalom (1983), who wrote the most widely used text on group psychotherapy, published his book *In-Patient Group Psychotherapy*. Although his Sullivanian model is quite different from mine, he came to many of the same conclusions:

1. Leadership must be positive and active.
2. Optimal structure must be provided.
3. Goals must be realistic.
4. Hostility and aggression should be downplayed and support provided.
5. Patients' concerns should be translated into an interpersonal problem that can be worked on in the group.
6. Each group meeting should be thought of as an entity unto itself (the Single Session group); it should stand alone with a beginning, middle, and end. Goals and structure should be appropriate for the particular individuals of each particular meeting.

Yalom also observed that turnover of patients in an inpatient setting— causing change of membership from one meeting to the next—was more disturbing to staff than patients. When he questioned fifty-one patients, they responded that turnover helped them: (1) deal with change; (2) work harder in group because there was less time; (3) have the benefit of new members' ideas; (4) be more altruistic; and (5) have hope for recovery (p. 78).

Yalom offers two structures depending on level of patient functioning. The higher functioning patients participate in an "agenda" group where they begin with a go-around. Patients state what they want to work on in the group meeting. Next, the leader helps the members work on as many agendas as possible in the allotted time. Then there is an evaluation and wrap-up.

The example that began this introduction came from an agenda-style group meeting. However, the staff of this setting found it necessary to modify the structure of each meeting in order to accommodate the natural flow better. As a consultant to the service, I felt that staff was adhering too rigidly to Yalom's prescription. Patients and leaders were often confused and overwhelmed by trying to figure out: (1) what is an appropriate agenda, (2) how to get *all* the patients to arrive at one, and then (3) how to help each person with their agenda. All of this had to be done in an hour. Leaders were so busy with these questions that they weren't free to use their intuition and creativity. A norm developed that if leaders deviated from the structure as I did in my opening example, they were delinquent.

Froberg and Slife (1987) in their article "Overcoming the Obstacles to the Implementation of Yalom's Model of Inpatient Group Psychotherapy" state that a number of therapists have abandoned the model because it is not practical. They feel that therapists are under a great deal of pressure during the "agenda filling" phase. They stress that agendas need to be fulfilled in order to give patients a sense of accomplishment. One solution is for the leader to generalize and find an agenda that includes most of the agendas presented: for example, responsibility for others or social isolation or low self-esteem. It is also helpful if patients have a good educative introduction to prepare them for the task at hand.

The structure that Yalom presents for lower-functioning patients is a series of exercises that forces limited interaction with others. These are similar to the ones I presented where patients close their eyes and then say what they have been seeing in the space around them (p. 157). Following are examples of the exercises Yalom uses:

- *Warm-Up Exercise.* Name part of the body that feels tight and relax it.
- *Structured Exercise.* Break up into partners. Tell your partner your best accomplishments. (Note the positive focus.)
- *Empathy Exercise.* Draw a name. Say how you imagine this person feels and why. Say one new thing you have learned about the person in group therapy.
- *Here-and-Now Exercise:* Complete the sentence, "The person who knows me best in the group is . . . ."

- *Tension Release Exercise:* One person leaves the room and changes appearance in some way. Others try to guess what change has been made (pp. 294–297). (This exercise is a beautiful Pre-Group exercise.)

PHASES OF GROUP DEVELOPMENT

The most exciting theoretical development in the group therapy field in the past nine years has been Beck and Dugo's (1981) work on phases of group development and leadership roles. Prior to this theory, most group analysts saw group process in terms of the relationship group members had toward the leader; that is, the glue that connects members to one another and makes it possible to form a group is their identification with the leader. In contrast, Beck and Dugo see the group's growth and movement as related to four different leadership roles that emerge in order to lead the group in resolving the group's four basic conflicts.

I allude to stages of group development in this book, suggesting that leaders be knowledgeable about stages of group development and look for them in the Single Session group. Each group meeting has a beginning, middle, and end, and different interventions are appropriate at each phase. Schutz (1966) named these phases: inclusion, control, and affection.

Beck and Dugo write that there are nine phases in group development and, as stated, four leaders that develop to lead the group in resolving the four basic conflicts. The first leader is the *Emotional Leader,* the member most invested in pursuing the task at hand. Emotionally involved and making himself most vulnerable, he is well liked and has status. He models the conflict between how close one can get with others without losing touch with his own needs.

The second is the *Task Leader,* usually the therapist. He takes care of the organizational and structural functions and models the conflict around power and control. How much power and control should each group member retain for himself and how much should he give over to the leader or other members?

The third is the *Defiant Leader.* He appears to be the least involved in the group and continually tests the limits. He models the conflict between distance versus closeness from the opposite direction of the Emotional Leader. How distant and nonconforming can a member be and still be accepted in the group?

The fourth is the *Scapegoat Leader.* This person appears to be attached to the group, attends regularly, and is always on time. He takes abuse and allows members to project their bad feeling onto him. He models the conflict around aggression. He forces members to deal with their aggressive feelings by being obnoxious. How should each group member deal with his own aggression? As members confront the Scapegoat Leader, he defends himself. In this process the members develop increasing clarity about how they want the group to be. As they sternly educate the Scapegoat Leader, they set standards for themselves. In each of the nine phases of group development, these leaders interact in a way that leads the group forward.

The application of this theory to ongoing outpatient psychotherapy groups is highly enlightening, but its usefulness to the Single Session inpatient group was not immediately apparent to me. However, in a recent conversation with these inventive theorists, I obtained some useful guidelines. According to their formulation, the inpatient group focuses on the first three phases of the group's development, which are similar to Schutz's phases. In the first phase people assess one another and, finally, contract to stay and work together. The second phase is one of competition, where hostility emerges in full force. These therapists refer to this phase as "the best known and least loved." In the third phase members are able to work together effectively on the task. It is a pleasant sharing phase.

Beck and Dugo feel that many of the problems that arise with inpatient groups are due to the group staying in Phase 2 — the most painful of stages for members and leaders. They recommend that a concerted effort be made to keep the Single Session group focused on Phase 1 issues: people getting to know one another and assessing one another. They agree that the severely disturbed have much to learn from Phase 1 issues and conflicts. Both Yalom's and my approach can be looked at in this light: encouraging here and now interaction and formulation of ideas as opposed to encouraging expression of hostility and confrontation.

There are opportunities on an inpatient service for there to be several meetings with some continuity of attendance. If there is a small percent of turnover, Beck and Dugo feel it is possible for the group to move ahead through developmental phases, provided the leader is active and structured, minimizing the rage that can develop in Phase 2. The group touches on competition issues but the gratification provided by the leaders tends to understimulate anger and the group moves on to the task. The task goals need to be concrete and limited. The structure may involve an exercise and discussion of it. Roles can be discussed in a cognitive manner.

Sometimes it is possible to have a closed group for three sessions. According to Beck and Dugo, this is all that is needed to move the group to a gratifying work position. The therapist would need to be highly focused to move the members through Phases 1 and 2 quickly, so that they can have some time in Phase 3, which, Beck says, "is a nicer place to be." If the group is opened up after three sessions, there will be continuity by old members teaching new ones.

If an inpatient therapist is skilled in leading groups, he might want to try using "the group within the group." Old members would form the "in group" or "fishbowl group" and new members would watch until they could grasp what was occurring and feel ready to participate. Beck and Dugo have recommended this technique to certain therapists and have found it successful. This approach seems to depend upon new members working through the first two phase issues silently and vicariously. They then join the group in the task. In my consultation work, I have found that any observer of a small group inevitably becomes powerfully involved in the process.

MEDICAL GROUPS

As was the case nine years ago, medical groups are markedly underutilized in the hospital setting. This fact remains so despite constant evidence of the efficacy of such groups. More articles have been published that illustrate the success of group intervention for patients with cancer (Hyland, 1984, Harris, 1985), eczema (Cole, 1988), rheumatoid arthritis (Strauss, 1986), asthma (Deter, 1986), bulimia (Huon, 1985, Connors, 1984), chronic pain (Herman, 1981, Moore, 1985, Spiegel, 1983), postmyocardial infarction (Horlick, 1984, Stern, 1983), strokes (Bucher, 1984), visual impairment (Evans, 1981, Oehler, 1980), and deafness (Bonham, 1981).

Although medical groups have not developed into cohesive programs within the hospital setting, *patient*-organized self-help groups have flourished in the community. Realizing and experiencing the powerful connection between self-esteem, recovery, and contact with others, patients began to organize and fill this need themselves. Many of the curative factors outlined in this book are realized in the self-help group: use of models, finding a valued role apart from physical prowess, the opportunity for altruism, exposure to an array of coping mechanisms, positive reinforcement for realistic goal attainment, education, and instillation of hope. Powell (1987) writes that the similarity of people's problems is strong enough to overcome many differences and that people gain new self-respect as they solve basic problems (p. 76). Riessman continues:

> When people help themselves—join together to deal with their similar problems, whether these concern mental health or the neighborhood— they feel empowered; they are able to control some aspects of their lives. The help is not given to them from the outside—from an expert, a professional, a politician. The latter forms of help have the danger of building dependence—the direct opposite effect of empowerment.

Empowerment increases energy, motivation, and an ability to help that goes beyond helping oneself or receiving help. (Powell, p. x.)

People report the same kind of relief referred to in this book (p. 162): They are not alone. For example, "Finally I knew I wasn't some kind of freak. It was a powerful healing experience to meet other victims and talk openly." "There is a feeling you get when you hear the others in group talking, a feeling that you recognize just what they're saying. And when you are talking, you can see that recognition in their eyes. That recognition is very important" (Eisman, 1988, p. 25).

As of 1984 there were 585,823 Alcoholics Anonymous members in the United States and 69,931 in Canada. The worldwide figure exceeded 1.1 million. Emotions Anonymous had 1,000 chapters in eighteen countries (Powell, p. 18). Lieberman and Borman looked at ten major self-help groups in 1982. Each one had grown 3 percent or more since 1976. AA had a growth of over 50 percent in six years with 30,000 chapters in ninety-two countries in 1978 (p. 31–32). There are self-help groups for almost all medical illnesses. In the Bay Area of San Francisco a 186-page directory of self-help groups is published. Many cities have self-help clearing houses to direct people. The California Self-Help Center at UCLA has a listing of more than 3,000 groups across the state. The groups are divided into four categories: those for physical and mental illness, those for addictions, those for coping with crisis or transition, and those for people who are "one step beyond" (relatives and friends).

Various authors agree that the rise of the self-help group is connected to the increasing numbers of chronically ill and to decreasing services. Albee (1985) clarifies that in the United States there are thirty-two million arthritics, twenty million people with high blood pressure, five million diabetics, ten million alcoholics, four million drug addicts, and many more millions suffering from other physical ailments. Jensen (1983) demonstrated that high risk male and female patients with chronic airway obstructions who participated in a self-help group were less likely to be hospitalized (20 percent versus 64 percent) and to be hospitalized for shorter periods of time (0.8 days versus 5 days) than a control group of similar others. Other researchers studying patients with cancer, arthritis, and ostomies have noted positive gains with self-help group attendance (Medvene, 1986).

The leadership of the self-help movement has made a clear distinction between what patients can offer one another and when professional input is needed. Lieberman notes that it is important that professionals only act as consultants to self-help groups so that creative lay leadership can flourish. It is interesting to see what patients themselves have come up with in the way of curative programs.

Meetings are usually highly structured. With the pooling of many members' experiences, a workable program is agreed upon. Members become clear about the progression that leads to recovery. These are often concretized into steps so that members know where they are in the progression and are rewarded for each step they achieve. "To reach people in . . . overwhelmed states, it is a tremendous advantage to have credentials that include personal experience with the trauma. With this kind of referent power, it is possible to be both caring and demanding" (Powell, p. 239).

The most widely used program is that of AA; other self-help groups have versions specifically designed for their problem. AA's twelve-step program is as follows:

1. We admitted we were powerless over alcohol—that our lives had become unmanageable.
2. We came to believe that a Power greater than ourselves could restore us to sanity.
3. We made a decision to turn our will and our lives over to the care of God as we understood Him.
4. We made a searching and fearless moral inventory of ourselves.
5. We admitted to God, to ourselves, and to another human being the exact nature of our wrongs.
6. We were entirely ready to have God remove all these defects of character.
7. We humbly asked Him to remove our shortcomings.
8. We made a list of all persons we had harmed, and became willing to make amends to them all.
9. We made direct amends to such people wherever possible, except when to do so would injure them or others.
10. We continued to take personal inventory and when we were wrong promptly admitted it.
11. We sought through prayer and meditation to improve our conscious contact with God as we understood Him, praying only for knowledge of His will for us and the power to carry that out.
12. Having had a spiritual awakening as the result of these steps, we tried to carry this message to other alcoholics and to practice these principles in all our affairs. (Courtesy of Alcoholics Anonymous)

What strikes me about these steps is their spiritual nature combined with self-responsibility. Spirituality and belief in a greater power can be employed in the construction of a wonderful narcissistic defense when such a defense is desperately needed. Alcoholics are known to use grandiosity as a narcissistic defense. Although it helps them feel better about themselves, it is maladaptive in that they don't accept the help they need. In the twelve-step program, people are encouraged to give up their grandiosity and move toward idealization—a defense that works to heal narcissistic wounds but connects individuals more to the people around them and the healing powers beyond themselves. As I note in this book (p. 156), when people are helped with their narcissistic defense work, other kinds of work can be demanded from them; in this case, it is self-responsibility.

The self-help dictum is "only you can do it, but you can't do it alone" (Powell, p. 77). The organizational goal of medical self-help groups is to minimize the physical disability, not accentuate it; to expand, not restrict normal social functioning. The optimistic message is "learn to live with it— well!" "Patients see real examples of what is possible, not just despite the 'disability' but perhaps because of it" (Powell, p. 244).

An equally important part of the process is the sharing of personal experiences in a nonjudgmental environment. In this book I describe certain "superstar" patients and my desire that they be used as leaders to teach others (p. 181). The self-help group format offers a perfect arena for many patients to model those patients who have made skilled and courageous recoveries.

LeMaistre (1985) is a single parent with a young child. She also has impairment of sight and muscular incapacity from multiple sclerosis. She manages to teach at Stanford University, help self-help organizations, practice psychology, and write. I was moved by these statements from her book, in which this superstar patient generously shares her insights and inspires others:

> To be psychologically well while physically sick involves the belief that your personal worth transcends physical limitations: you need positive self-esteem for true adaptation. This belief in your self-worth rarely emerges until what you have lost and grieved for stands second in importance to precious moments of inner peace and joy. . . . You are not alone—none of us is alone—we may not know each other yet, but there are kindred spirits. A single treasured personal relationship makes the path bearable. (pp. 15, 157)

SOCIETY AND RESPONSIBILITY

In my final chapter, on cost containment, I begin to make the connection between hospital ills and those of society. Sometimes it seems as though hospitals are supposed to do it all: take care of all the casualties and also prevent them from occurring. Hospitals take on a "bottomless pit" situation, which only leads to frustration.

Erickson (1980) is one of the few theorists who tried to make the overwhelming connection between society's ways (for example, norms rewarding how well a Japanese woman bows) and historical forces (for example, war) on the formation of psychic structure. He posits that the psyche is formed around what the child perceives as reinforcements to his self-esteem. The psyche assumes a certain predictability and continuity. If one learns from society that one is rewarded and can achieve status through the accumulation of material wealth, one counts on that standard continuing throughout life. One can imagine the psychic chaos that results as people move from one culture to another or as one's own culture changes so fast that there are "generation gaps," or as natural or man-made disasters occur that suddenly change how one acquires self-esteem points.

Let me remind the reader that self-esteem is the bedrock of psychic structure. If cracks develop, health becomes endangered (Erickson, p. 3). The seriousness of this happening is poignantly illustrated by the men who are members of extreme Muslim sects and volunteer for suicide missions. These are men of low self-esteem who have an opportunity to be heroes (*Holy War/Holy Terror,* documentary, Frontline Series). They literally die in order to win the self-esteem points necessary for psychic survival.

California has made an initial step to bridge the gap between government and social ills and delivery of health care. In 1987, Resolution Chapter 77 was passed by the state legislature. The resolution states that there is a connection between self-esteem, self-responsibility, and societal institutions. The assumption is that if people had better self-esteem they would be more responsible citizens and contribute to institutions rather than drain them. Funds were allocated to study what contributes to self-esteem of children, for example, a noncritical approach to education. Other areas that would be researched as to how they connect with self-esteem and personal and social responsibility were crime and violence, alcoholism and drug abuse, welfare dependency, children failing to learn in schools, teenage pregnancy, child and spousal abuse, and recidivism. The committee itself was to be composed of people from the fields of law enforcement, corrections, mental health, social science, education, religion, and organizational development.

Some of the quotes from this committee and its tasks could easily have been incorporated in this book.

Our sense of self-esteem has a profound influence on our ability and capacity to function effectively. It can be likened to a barometer that is linked to one's energy, emotions, and creativity. As the barometer of self-esteem rises, typically so does our creativity, openness, enthusiasm, energy, and capacity to cope with the vagaries of life. . . . Self-esteem is that portion of our sense of self which reflects the value we place on ourselves. These positive and negative values are attached to the various characteristics, skills, and roles, which in total give each of us our sense of self. The values we place on each aspect of our sense of self are derived from the feedback we receive through our lives in regard to our performance in life. The most influential source of feedback to us is from the people who are important to us. Four factors have been identified that must be operating in our lives if we are to have a high sense of self-esteem. They are . . . Connectiveness . . . Uniqueness . . . Power . . . Models. (Bean and Clemes, 1988)

Although there is criticism of the committee and many find it laughable, it is at least a recognition on the political level that there is a connection between basic self-esteem and personal and social responsibility, and that our institutions can foster or damage the mental health of our children.

SUMMARY

I have described how a positive approach to treating medical patients and severely disturbed psychiatric patients has persisted and developed over the past nine years. A self psychology approach to treating these populations continues to be valid. Since these patients often receive exposure to group therapy on an inpatient service, appreciation for what can be accomplished in the Single Session group is paramount. Yalom (1983) and Beck and Dugo (1981) have contributed to this understanding.

The profundity of the notion of self-esteem as the bedrock of psychic structure and mental health has been recognized in the community. Self-help groups are growing in membership so that thousands of people can be more connected with others and feel better about themselves. The State of California has funded a committee to look at places where children's self-esteem can be fostered, the assumption being that with increased self-esteem comes greater social and personal responsibility.

I would like to take this opportunity to thank all of the professionals who have bought this book, read it, and used it. Many of you have taken the additional step of giving me feedback, which has helped me to learn continually. I trust this communication will continue.

Elaine Cooper Lonergan, M.S.W., Ph.D.
Langley Porter Psychiatric Institute
Adult Outpatient Department

REFERENCES

Albee, G., 1985. The answer is prevention. *Psychology Today, 19*(2):60–66.

Alcoholics Anonymous. Inter-County Fellowship, 1046 Irving Street, San Francisco, CA 94108. 415-661-1828.

Bacal, H., 1985. Object-relations in the group from the perspective of self psychology. *International Journal of Group Psychotherapy, 35*(4):483–502.

Basler, H. D., Brinkmeier, U., Buser, K., et al. 1982. Psychological group treatment of essential hypertension in general practice. *British Journal of Clinical Psychology,* pp. 295–302.

Bean, R. & Clemes, H. California Task Force to Promote Self-Esteem and Personal Social Responsibility, 1130 K Street, Suite 300, Sacramento, CA 95814.

Beck, A. & Dugo, P., 1981. A study of group phase development and emergent leadership. *Group, 5*(4):48–54.

Blanchard, E. B. & Schwartz, S. P., 1987. Adaptation of a multicomponent treatment for irritable bowel syndrome to a small group format. *Biofeedback, 12*(1)63–69.

Bonham, H. E., Armstrong, T. D., & Bonham, G. M., 1981. Group psychotherapy with deaf adolescents. *American Annals of the Deaf, 126*(7):806–809.

Bucher, J., Smith, E., & Gillespie, C., 1984. Short-term group therapy for stroke patients in a rehabilitation centre. *British Journal of Medical Psychology, 57*:283–290.

California Self-Help Center. 405 Hilgard Avenue, UCLA, Los Angeles, CA 90024. 213-825-1799.

Cole, W. C., Roth, H. L., & Sachs, L. B., 1988. Group psychotherapy in the medical treatment of eczema. *Journal of American Academy of Dermatology,* pp. 286–291.

Connors, M. E., Johnson, C. L., & Stuckey, M. D., 1984. Treatment of bulimia with brief psychoeducational group therapy. *American Journal of Psychiatry, 141*(12):1512–1516.

Deter, H. C., 1986. Cost benefit analysis of psychosomatic therapy in asthma. *Journal of Psychosomatic Research, 30*(2):173–182.

Dittes, J. E. & Kelley, H. H., 1956. Effects of different conditions of acceptance on conformity to group norms. *Journal of Abnormal and Social Psychology, 53:*100–107.

Eisman, C., 1988. Getting the most from the self-help network. *The Almacon,* pp. 24–27.

Erickson, E., 1980. Ego development and historical change: clinical notes, Saul Scheidlinger (ed.) in *Psychoanalytic Group Dynamics.* New York: International Universities Press, pp. 189–212.

Evans, R. L. & Jaureguy, B. M., 1981. Group therapy by phone: a cognitive behavioral program for visually impaired elderly. *Social Work Health Care,* 7(2)79-90.

Feilbert-Willis, R., Kibel, H., & Wikstrom, T., 1986. Techniques for handling resistances in group psychotherapy. *Group, 10*(4):228-238.

Froberg, W. & Slife, B., 1987. Overcoming obstacles to the implementation of Yalom's model of inpatient group psychotherapy. *International Journal of Group Psychotherapy, 37*(3):371-388.

Grunebaum, J. & Solomon, L., 1987. Peer relationships, self-esteem and the self. *International Journal of Group Psychotherapy, 37*(4):475-513.

Haehn, K. D., 1985. Psychological approaches to improve patient compliance. *Journal of Hypertension (suppl.), 3*(1)61-64.

Harris, L. L., Vogtsberger, K. N., & Mattox, D. E., 1985. Group psychotherapy for head and neck cancer patients. *Laryngoscope, 95*(5): 585-587.

Harwood, I., 1983. An application of self-psychology concepts to group psychotherapy. *International Journal of Group Psychotherapy, 33*(4):469-488.

Herman, E. & Baptiste, S., 1981. Pain control: mastery through group experience. *Pain, 10*(1):79-86.

Horlick, L., Cameron, R., Firor, W., et al., 1984. The effects of education and group discussion in the post myocardial infarction patient. *Journal of Psychosomatic Research, 28*(6):485-492.

Huon, G. F. & Brown, L. B., 1985. Evaluating a group treatment for bulimia. *Journal of Psychiatric Research, 19*(2-3):479-483.

Horwitz, L., 1984. The self in groups. *International Journal of Group Psychotherapy, 34*(1):519-540.

Hyland, J. M., Pruyser, H., Novotny, E., et al., 1984. The impact of the death of a group member in a group of breast cancer patients. *International Journal of Group Psychotherapy, 34*(4):617-626.

Jensen, P., 1983. Risk, protective factors and supportive interventions in chronic airway obstruction. *Archives of General Psychiatry, 40*(2):1203-1207.

Josephs, L. & Juman, L., 1985. The application of self psychology principles to long term group therapy with schizophrenic in-patients. *Group, 9*(3):21-30.

Katz, A., 1987. *Partners in Wellness — Self Help Groups and Professionals.* Sacramento, CA: Office of Prevention, State Department of Mental Health.

Kohut, H., 1981. The bipolar self: panel report. *Journal of the American Psychoanalytic Association,* p. 29.

Leavitt, H. J., 1951. Some effects of certain communication patterns on group performance. *Journal of Abnormal and Social Psychology, 46*:38-50.

LeMaistre, J., 1985. *Beyond Rage: The Emotional Impact of Chronic Physical Illness.* Oak Park, IL: Alpine Guild.

Lieberman, M., Borman, L., & Associates, 1982. *Self-Help Groups for Coping with Crisis.* San Francisco: Jossey-Bass.

McGrath, J., 1984. *Groups: Interaction and Performance.* Englewood Cliffs, NJ: Prentice-Hall.

Medvene, L., 1986. Selected highlights of research for effectiveness of self-help groups. California Self Help Center, UCLA.

Moore, J. E. & Chaney, E. F., 1985. Outpatient group treatment of chronic pain: effects of spouse involvement. *Journal of Consultation and Clinical Psychology, 53*(3):326–334.

Oehler-Giarratana, J. & Fitzgerald, R. G., 1980. Group therapy with blind diabetics. *Archives of General Psychiatry, 37*(4):463–467.

Pepinsky, P. N., Hemphill, J. K., & Shevitz, R. N., 1958. Attempts to lead, group productivity and morale under conditions of acceptance and rejection. *Journal of Abnormal and Social Psychology, 57*:47–54.

Pyle, R. & Mitchell, J., 1985. Psychotherapy of bulimia: the role of groups, W. Kaye & H. Gwirtzman (ed.) in *The Treatment of Normal Weight Bulimia.* Washington, DC: The American Psychiatric Press.

Peled-Ney, R., Silverberg, D. S., & Rosenfeld, J. B., 1984. A controlled study of group therapy in essential hypertension. *Journal of Medical Science, 20*(1):12–15.

Powell, T., 1987. *Self-Help Organizations and Professional Practice.* Silver Spring, MD: National Association of Social Workers.

Project of the Bay Area Self-Help Clearinghouse, *Whole Self-Help Directory.* San Francisco: Mental Health Association, 1985.

Schachter, S., 1951. Deviation, rejection and communication. *Journal of Abnormal and Social Psychology, 46*:190–207.

Schutz, W., 1966. *The Interpersonal Underworld (Firo).* Palo Alto, CA: Science and Behavior.

Shaw, M. E., 1959. Some effects of individually prominent behavior upon group effectiveness and member satisfaction. *Journal of Abnormal and Social Psychology, 59*:382–386.

Spiegel, D. & Bloom, J. R., 1983. Group therapy and hypnosis reduce metastatic breast carcinoma pain. *Psychosomatic Medicine, 45*(4):333–339.

Stern, M. J., Gorman, P. A., & Kaslow, L., 1983. The group counseling-versus exercise therapy study: a controlled intervention with subjects following myocardial infarction. *Archives of Internal Medicine, 143*(9): 1719–1725.

Strauss, G. D., et al., 1986. Group therapies for rheumatoid arthritis: a controlled study of two approaches. *Arthritis-Rheumatism, 29*(10): 1203–1209.

Toseland, R. & Siporin, M., 1986. When to recommend group treatment: a review of the clinical and the research literature. *International Journal of Group Psychotherapy, 36*(2):171–199.

WGBH Boston. Frontline Series, *Holy War/Holy Terror*. Aired on KQED San Francisco, June 1986.

Weinstein, D., 1987. Self psychology and group therapy. *Group*, *11*(3):144–154.

Wilson, A., 1982. Treatment of the narcissistic character disorder in group psychotherapy in the light of self psychology. *Group*, *6*(3):6–10.

Yalom, I., 1970. *The Theory and Technique of Group Psychotherapy*. New York: Basic Books.

Yalom, I., 1983. *In-Patient Group Psychotherapy*. New York: Basic Books.

Part I

THE NEED FOR
GROUPS IN MEDICAL
AND PSYCHIATRIC
SETTINGS

Chapter 1

Treating the Whole Patient

SELF-ESTEEM REPARATION

When people have a physical or severe psychiatric illness, they suffer from wounded self-esteem; when self-esteem is threatened, the stability of the psyche–soma system is threatened. Loss of self-esteem interferes with the patient's recovery, ability to cooperate with medical staff, and relationship with family and friends. Thus therapeutic technique must first and foremost be utilized to help hospital patients with the repair of damaged self-esteem, the buttressing of crumbling self-esteem, and the boosting of low self-esteem. Hospital-based group intervention can be an extremely effective method of healing wounded self-esteem. It can encourage patients to participate in "self-soothing" activity. Patients should get a "dose" of positive self-esteem with each group visit. This book discusses the theory and technique of "self-esteem reparation" group intervention within medical and psychiatric settings, and provides a guide on how to begin and maintain such groups.

Self-esteem reparation group work with medical and psychiatric patients focuses on the strengths of the individual, respecting ego defenses rather than eliciting irrational anxiety or frustrating the patient. This does not mean that the group leader gives false reassurance or unwarranted praise. Rather, the leader encourages the patient to reflect on his or her genuine strengths and progress. This approach recognizes an individual's capabilities, and with that recognition self-esteem is elevated.

Stolorow and Lachmann (1980, p. 12) define self-esteem as "the positive affective coloring of self-representation." They refer to Hartmann's definition of self-representation: the unconscious, preconscious, and con-

3

scious representations of the bodily and mental self. Severely disturbed psychiatric patients have long-standing self-esteem problems; a positive self-image (self-represenation) was never solidified. As a result, they have the lifelong narcissistic task of helping themselves feel better. Stolorow and Lachmann state that a task is narcissistic to the extent that it buttresses threatened self-representation; the cohesiveness and stability of self-representation is the structural foundation upon which self-esteem rests. "When self-esteem is threatened, significantly lowered, or destroyed, then narcissistic activities are called into play in an effort to protect, restore, repair and stabilize it" (Ibid., p. 21). Self-esteem reparation group activity can help severely disturbed patients with their narcissistic task. These patients have strengths which can be elicited and supported in behalf of their own recovery. They can also be helpful to other group members.

No matter how emotionally healthy they are, people will experience a blow to self-esteem with medical illness. As their body is theatened, so is their self-esteem. The unconscious makes a primary connection between physical well-being and personal worth. Fenichel writes: "The first supply of satisfaction from the external world, the supply of nourishment, is simultaneously the first regulator of self-esteem" (1945, p.40). When people become physically ill they may experience a loss of face and may fear that they have done something wrong to deserve their misfortune. "Why me?" they ask; or, "Am I being punished?" "What did I do wrong?" Strain and Grossman (1975) delineate the troubles medical patients face: a basic threat to narcissistic integrity; fear of strangers; separation anxiety; fear of losing love and approval; fear of losing control of developmentally achieved functions; fear of losing or injury to body parts; and guilt and fear of retaliation. Group intervention designed to address these fears is an effective method of expediting self-esteem recovery and encouraging patient's active participation in the healing process.

THE COMPLEX WHOLE

In order to do justice to the topic of how to begin and maintain groups in medicine and psychiatry, one should thoroughly review the context in which these groups take place. The most immediate context is the medical complex. The organization, with its structure and values, affects the formation and maintenance of the groups. This includes the leaders of the group and their orientation, role in the organization, status, etc. One looks at the individual involved: the patient's history, culture, current living situation, and emotional state. As one attempts to diagnose the illness, whether in medicine or psychiatry, the line might seem fuzzy; it is likely that the patient has both medical and psychiatric symptomatology.

One proceeds to look at the society within which the individual, the group, and the institution operate, for it too will impinge upon and affect the group; for example, the status that each member has in the society or the role function that each is expected to fulfill will be reflected in the group. Then one proceeds to look for significant historical events such as wars, separations, and reunions caused by political events, which affect the individuals involved (patients and staff), and periodic funding shifts, which affect the organization.

The reader may find this list overwhelming; others may find it oversimplified. Within the confines of this book, all of these areas cannot possibly be explored. Furthermore, there are limitations to our knowledge. However, this is a quandary we all face as we try to master clinical understanding and skill. One reasonable solution to this quandary is to narrow the field of inquiry so as to improve our ability to manipulate and comprehend its contents.

In researching the literature in preparation for this book, it became apparent that much of what I have stated has been said before. I selected from the literature, and from my own experience with more than 3,000 patients and relatives—who participated in groups composed of severely disturbed psychiatric patients, medical patients, drug addicts, and the aged—those concepts and techniques that have been particularly helpful to me and my students in beginning and maintaining such groups.

Even though it is necessary to limit the material covered in this book for the purpose of clear presentation, it is important to remember that there is a larger context in which the concepts and prescriptions presented in this book take place. Two useful conceptual schemes attempt to do justice to the existence of the broad, encompassing "whole": one is systems theory (Durkin, 1975), and the other is the scientific methodology espoused by Karl Popper in his books, *Logic of Scientific Discovery* (1959) and *Objective Knowledge* (1972). Both of these philosophical frameworks have influenced the writing of this book.

SYSTEMS THEORY

Systems theorists think that all of the sciences should work together in some way; they should integrate their knowledge and develop a common language in which to communicate. Since each science is approaching an understanding of *one* area of existence, and since all the areas of exploration (the physical and social sciences) are interconnected, the lack of communication among the disciplines results in a dearth of knowledge about the effects of one area on another.

Systems theory takes the language of biology, which refers to living systems that are "open" (constantly changing), and applies this terminology and conceptualization to individual, group and family psychology. Systems theorists can conceptualize the broader whole by diagramming the individual, group, agency, leader, and social systems and analyzing how each system affects the others. These theorists tend to focus on "boundarying," which is the way living systems (which includes the individual, the group, the family, and society) control what they take in and what they let out in order to maintain optimum homeostasis. They can extend their analysis to include inner psychic systems, such as the ego, id, and superego, or go to the more general extreme and include world systems.

Even within the mental health field we break down areas of inquiries and often proceed to think and act as though they are, in fact, isolated entities. For example, we separate medical and psychiatric patients as though they really are two distinct groups. We tend to forget that we have made an artificial separation for our convenience and our sanity. We have done the same in separating "individual" and "group" psychology as though the two could really be separated.

Beginning with Freud, who acknowledged that individual and group psychology could not be separated (Scheidlinger, 1980), many theorists and practitioners have tried to cut through the limitations of these breakdowns. The increasing numbers of individuals in an infant's life (group exposure) helps the infant to modify its narcissism and to become a part of a community which is crucial to healthy personality development. Wolberg (1977) expands upon this line of thought in her article on projective identification. Erikson (1980) writes about the effect society and history have on character development.

Throughout the years, professionals have made attempts to integrate the fields of psychiatry and medicine, both theoretically and practically. Periodic attempts are made to hospitalize medical and psychiatric patients on the same floor. We tend to go in swings, first seeing all people the same—medical and psychiatric patients—and gradually becoming painfully aware of their differences and separate needs, then discovering specialization and developing skills responsive to "differences," gradually losing sight of similarities, then once again becoming aware of similarities and the limitations of specialization, and so forth. In 1963 the Joint Commission on Mental Health insisted that community hospitals provide for the psychiatrically ill and not immediately isolate them in mental hospitals far from the community (Detre, Kessler, and Jarecki, 1963).

Ironically, most community hospitals isolate medical from psychiatric patients *within* the hospital, and the idea is perpetuated that they really are two distinct groups.

People tend to "externalize" for comfort and categorize for simplicity. For example, at a workshop I gave on groups for medical patients, the audience was commenting on and asking questions about "them." One physician in the group said, "Aren't we really talking about *us*? How many of us haven't been or won't be in a hospital?" Reding and Maguire (1973) reported an experience where medical and psychiatric patients were hospitalized on the same unit. They wrote that they had found no prior reference in the literature to this kind of experimentation. It was a positive experience, where length of hospital stay was shortened for the psychiatric patients. The medical setting was soothing for the psychiatric patients, and the psychiatric patients were helpful to the medical patients. I know of two recent programs where similar attempts are being made successfully.

In this book I suggest an interdisciplinary team approach as a way of reaping the benefits of specialization while still keeping the "whole" or "total" person in focus. Auerswald (1968) feels the team approach is too limited. "Only those concepts that pose no serious challenge or language difficulties are welcomed . . . . Interfaces between the various arenas of systematic life operation (e.g., biological, psychological, social or individual, family, community) represented by various disciplines are also ignored." He advocates the "ecological" approach, which would include more of the sciences. (Although I agree with him, I think that at this point the team approach is a practical way to begin moving in the right direction.) Devereaux (1949) thinks that an anthropologist should be added to the treatment team, since culture plays such a strong role in the extent and kind of mental illness that exists in varying populations. The anthropologist would dispense individualized "social-therapy" prescriptions.

The reader may already see that even systems theory is only a beginning attempt to recognize, appreciate, and understand the whole. We have just begun to envision the implications for treatment interventions in individual and group therapy if we consider all the impinging systems. Any attempt to categorize various systems or ingredients of systems seems oversimplified, no matter how long the lists may be. Certainly there are many parts we have yet to discover—parts that are out of our awareness. Here is where Karl Popper's approach is helpful.

KARL POPPER

The philosopher Karl Popper has an approach to learning and validation that I find useful. The concept of truth is regulatory rather than absolute. We can never completely know the truth because that is inherently beyond our capacity. We can only form hypotheses. We can test our hypotheses and modify them according to the results, test again, and repeat the cycle. Each cycle brings us closer to the truth, and this should be the aim of all science. He makes the following criticism of social theory (such as systems theory) and its predictive value: "If there is such a thing as growing human knowledge, then we cannot anticipate today what we shall know only tomorrow" (1957, p. x).

This philosophy has been valuable to me as a supervisor. Students want to know what is "right" and what is "wrong" in making treatment interventions. The reality is that no supervisor knows the answer to that question because each individual and situation is different and the supervisor is one step further removed. (Systems theorists have said that by definition when you analyze an event you are dealing with the past.) I encourage trainees to make guesses about what is going on with the patient and group according to both the theory they have learned and their intuition, to test out the guesses by making an intervention—verbal or nonverbal—and then modify the guess according to the result. Even if the truth cannot be known, we are always faced with choices, and these choices should be derived from an empirical approach to problems. Our preference for diagnosis and therapy can be based on informative hypotheses about problems to be solved, followed by the testing of these hypotheses.

The examples in this book are the result of this approach. Very often my guesses and those of my students were very much off base. Those experiences are shared with the reader. This book presents techniques that worked and didn't work in forming and maintaining groups in psychiatry and medicine.

ANALYTICAL VERSUS SUPPORTIVE GROUP INTERVENTION

Hospital group intervention can include: (1) the open, "single-session" turnover group and (2) the long-term or short-term therapy group. In the former, supportive technique (self-esteem reparation) is the most appropriate, since there is such a time limit that in-depth personality reconstruction is impossible. In the latter, technique designed to alter personality (psychoanalytic, interactional, insight-oriented group therapy) may be employed.

Table 1-1 compares the two extremes of analytical and supportive group therapy, that is, the therapy group composed of neurotics who profit from regression, and the single-session turnover group that commonly takes place in a hospital. There are many therapy groups that fall between these extremes: for example, the long-term groups composed of post-hospitalized mental patients or addictive personalities where supportive techniques are indicated but where one would want to limit the turnover in the group.

There are patients in long- and short-term groups who benefit from an approach that utilizes members' anxiety and discomfort, but this book will not deal with these types of groups or patients. However, it is important for the reader to remember that the struggle to maintain self-esteem is a universal one. People with intact self-esteem will question their worth when faced with a crisis (such as loss of job). Thus patients participating in analytic group therapy may backslide at times, and the therapist then has to employ self-esteem reparation technique. Freud stated that when the anxiety level is too high, psychoanalysis stops. The analyst has to employ supportive techniques temporarily until self-esteem is elevated and anxiety lowered.

Is the single-session turnover group considered group therapy? If "group therapy" is defined as treatment designed to alter personality, it is not. However, this book illustrates how and why these brief group experiences are therapeutic. They have an important place in group work in medical and psychiatric settings.

Group therapists voice concern over dropouts in long-term group therapy. There seem to be many people who, after joining a group, cannot tolerate it or are not suitable. Yalom writes: "The irony is that these patients whose attrition rate is so high are the very ones for whom a successful group experience could be particularly rewarding" (1970, p.168). Many of these dropouts respond to supportive group intervention (single-session group) or supportive group therapy (long- or short-term group). They certainly do well when included in the single-session turnover group that takes place in a hospital during a crisis. In fact, most participants in such groups have never tried group therapy, even though many have had emotional problems. Many dropouts could also tolerate long-term group therapy where technique was supportive of self-esteem and ego strength. In this book there are many examples from long-term groups of severely disturbed patients where supportive technique is employed and emotional growth takes place. Patients change their self-destructive behavior and voice greater satisfaction with themselves and their lives.

Social group work has a long history of supportive group intervention. Social workers have gone into communities, found natural groups, and adapted technique to meet each group's needs. They have practiced in

TABLE 1-1
Analytical and Supportive Group Therapy

	Analytical Group Therapy	Supportive Group Intervention
Selection of members	Much care is taken in composing group; severe pathologies are excluded; effort is made to prevent dropouts.	Almost everyone is included.
Preparation of members	Much individualized preparation of member before joining group; usually a number of individual sessions.	Only preparation may be conveying to patient that he or she is expected to attend group; can be a few minutes.
Length of group	Long-term: an indefinite number of sessions.	May be for one session only.
Membership turnover	Ideally, only on rare occasions and when members have worked through their problems.	May have different members each week.
Technique	Facilitation of regression; periodic instillation of anxiety and frustration.	Build self-esteem; reinforce ego strength; reduce anxiety and regression.
End result	Character change: patient will not feel better after one meeting but over time will change long-standing patterns of behavior.	Person feels better about self after meeting; immediate feeling of relief.

many different settings, always focusing on and enhancing ego strength. Unfortunately, this literature has not been fully integrated or appreciated within the mainstream of the discipline of group therapy.

THE SINGLE-SESSION TURNOVER GROUP

One of the surprises in store for me as I worked with hospital groups was the success of the single-session or open group with constant turnover. For example, on an inpatient medical floor where the average length of hospital stay was 11 days, patients may attend one or two group meetings. In the outpatient department, a waiting-room group might be held while people were waiting for clinic appointments. A creative staff person would bring two or more people together spontaneously because at a particular moment they were struggling with the same issue. Working in this way takes a leader who is skilled and comfortable with groups; traditional training in group therapy is often not adequate preparation to lead this kind of group. In a survey conducted in the Northeast on groups in maternal and child health, Poynter-Berg (1979) found that 68 percent of the groups were "open," and group leaders expressed discomfort with their lack of knowledge in leading this kind of group. "Single-session groups require specialized skills on the part of the leader—tuning in to the group members' needs, contracting, getting into the work, and termination—all in one or two hours" (Poynter-Berg and Weiner, 1979, p. 37).

THE VALUE OF THE SINGLE-SESSION GROUP

Many of us have made the assumption that the problem with hospital groups in medicine and psychiatry is that they are not long-term and closed. Poynter-Berg (1979) mentions the "mystique of long-term treatment," and Youcha writes:

> A myth exists . . . that the only "real therapy" is insight therapy, and anything else such as activity or discussion is for those who are low on the hierarchal totem pole. This has proven disastrous for the severely disturbed patient, since the more experienced and trained professional will not deign to engage in a treatment approach which is below his dignity but is nevertheless the kind of treatment which may be best for the patient. (1976, p. 135)

We therefore knock our heads against a wall trying to make groups long-term and closed instead of appreciating the value of the single-session turnover group, which patients seem to respond to readily. These groups may not meet the group leader's needs because of their expectations and training, but they certainly seem to meet the patients' needs. Why? How? What have we underestimated? The answer to this question may be:

1. The curative power of group interaction when a patient has been socially isolated.
2. The power of group interaction in treating self-esteem.
3. The greater tolerance for differences between people during a crisis.

If we go back to Freud's statement, we can view social interaction as a basic human need of which many of these patients are deprived. Consequently, just one structured, positive group experience can bring temporary relief. Also, we probably underestimate the damaged self-esteem many of these patients experience and the power of positive group interaction in treating self-esteem. Even if people with low self-esteem come to only one meeting, much can be accomplished in helping them feel better about themselves (see Chapter 8 on treating wounded self-esteem). Part of the power of positive group intervention is that it can humanize the hospital experience and thus elevate people's self-esteem. When groups facilitate communication between patients and staff, aid in patient education so that people can take more responsibility for their self-care, and help team members work together, not only does group intervention help patients feel better about themselves but the quality of the medical care they receive improves. All of these points are elaborated upon and illustrated in the text of this book.

COMPOSITION OF THE GROUP

When Yalom (1970) and Gitterman (1979) give prescriptions for forming groups, they suggest an optimum amount of heterogeneity and homogeneity in composition: enough homogeneity for commonality and enough heterogeneity for spontaneity. I agree with these formulations and encourage them; but in many of the groups we are talking about, I believe there is more "crisis" involved than is realized. Because of the immediacy of many people's problems, the groups can tolerate more heterogeneity. This is certainly true in a medical setting and in an acute psychiatric-care facility. This book gives examples of very unlikely combinations of people working together in group meetings.

Despite the poor prognosis based on such a composition, the meeting may evolve into a cohesive group experience where some of Yalom's (1970) curative factors are operative: universalization, instillation of hope, imparting of information, altruism, imitative behavior, and catharsis. In psychiatric settings, groups have been formed from waiting lists— with positive results. In medical settings, groups have been spontaneously formed in waiting rooms as people are waiting for clinic appointments.

Populations who were formerly seen as unsuitable for psychotherapy are now viewed as treatable in groups, and positive results are being reported in the literature. For example, Allen (1976) and Monaster (1972) write about their groups with senile patients. Cook (1975) led an inpatient group for aphasic patients. Payn (1974) led groups in an outpatient department for psychiatric patients who were viewed as unsuitable for ongoing psychotherapy and only came to the clinic for medication. Instead of spending ten minutes with each patient writing a prescription, he put the patients assigned to him together in one room and wrote out the prescriptions with everyone present. Eventually, these socially isolated, withdrawn, and delusional patients began recognizing each other and talking together. I once formed a group of all the outpatients whom the psychiatric residents rejected for their therapy groups. My co-leader called it the garbage-pail group. It became cohesive and outlived many of the resident's groups.

CONTINUITY

Shulman writes, "The ability of group members to work effectively, with feeling, in a single-session large group, when the proper conditions are set by the worker, has never ceased to amaze me" (1979, pp. 267-8). He suggests that each meeting be looked at as a small group, with stages of group development taking place within one meeting. Timing of interventions is crucial, and the leader should allot time periods for each stage: tuning in, contracting, work, and termination.

Bailis, Lambert, and Bernstein (1978) write about the continuity that evolves in an open group where there is constant turnover. This is a mysterious phenomenon that many of us have observed. How is it that groups of changing membership can act as a unit from one meeting to the next? Of course, the evolution of the group is not as rapid as if the membership were constant (this is not to say that all groups with stable membership evolve), but it *can* evolve. The authors explain this phenomenon as the transmission of norms from one generation to another. All it takes is one or two members being carried from one meeting to the next, or some contact between old and new members between group meetings, for norms to be transmitted. This is a small example of a universal historical phenomenon where people are designated to transmit information from one generation to another in order to assure continuity. Perhaps the need for continuity is basic to human nature.

TECHNIQUE

Technique for long-term groups has to be modified in order to make the best use of the single-session group. Goals have to be appropriate and limited. Shulman (1979) writes that a manageable agenda is needed so that the leader and the group are not under pressure to zoom ahead. In each meeting the leader has to focus on a commonality. If the group is very heterogeneous, the focus may be quite broad, such as "coping with hospitalization." The more homogeneous the group, the more specific the focus can be, such as "coping with a heart attack." How this becomes operational will be evident in the examples given in this book.

SUMMARY

This book will deal with the practical and theoretical issues of beginning and maintaining hospital groups. Chapter 2 presents a brief overview of research in the field. Part II discusses various aspects of setting up such groups, especially the importance of recognizing, understanding, and being sensitive to the complexities of the system of the particular medical or psychiatric setting. A hospital group is intimately connected to everything else that goes on in a hospital. Supervision of groups and group leaders is no more isolated from the ongoing operation of the hospital than the group itself is. This is discussed in Chapter 3.

The training and preparation of group leaders is outlined in Chapters 4 and 5. Change is often difficult, and leading such groups can often elicit fear in the leader. The leader's attitude is crucial in maintaining a hospital group, and this is discussed at length. The importance of interdisciplinary teamwork is discussed throughout the book as a whole and highlighted in Chapter 6.

Treating patients' wounded self-esteem and eliciting coping devices are the topics in Part IV. The method promulgated is a supportive one: Patients' ego strengths are reinforced, and technique fostering regression, frustration, or confrontation is discouraged. Most of the people participating in these groups are severely disturbed psychiatric patients or medical patients who have chronic emotional problems or who are in a state of crisis because of the sudden onset of severe illness. They may participate in long-term outpatient groups or in single-session turnover inpatient groups. The hospital experience from the patients' point of view and the overall value of groups for patient rehabilitation are dealt with in Chapters 10 and 11.

The final section of the book looks at groups from the perspective of cost-benefit analysis.

Chapter 2

Research on Group Intervention

In order to put the theory and practice presented in this book in a proper context, it is helpful to review the history of hospital groups and the literature. Literature on groups for psychiatric inpatients is abundant, and efficacy studies have demonstrated the positive effects of group therapy for the severely disturbed. Literature on medical groups is more scarce and spread out.

The first recording of group therapy sessions was in 1905 when an internist, Joseph Henry Pratt (1963), held classes for his tuberculosis patients; he discovered that his patients not only got information about their disease but benefited from mutual support as well. Other medical doctors began to follow his example. However, for some reason, use of groups did not continue to develop in medicine. Instead, psychiatrists such as Lazell, in 1921, and Marsh, in 1931, began using group methods with psychotics (Anthony, 1971). During World War II, group therapy flourished as a means of treating large numbers of people with mental health problems and became more sophisticated as a treatment tool. It is interesting to note that the earliest experimentation in group intervention was with medical patients and schizophrenics—the primary subjects of this book.

EFFICACY STUDIES ON GROUPS IN PSYCHIATRY

The efficacy of group treatment has been demonstrated and developed in the practice of psychiatry. Group workers have shown how the hospital milieu can be assessed and manipulated in order to understand and treat

15

the patients better (Weiner, 1959; Weisman, 1963). Short-term and long-term group treatment have been seen as the treatment choice for schizophrenics in both inpatient and outpatient settings. Research has documented the value of such groups. Youcha (1979, personal communication) at Bronx State Hospital has demonstrated that schizophrenics attending outpatient groups were hospitalized less frequently and for shorter periods and used less medication. O'Brien (1975) also got these results, with the addition that the patients' social functioning improved. Studies of schizophrenics (Parloff and Dies, 1977) and psychiatric inpatients (Houlihan, 1977) showed faster progress among those receiving group therapy than among those not receiving it. There are many more studies, but because "the truth" is so hard to define and prove, the research does not begin to document what professionals have observed and experienced as to the potential of therapeutic group intervention. William Powles (1980) in an institute at the A.G.P.A.*, 1980, stated that group therapy was not a science based on the collection of rigorously tested data but a craft that is taught by apprenticeship (Annual Conference, Institute on Supervision, 1980).

EFFICACY STUDIES ON MEDICAL GROUPS

The picture of group practice in medicine is quite different from that in psychiatry, despite the powerful rationale for the use of group intervention. Literature on the subject is spotty and undeveloped. A popular book on "liaison psychiatry" does not mention group once (Strain and Grossman, 1975). Eisenberg (1980) writes: "Host resistance to pathogenic agents is weakened by social stress and strengthened by social support. . . . The probability of resolving the patient's difficulties will be enhanced by targeting treatment measures at the social components of the illness experience as well as the pathophysiology of the disease process"(p. 277). He continues " . . . inadequate social support is analogous to nutritional deficiency. One cannot write a prescription for spouses and friends . . . yet we can work to improve 'the fit between individual needs and network support structure'" (p. 284). He outlines a number of panaceas for this problem, including the self-help group, but does not refer to the potential of groups led by professionals and integrated into the delivery of medical care. Yet there are a number of journal articles on groups which described them as helpful for treatment of patients with specific disease entities: cancer (Trachtenberg, 1973), postmyocardial infarctions (Fisher

*American Group Psychotherapy Association

and Laufer, 1977), end-stage renal disease (Lubell, 1976) or on specific services: pediatrics (Adams, 1976), rehabilitation, (Oradei and Waite, 1974), primary care (Brickner, 1978), private medicine (Yalom and Greaves, 1977). In *Coping with Physical Illness* Moos (1977) writes of the value of self-help groups. Social workers have written articles documenting the need for use of community meetings on medical inpatient floors (Hallowitz, 1972), and stating the rationale and potential for medical hospital groups (Harm and Golden, 1961). Apaka and Sanges (1962) write of the importance of involvement of the interdisciplinary team and of groups becoming integrated into the ongoing delivery system. In *Newer Dimensions in Health Care*, Brown (1961) suggested that groups be used comprehensively in the hospital setting to give patients the opportunity for peer support, social activity, and mutual aid, cutting through patients' feelings of isolation and helplessness. Frey (1966) elaborates on these themes in an informative survey of groups in hospitals.

While these articles represent the beginnings of a collection of data, none of the authors combine a theoretical basis for a hospital group program with clinical experience from a variety of groups dispersed throughout a general hospital and integrated into the ongoing delivery system of medical care. Frey reports that only one group surveyed in the Northeast had another team member as a co-therapist (not part of program, illustrating how groups can be isolated and not integrated into the hospital system). The groups were usually isolated from the rest of the team's work. Recently, two primary care programs have tried to develop group programs for a variety of outpatients; these groups are integrated into the mainstream of the delivery system (Brickner et al., 1978). Coven, from St. Vincent's Hospital in New York City, has published an article in the International Journal of Group Psychotherapy. Schniewind and Needle (1978) have instituted some life-stage groups in their program.

Some efficacy studies have been done testing the value of group therapy in a medical setting—particularly how it affects course of disease. Schniewind and Needle summarize these studies:

> Group psychotherapy had its origin in primary health care with a "tuberculosis class" started in 1905 by an internist, Dr. Joseph Henry Pratt (1907). An average of 15–20 of his patients met every Friday at the hospital for a "social hour." The class was led by a physician and a volunteer "friendly visitor." Most of the 52 participants in the first two years improved or had their disease arrested.
>
> A few selected reports from the recent literature give an idea of what can be accomplished by the group psychotherapy of problems

common to primary health-care settings: obesity, asthma, myocardial infarction, death and dying, and psychosomatic illness.

Wollershiem (1970) studied 79 overweight female students. Twenty patients were assigned to each of three treatment categories: (1) social-pressure groups for 20 minutes, (2) nonspecific group therapy for 90 minutes, (3) focal-learning therapy for 90 minutes. Nineteen patients were in a control group. Each group consisted of five patients and one therapist, and met for ten sessions. The women in all three treatment groups lost weight, and in the latter group a change in eating behavior was observed. Women in the control group gained weight.

Two excellent papers present the results of long-term group psychotherapy with asthmatic patients. Groen and Pelser (1960) describe two groups led by an internist under psychiatric supervision. Patients in the therapy groups, which met twice a week, did better psychologically and medically than the controls. Sclare and Crocket (1957) report experience with a group of asthmatic women which met one hour a week for two years. The average number of patients per session was 4–5. Of the 25 patients who attended, nine dropped out in less than five sessions. Some patients came regularly over long periods, others came irregularly, some came in spells alternating with periods of absence. They concluded that group therapy does not have a specifically beneficial effect on asthma *per se* but that improvement in certain measured psychological and interpersonal factors contributed to better medical management.

A large sample of post-myocardial-infarction patients were studied by Ibrahim et al. (1974). One hundred eighteen patients were assigned sequentially, 12 at a time, to group therapy or to control status. Five groups, and five control cohorts were thus formed. The therapy groups met for one and a half hours weekly for one year, and were led by one clinical psychologist who fostered interaction and encouraged exploration of emotions and attitudes. They oriented their research around five questions: (1) Will patients who have had a myocardial infarction accept group psychotherapy? Of 140 patients approached by the CCU nurse, 118 or 84 percent accepted. (2) Will their physicians give permission? All physicians approached did. (3) Can these patients participate regularly in this extended form of psychotherapy? The dropout rate was only 16 percent for both the therapy and the control cohorts. (4) Will the patients demonstrate an increase in adaptive behavior to life changes? At the end of the year patients in the therapy groups had a much more positive outlook and did not demonstrate the increased social alienation shown by the controls. (5) Will group psycho-therapy affect the outcome of their heart condition? The percent of patients rehospitalized was the same for both samples. However, group patients stayed an average of 26 days compared to 36 days for the controls. There was no significant difference in any physiological parameters. The one-year survival rate was greater for the group patients, but significant only at the .07 level.

Not all group work with medical patients results in improvement. An interesting short clinical note on nine hypertensive women who attended 4 to 26 group-therapy sessions reports a statistically significant increase in both systolic and diastolic blood pressure. Patients in the control cohort showed a decrease in blood pressure on medical management alone (Titchener, Sheldon, and Ross, 1959). These findings need to be replicated in a larger sample, but may point to a relative medical contraindication for group psychotherapy.

Yalom and Greaves (1977) report on four years of experience as leaders of a group for patients with metastatic cancer. Over 40 patients attended at least one meeting, 20 of them came regularly. Average attendance was 6–7, which they considered an ideal size. Twelve group members died. Because of medical staff interest in learning about how people face death, there were often one or two additional "therapists" at each meeting. Patients encouraged this, and benefited from helping each other.

Patients with classical psychosomatic illness are often seen together in groups. Several experienced authors recommend mixing patients with various psychosomatic problems, medical illness, and neuroses (Brautigam and Ruppell, 1977; Stein, 1971; Garma, 1973). In primary health-care settings, neurotic patients with life-stage problems similar to those being faced by medical patients can be placed in the same group. Broadening the selection criteria in this manner has an additional practical advantage of making it easier to assemble a critical mass of patients in a short enough time to actually start a group.

With one exception these studies illustrate positive effects of group intervention for obese, asthmatic, and cardiac patients. Patients were easier to manage, had shorter rehospitalizations, and were more positive in attitude (less depressed). Although compliance with the medical regimen wasn't uniformly studied, the studies lead one to believe that group intervention could improve compliance. Compliance is of great concern to the medical profession today. The solution to the problem often involves the doctor, nurse, or social worker sitting down and talking with one person after another. These attempts are successful, but if group attendance could accomplish the same thing, it is a wasteful use of time. People leading groups of medical patients have observed that medical patients become more compliant, but it has not been rigorously tested with patients of varying chronic diseases (Coven, 1980).

Medicine is behind psychiatry in its efficacy studies on group intervention and effect on course of diagnosis and treatment, but that does not make groups in medicine less therapeutic: It simply means that they have not been as well researched. Even in psychiatry, more research is needed to test efficacy of groups. For example, practitioners have observed that posthospitalized schizophrenics attending group therapy take less medication and stay on jobs longer. This is in the process of being researched (Sands and Radin, 1978).

RATIONALE FOR MEDICAL GROUPS

The intimate and complex relationship between soma and psyche has been well documented in the literature (Usdin, 1977; Eisenberg, 1980; Engel, 1976). It is also well accepted that optimum delivery of medical care includes treatment of the total patient (Cooper, 1976; Cooper and Cento, 1977; Delbanco, 1975). Studies have shown how emotions, particularly anxiety and depression, affect the recovery of the medically ill (Hackett and Cassem, 1974; Kennedy and Bakst, 1966).

A comprehensive hospital-based group program is one means by which the traditional mind–body split in medicine can be modified; it is a means through which the total patient can be treated efficiently and effectively. A hospital population lends itself to a wide variety of opportunities for group intervention: inpatient and outpatient, private and teaching services. Groups can be short-term and long-term, homogeneous and heterogeneous in terms of medical diagnosis, and composed of acutely and chronically ill patients. Selection of group intervention will involve availability, capacity, and motivation of staff and patients.

As noted earlier, the usual hospital division between psychiatry and medicine is an arbitrary one. Nason and Delbanco (1976) reported a study by Weiss and English in 1949 where at least 50 percent of an outpatient medical population had symptoms and functional illness secondary to emotional and social problems. Panepinto and Kohut (1971) documented the large percentage (53 percent) of alcoholics among an inpatient general-medicine population. Valliant (1979) followed 59 men who rated high on mental health and compared them to a control group; only 2 became chronically ill or died by the age of 53.

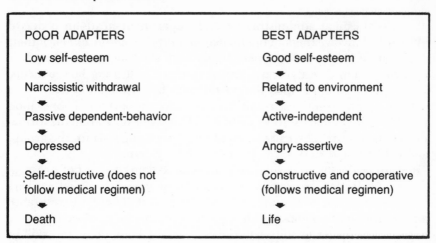

POOR ADAPTERS	BEST ADAPTERS
Low self-esteem	Good self-esteem
↓	↓
Narcissistic withdrawal	Related to environment
↓	↓
Passive dependent-behavior	Active-independent
↓	↓
Depressed	Angry-assertive
↓	↓
Self-destructive (does not follow medical regimen)	Constructive and cooperative (follows medical regimen)
↓	↓
Death	Life

FIGURE 2-1. *Qualities observed in adaptation to illness*

As I first glimpsed a general-hospital population, I was struck by the large numbers of people who were in need of sophisticated and professional emotional support. Two groups of medical patients have stood out for me: those who are very disturbed and withdrawn, and those who were "superstars," coping with a catastrophic illness impressively well. One group was headed toward death and one toward life. Figure 2-1 includes the observable qualities of each group; most people fall in between these extremes.

A HOSPITAL-BASED GROUP PROGRAM FOR MEDICAL PATIENTS

In 1959, the efficacy of groups was demonstrated at St. Vincent's Hospital in New York City when a federally funded demonstration project was introduced in the psychiatry division by the department of social work. The director, Hazel M. Halloran, wished to expand the program in order to use the group modality to help meet the educational and emotional needs of patients in the general hospital division. In 1975, I was hired as group-work coordinator to develop, supervise, maintain, and coordinate this program.

The program developed slowly, as it was first necessary to gain the trust of prospective leaders and administrative, medical, and nursing staff in the various divisions of the general hospital. The associate director of the department of social work, Susanne A. Kohut, and I met with medical directors, hospital administrators, and department heads in order to inform and involve them in the formation of the program and elicit their cooperation. Support from interdisciplinary staff was later enlisted by involving them directly in the group and demonstrating how patients' group participation helped the staff deliver better medical care.

Group leaders got best results in obtaining support and cooperation from interdisciplinary staff when they: (1) involved key staff in the formation of the group; (2) spent sufficient time preparing staff for the group; and (3) educated staff to the purpose of the group.

Group leadership was voluntary. I began to gain the trust of prospective group leaders by working with the most motivated social workers rather than trying to win over the most reluctant. There was resistance among the staff to form groups because of heavy caseloads, former negative group leadership experiences, lack of knowledge and skill in group leadership, and hesitation in working with an additional supervisor (group leaders continued with their casework supervisors and came to me for supervision only in group work). As the first motivated group leaders had rewarding group leadership experiences and developed confidence in my supervision, more staff volunteered to lead groups. Ultimately, 21 M.S.W.s, 4 B.S.W.s, and 11 fieldwork students became group leaders over a period of 32 months.

Most group leaders volunteered because they wanted a good learning experience. I kept this in mind in selecting the group to be formed. Every effort was made to select a group that reflected the interest of the leader and that had the best chance for good attendance (large numbers to draw from and an available, motivated population). Even with this effort, some groups failed to thrive and morale of leaders became a problem.

There were 17 inpatient groups, including groups for patients hospitalized on general-medicine floors (private and nonprivate), patients who were severely ill with progressive deterioration, nursing-home candidates, children, stroke victims, post–myocardial-infarction (heart-attack) patients, open-heart-surgery patients, burn patients, and relatives of severely ill patients.

There were 12 outpatient groups for patients with ongoing medical problems who required self-care (for example, people with diabetes and hypertension), prenatal patients, stroke victims, asthmatic children, cystic fibrosis patients, cancer patients, and parents who had chronically ill or disabled children. Three groups combined inpatients and outpatients; they included groups for dialysis patients, patients with gastrointestinal problems, and hemiplegics.

Table 2-1 shows the number of groups and attendance in the first 32 months of the program. The figures reflect the slow beginning of the

TABLE 2-1
Hospital-based Group Program for Medical Patients over 32 Months

	No. of Meetings			Attendance Per Group			Attendance Per Meeting		Majority Attended: No. of Meetings		Most Meetings Attended		Age Range
	Total	Avg. No.	Range	Total	Avg. No.	Range	Avg. No.	Range	Avg. No.	Range	Avg. No.	Range	(Yrs.)
Inpatient (N=17)	378	22.5	3-63	1200	70.5	6-215	3.9	2-6	1.4	1-2	4.8	1-12	3-92
Outpatient (N=12)	535	44.6	9-108	522	43.5	6-205	3.6	2-7	7.0	1-25	17.8	4-73	6-80
Combined In- and Out-Patient (N=3)	68	22.6	20-28	66	22	5-53	2.7	2-3.2	3.5	1.5-6	11.6	7-16	20-84
Total (N=32)	981	30.6	3-108	1788	55.5	5-215	3.7	1.6-7.1	3.6	1-25	11.5	1-75	3-92

program and results of the more developed group program after some learning from mistakes and trust by the hospital network was established. Ages of members ranged from 3 to 92.

As is evident in the table, there were more inpatient groups than outpatient and more than twice the number of patients attended them. These inpatient groups tended to have a high turnover, and the leaders, who for the most part were assigned exclusively to the inpatient service, did not continue with them as long as the outpatient groups. The average attendance at meetings was similar for both types of group. (The average is low and illustrates that we have much to learn!) The outpatient groups tended to meet for longer periods of time with fewer patients attending during the life of the group. Outpatient groups had more consistency of membership and were more "closed" than inpatient groups.

The results of this program are incorporated throughout this book. In summary, the groups: (1) enhanced self-esteem of patients, contributing to better morale and capacity for self-care; (2) cut through patients' depression, withdrawal, feelings of helplessness and anxiety; (3) helped to positively change the atmosphere of a floor or clinic; (4) encouraged patients to be assertive with staff and with one another; (5) helped the team learn about basic characteristics of a given population; (6) facilitated patients' education in regard to their illness; (7) helped the interdisciplinary team communicate and work together; (8) elicited new information from patients that was crucial in making treatment plans; and (9) identified patients who had not previously been recognized by staff as needing special help.

Part II

HOW TO BEGIN GROUPS IN MEDICAL AND PSYCHIATRIC SETTINGS

Chapter 3

Working within the System

What is "the system?" First of all, it is the entire institution or setting within which the group takes place. It includes the structure of administration and funding sources; the hierarchy within the agency, both formal and informal; the structure of the floor, clinic, or department within which the group operates, as well as the department of which the group leader and supervisor are a part. John Muir, the great naturalist, summed it up well: "When we try to pick out anything by itself, we find it hitched to everything else in the universe" (1916, p. 211). Both the supervisor and the group leader have to begin by understanding and working within the hospital system.

ANALYZE THE SYSTEM

When Frey (1966) did her survey of hospital medical groups in 1966, she found some talented social group workers who were sensitive to systems networks and teamwork. The literature already reflected concern over the hospital system and how it affected the recovery of the patient. Frank (1952) wrote that the group therapist should be cognizant of the hospital society and work with it. Galinsky and Galinsky (1967) studied three organization styles in mental hospitals: custodial, individual treatment, and milieu treatment. They looked at power structure, staff practices, sanctioning power, and belief systems. They found that the patient subsystems reflected the hierarchal structure of staff. Patients in custodial hospitals had peer groups which were rigid, with minimal supportive interaction. This was in contrast to the milieu hospital where peer

27

groups and staff had positive interaction. Astrachan et al. (1970) reported on a day hospital that was designed according to system theory concepts.

Accurately analyzing a hospital system and its problems is difficult. Berne (1966) suggests that the group leader make an authority diagram. Kernberg (1978) believes that too often we ascribe problems to the leader when, in fact, the problem is that the assigned task is impossible to perform (for example, "curing the patient"). He feels that the following should be looked at: (1) the nature of the task and its constraints; (2) the optimal administrative structure required for the task; (3) the nature and amount of authority functionally required by the leader; (4) the leader's technical and conceptual skills and liabilities; and (5) the leader's personality characteristics, which might be involved in the problem.

In order to form a group in a hospital, one is totally dependent on many people's cooperation: interdisciplinary colleagues, administrators, supervisors, and patients. To ignore this fact is to sabotage one's own work. Yet for some it is not a pleasant reality to face; many of us would prefer to think of ourselves as autonomous rather than as part of an interdependent network.

Like many others, I had to learn about my dependence on others the hard way. I was a consultant on a weekly basis to an agency in which I had enjoyed high status and respect. Staff members seemed to be highly appreciative of what I had to offer. I was outside the system, giving feedback, and I was seen as a "gift" and not as a threat. When I accepted a position as a full-time staff member and tried to fulfill my assignment as supervisor and administrator, I found myself working within the system. Although I needed the support of the male director, my insensitivity to the intense rivalry in this system for his support rendered my job extremely difficult.

At my next job, which involved developing a group program for medical patients, I knew that I had to form relationships with every key staff member—something I had not done in my former position. First came my immediate supervisor (without her cooperation I could be bogged down by administrative detail); then those who supervised staff that would work with me (without their support I would have no one to supervise); then, the trainees themselves (without their motivation I would have no group leaders); then, the interdisciplinary team (without their cooperation we would have no patients for the group); and finally, administration (they would provide space, funding, publicity). I began my new job by meeting with one person after another. The associate director of the department arranged for me to meet with every medical director, department head, and appropriate adminstrator.

ELICIT STAFF SUPPORT

It is important not to be in a hurry to start a group or a group program. The initial discussions with key people are a crucial part of beginning. In fact, it *is* beginning. It is as crucial as setting the stage for a theater production.

During these initial meetings, group leaders have to have a sense of humility, patience, and flexibility. They cannot be narcissistically tied to their original ideas; they must be able to modify their ideas in accordance with staff and group members' contributions. From the beginning, leaders have to view the group as a "shared" group. If interdisciplinary staff participate in the formation of the group in the thinking stage, they will also have an investment in the group, and the group will reflect their ideas as well as those of the leaders.

Borriello, in working with psychiatric patients, writes that a group is doomed if the system is not analyzed and staff support not elicited. "The therapist must present his group therapy as supportive of what staff is already doing, not as something that will supercede or replace staff's activities" (1976, p. 101). Apaka and Sanges (1962) describe how a group leader started with a relatives' group in a medical setting because this would be least threatening to medical staff; the group leader was a social worker, and the doctors had gotten used to them working with relatives. To start with a patient group would have meant introducing medical staff to two new concepts. Winder and Medalie (1973) found that the parents were an important part of the system that they had ignored in forming a group for cystic fibrosis teenagers. They concluded that in future groups they would have more ongoing communication with parents so that their group would not be sabotaged.

The leader has to appreciate that a group means a change in the system. When one thing changes in a system, everything else must change as well. This means that every person the leader engages will have to experience change, and this can be threatening. In a medical setting doctors may see the group as diminishing their control of the patient. Nurses may see group attendance as taking time away from other important patient activities such as sleep and rehabilitation.

Staff may also be afraid that: (1) patients will hurt each other in the group, (2) misery does *not* like company, (3) group participation will increase patients' depression, (4) they will be "bad-mouthed" in the groups, and (5) negativity will be contagious, and there will be patient rebellion and more malpractice suits.

These fears, which will be discussed in this book, are not unfounded and should be taken seriously. The new leader has to attend to them in the preparatory discussion as well as in ongoing meetings with the interdisciplinary team. In fact, the new leader may have such fears as well.

A helpful approach is for the leader to learn from each person in the preparatory sessions. The leader may ask certain questions:

1. What is the person's job like?
2. What role does the person play in the institution?
3. What need, if any, does this person see the group fulfilling?
4. What kind of group would help this person in the performance of his or her job?
5. Would this person like to visit or participate in the group?
6. Would periodic reports of the group be helpful?
7. What does this person think would be a good place, time, and day for the group?
8. What would be the best way to continue communication?

Once leaders establish the need for the group and how the group is going to help the person being engaged, they can ask for something in return. The discussion should end with a contract where both parties benefit. For example, the leader will help a medical doctor deal with noncompliant patients by having them in a group, and the doctor will agree to encourage patients to attend the group and ask them about the group after they have attended. The leader will report the content of the meeting to the doctor, who promises to read the leader's notes each week.

OBTAIN SANCTION

Group leaders often underestimate the profundity of what they have to offer. It is important that they see (or make explicit) the relationship between the goal of the group and the goal of the agency (Gitterman, 1979). In a psychiatric setting the leader has to understand and be able to communicate how group attendance will help the schizophrenic recover: more explicitly, *how group interaction helps break through narcissistic withdrawal* (see Chapter 8). Groups formed in a general hospital have to be directly connected with the effort to speed patients' *physical* recovery. People contract with a medical hospital to get help with their physical health; groups that are seen as enhancing emotional health without affecting physical recovery are not appropriate in a medical setting. With the formation of each group, the leader has to answer to the question, "How does this group help the physical recovery of its membership?" or "Where does the hospital need help in improving the medical care it provides?"

There are certain areas where hospitals have particular difficulty administering optimum medical care. For example, administration is often in need of a feedback mechanism from the population it is serving. The group can serve this purpose. In one instance, when administration was thinking about making a service coed, they asked the group leaders to elicit feedback from patients on this idea. The patients' response was more positive than negative, and the plan was implemented.

Shulman (1979) feels that the group is an ideal place for patients and staff to communicate better. He gives an example where a doctor comes to a medical group and answers patients' questions, with positive results. Patients said that they did not ask questions of doctors outside the group because the doctors were too busy and they were more afraid of the answers. In another example, nurses shared their frustrations in response to patients' complaints. It furthered understanding between staff and patients. Weisman (1963) described how a group worker on a psychiatric unit helped mediate when the hospital's goals and patients' goals were in conflict. Lipton and Malter (1971) stress the importance of the group worker being able to identify with both patient and administrative systems in order to succeed in the mediator role.

Another frequent area of frustration for hospital staff is noncompliance of medical patients. Coven (1981) describes the frustration staff feels:

> Physicians' notes frequently mentioned "depression" or "anxiety"; yet both doctors and nurses admitted to feeling much more upset about the depression or anxiety than the patient did. "Patient not complying!" "Patient says she just cannot lose weight!" and "Patient says he cannot cook without salt!" were frequent chart entries (p. 101).

She presented group treatment as a way of helping staff with this difficult population.

OBTAIN VERTICAL AND HORIZONTAL SANCTION

Gitterman (1979) mentions the need for vertical and horizontal organizational sanction. These are crucial. Some of the most difficult situations in beginning groups have arisen out of neglect of these areas. In one instance, the leader of a parents' group arranged for a volunteer to babysit. She assumed that the volunteer could take the children to the cafeteria during the group session. Although the supervisor met with the director of nutrition when forming the group program, the head of the cafeteria was not included in the planning process of this group. As it turned out, the children were not welcome in the cafeteria; however, if the nutritionist had been included in the formation stage of the group, she would probably have been accommodating.

Two groups that I supervised in a general hospital failed because we had not properly analyzed the medical hierarchy. In both instances we got approval for the groups from the medical directors, and we assumed their approval would filter down to the attending staff. We learned that the directors were not the true leaders of the department but that an attending physician was the real source of power and leadership. The attending physician insisted on termination of the group. Had we engaged him in the planning stage, the group would have reflected his needs and he would have been more likely to "own" it.

The groups with private patients at St. Vincent's Hospital became possible because supervisors and group leaders were successful in obtaining vertical sanction from the true leader of the department. Prior to the group, private doctors on this service would not agree to social workers routinely seeing their patients; social work contact had to be through referral. The former medical director, Dr. William J. Grace (now deceased), was extremely experienced and respected. He was struggling with how to meet the emotional needs of his patients so that their physical recovery would be improved. He agreed that groups could help him achieve this goal and invited me to a meeting with his attendings, where he voiced his enthusiasm. Slowly, private doctors began to agree to their patients coming to the groups.

One example illustrating the importance of horizontal approval is an inpatient group where in one meeting there were 14 interruptions by nursing staff. We concluded that the nursing staff may have had a need for the social worker's attention, since many of the nurses on this floor were young and inexperienced. The social worker began meeting with them and helping them with their overwhelming feelings toward the patients. Interruptions of the group stopped, and some nurses began to participate.

Another example of need for horizontal approval occurred in an outpatient group of working, posthospitalized mental patients. One patient lost her job: Her self esteem was greatly affected and she needed another job desperately. She competed in the job market and had one rejection after another. It became obvious that she needed a special placement, which could only be arranged through a vocational counselor. This patient needed more than the group therapist's therapeutic skills. The leader was dependent on her team members: the doctor for prescribing medication and the vocational counselor. Without their help, this group member would have continued to regress.

COMMUNICATE WITH STAFF

Because the leader is dependent on key people in the hospital, it is important to conduct ongoing communication with team members in every medium possible. Usually this takes the form of: (1) written communication through "memos," (2) formal verbal communication through attendance at staff meetings, and (3) informal verbal communication. One form of communication should not exclude the other.

WRITE A MEMO

A memo introducing the group to staff is a formalization of what has been decided upon in the preparatory sessions. The memo should include: time, day, place, number of group sessions; description of eligible population; rationale for the group, including its relationship to medical or psychiatric care; focus and goal of the group; when and how evaluation of the group will take place; referral procedure; how ongoing communication with staff will take place; the kind of help and support the leader wants from staff.

The memo should go out to all people seen in preparatory discussions, as well as key people in the vertical and horizontal structure. It is often hard to know who all these people are, but it pays to make an extra effort to find out. No matter how thorough you are, you may leave out someone important, only to have them sabotage your group or take much of your time as you try to gain their support.

Timing of the memo is important. In a few instances at St. Vincent's Hospital, we were lax about sending out the memo before the group started, thinking that we had approached everyone verbally anyway. The results were disastrous, and in one instance a group was forced to terminate. It pays to be conservative and overly cautious in a setting that is so complex and often beyond the range of our understanding.

OBTAIN PRIVATE PHYSICIANS' APPROVAL

It is often difficult for the group leader in a medical setting to communicate with patients' private doctors, who are frequently not on the service at the same time as the group leader. Yet such communication is crucial because the doctor is often the most important relationship in the patient's life; the doctor has power and status in the hospital hierarchy; and the doctor traditionally assumes responsibility for total care of the patient (including his or her emotional needs) and therefore may be quite possessive of the patient.

To: Attendings, residents, interns, nurses in general medicine clinic

From: K. N., Department of Social Work

Re: Hypertension group

Many patients in the Adult General-Medicine Clinic have been diagnosed as hypertensive. Problems such as failure to follow medications and diet are frequently seen in such patients. Side effects of certain prescribed medications may also influence the patient's decision to disregard a medical regimen. Denial and other emotional responses such as sadness, anger, and guilt are often associated with hypertension. It is my belief that patients with hypertension can be helped to deal with many of the problems associated with their illness within a group situation. In the group, patients might be able to discuss the nature and treatment of high blood pressure, explore their emotional responses to chronic illness, and have the opportunity to share with other group members the experience of a common illness. It is my hope that the group will become an effective method of patient education, giving a sound, informative groundwork for understanding the illness and creating a peer support system to help meet some of the patients' emotional needs. Interdisciplinary staff participation is encouraged, particularly in dealing with patients' concerns about the nature of treatment of hypertension.

The group will begin on Friday, March 18, and will run for a six-week period, at which time its usefulness will be evaluated by patients and staff. Meetings will take place from 12:45 to 1:45 p.m. in the Social Service Department, third floor, Lowenstein Building. Patients will be requested to register at the clinic desk, making clinic staff aware of their presence at group. By doing so, patients will be assured of seeing the doctor on a first-come first-served basis at the conclusion of group meetings. Referrals for group will be accepted from nurses and doctors in the clinic. The patients will be prescreened by me. Criteria for selection of patients to group are an established diagnosis of hypertension, an ability to communicate, and an interest and willingness to invest specific time.

I welcome suggestions and comments from staff at any time. Your support in facilitating group attendance will be greatly appreciated.

FIGURE 3-1. *Memo to staff from group leader*

To: Department of Medicine

From: J. Q., Department of Social Work
      E. P., Department of Medicine

Re: Post–Myocardial-infarction Group

In response to attending physicians' interest in the potential of groups to help their patients adjust to their illnesses, we are beginning a group program on the private service by offering a group to patients who are recovering from myocardial infarcts. Only a limited number of patients will be invited to attend this trial group because of the extensive time that such a group requires. The group is tentatively planned to meet once a week through July and August.

The intent of the group is to encourage patients to communicate with hospital and staff and each other about fears, anxieties, and questions that cardiac disease has created for them. So much of today's literature has stressed the importance of the psychosocial aspects of cardiac disease and urges that staff combine areas of expertise in dealing with these patients. Defensive denial will not be challenged in the group. Instead, we wish to allow patients the opportunity to provide emotional and social support for each other, breaking through feelings of isolation.

Every effort will be made to personally contact private physicians whose patients will be involved in the group. However, as this contact is not always possible, notes will be left on the patients' charts indicating our intent to include the patient in the group and to communicate pertinent information about his behavior in the group.

We welcome feedback from any interested staff. Mrs. Q. can be reached at Ext. 82, and Dr. P. can be paged.

FIGURE 3-2. *Memo to attending physicians from group leaders*

In beginning a group program, it is often necessary to get permission from the doctor for the patient to attend the group. In an open-ended inpatient group where membership changes each week, the leader may have to communicate with a number of different doctors each week. This can be a tedious and time-consuming process, since it may include one or more of the following tasks:

1. Administrative permission, whereby the medical director or hospital administrator gives permission to the group leader to work with all private patients (even if this sanction is operative, the adminis-

tration often wants to elicit permission from physicians so as not to alienate them and assure fuller cooperation).

2. Overall permission, whereby the doctor gives the leader permission to screen all of his or her patients.
3. Phone calls to every doctor every week eliciting permission.
4. A brief note on the medical chart, asking the doctor to check whether his or her patient can attend.
5. A letter on the chart, explaining the purpose of the group and asking if patient may attend.

The reader may already know or guess how cumbersome it is to get the physician's approval for each person who attends the group. A talented potential group leader with a heavy work load may refuse to have a group with private patients solely on this basis. Sometimes notes are left on the chart and not seen or responded to by the doctor. The leader may then telephone, only to find that the doctor is not available. How can these difficulties be minimized?

The group leader with good collaborative skills can eventually form a relationship with a doctor, resulting in an "overall permission." Sometimes a doctor will give consent because colleagues report good experiences with the groups. But this takes time; until then, notes or letters usually have to be left on the medical chart.

It is a help if letters or notes are typed and copied in bulk, so that each week the leader can bring a stack of letters to the floor and put them on charts of suitable group candidates. The letters should have a space where the date, name of doctor, and name of patient may be written in. The doctor's task is simplified if there are "I approve" or "I disapprove" boxes to check and initial.

The letter needs to be put where it is highly visible. It should be put in front of the chart or, if filed inside, placed by the progress sheet which the doctor is going to write on. Letters can be filed in the chart *after* they have been checked.

Steps to counteract the problem of doctors' not signing the letters include administrative approval of attendance; head-nurse screening; and leader's reinforcement of doctor's signing the letters.

Some medical directors will allow the group leader to add a clause such as: "If you do not initial this letter or check a box, I will assume you give permission for attendance." Sometimes medical staff will not trust the social work leader's screening capacities but will trust the head nurse's judgment. Often the head nurse, who knows the doctors, will assume responsibility for selecting patients for the group and placing them in the group. If the head nurse is a co-therapist, the problem of recruitment is lessened considerably. Many doctors are more comfortable trusting their patients with nurses than with social workers, psychologists, or psychiatrists. At other times social workers are less of a threat than psychiatrists because the psychiatrist often comes in as a consultant and is not part of the ongoing treatment team, and because patients may get the message that they are sick emotionally and need group therapy.

When a doctor overlooks signing a note of permission, the leader must be sure to let the doctor know the importance of signing the note in the future. When the leader telephones the doctor for permission, the leader can briefly explain the difficulty of making calls each week before the meeting. When the doctor does sign the form, the leader can reward the doctor for this act by voicing appreciation. Repetition and reinforcement can be helpful in changing physicians' behavior.

Figure 3-4 is an example of a more formal letter. Note that the director of medicine has signed the letter. It is always helpful to let the private doctor know that top administrative personnel support the group. Note also that in this particular group the head nurse and social worker on the floor are co-therapists.

At St. Vincent's Hospital most doctors checked the first box after the first year. Occasionally doctors checked the third box but it was rare for doctors to check the second box. Eventually the letter becomes a formality in that permission is not required, but it serves another important purpose: It is a way of reminding doctors that the group is taking place and their patients are participating, so that they will remember to discuss the group with their patients.

I would like to invite _____ to attend the orientation group that meets on Thursday afternoon at 1:00 p.m. on Smith 8. The group will help to orient children to hospital routine, as well as allow the children to interact with their peers.

Please let me know if you would like your patient to attend the group by checking the box below. If neither box is checked, I will assume your permission is granted.

☐ Yes, you may invite my patient to the group.

☐ No, you may not invite my patient to the group.

FIGURE 3-3. *Chart note from group leader to attending physician*

Date:

Dear Dr. _____ ,

The supportive group for patients recovering from myocardial infarcts continues to meet on Cronin 7, Wednesdays, at 11:00 a.m. L. H., R.N., and F. A., M.S.W., co-lead the group.

From our point of view, these weekly meetings prove to be helpful as an opportunity for patients to: communicate feelings and concerns; be educated about the illness, treatment, and process of recovery; receive mutual support; and share different modes of coping.

Often patients reveal information about themselves in the group that is helpful to the doctor in planning comprehensive treatment for the patient. After each meeting, Mr. A. will write a summary of the patient's participation on a social work grey sheet which will be filed in the chart.

We would like your patient _____ to attend the group this week. All attendance is voluntary. *Please check one of the boxes below and initial.*

    ☐ I *approve* of the patient attending the meeting.

    ☐ I *disapprove* of the patient attending the meeting.

    ☐ The head nurse should use her discretion on the day of the meeting, since patient's course of recovery is presently uncertain.

As always, we thank you for your interest and cooperation.

_____   _____   _____
Head Nurse   Social Worker   Director
                                      Department of
                                      Medicine

FIGURE 3-4. *Formal letter to attending physician*

REACH OUT TO STAFF IN OTHER WRITTEN FORMS

Group leaders can use a written format in a variety of ways. In a hospital setting it is nearly impossible to over-communicate. Each leader will have his or her own unique way of reaching out to staff on all levels. Figure 3-5 is a sample of an annotated bibliography that was distributed to team members as a means of orienting them to the value of group treatment for emotionally disturbed, noncompliant medical patients. In Figure 3-6, Chetrick and Woods (1979) attach to their memo regarding the goals and values of groups for the relatives of burn patients an excerpt from an article.

COMMUNICATE VERBALLY

The group leader should seize any opportunity for formal or informal communication. Gifford, Landis, and Ackerly (1953) describe how they integrated their group work into the ongoing functioning of a psychiatric unit: The group leaders participated in patient rounds and all administrative meetings. Many group leaders discuss the formation of new groups in rounds or weekly interdisciplinary staff meetings. In order to win private doctors' support for groups in a general hospital, I attended their monthly business meetings periodically. As a way of getting greater support from house staff, I attended the residents' orientation and administrative meetings. In a group for working schizophrenics where referrals came from vocational counselors, the therapists met with a large group of vocational counselors and their administrators and presented content from beginning group meetings.

Often informal communication is the most powerful. The best interdisciplinary co-leadership teams I have seen were leaders recruited through friendships. Sometimes the leader can win the support of staff members negative to groups by spending time with them and talking about something totally different. Group leaders can use all of their therapeutic skills in eliciting cooperation by viewing the entire system and its parts (who are people) as their client. I have often felt that actually leading the group is the easiest part of maintaining a group in a hospital setting.

One of the primary purposes of the group is to elicit feedback and information from the patient so that diagnosis and treatment will be enhanced. On an inpatient service this benefit cannot occur unless leaders communicate with the team immediately after the meeting and before the patient is discharged. If this cannot be done verbally, it has to be done in writing. It is also useful for leaders to document their work in the medical chart, thus accounting for their time and quality of work. However, it is not uncommon for a leader to write a summary on a patient and file it in the chart where interdisciplinary staff never see it. If the note is placed in front of the chart or on the progress sheet, staff will see the note and be able to use the information.

The reader may be concerned about confidentiality. Should the group leader share with staff what a patient reveals in the group? Interestingly, out of 3,000 patients and relatives who participated in 1,400 group

Bibliography (Distributed by Carol R. Coven)

Cooper, Elaine J. 1976. Beginning a Group Program in a General Hospital.
   Group: news journal of the Eastern Group Psycho. Society.6-9:9.
"The success of our program has been facilitated by nurses, doctors, and
social workers working together; support from the department's
administrative and supervisory staff; and supervised group leaders who are
intelligent, motivated, creative, and courageous. . . .This program has
demonstrated the effectiveness of groups being integrated into the medical
treatment plan and having direct input from the interdisciplinary team."

Lonergan, Elaine Cooper. Group for Medical Patients: A Treatment for
   Damaged Self-Esteem. *GROUP*, Summer, 1980, 4(2):36-45.
"But what about the patient in this process? Despite the fact that groups
are . . .focused on hospitalizations or illnesses, patients found themselves
interacting with peers and their 'old self' emerged. Without realizing it, they
seemed to momentarily forget their illness and be 'themselves.' When this
happened the patient became more than a 'sick' person but a person who
had a long history, with unique characteristics and interpersonal skills, and
someone capable of contributing to one's fellow man."

Coven, Carol R. Fantasy to Reality: Beginning Group Treatment in the
   Medical Clinic. Unpublished.
"Group has developed into a critical and exploratory support system for
people who previously had little contact or in-depth interaction with other.
. . .In group it has become less frightening for these patients to face the
despair/hope dichotomy of their illnesses . . .and the importance of their
emotions in physical health."

Schniewind, H. E. 1976. A Psychiatrist's Experience in a Primary Care
   Setting. *Internat. J. Psychiat. in Med.* 7(3):235.
"A group-therapy program, developed with one of the social workers, is
one of the primary ways in which direct psychiatric service is made
available to the Center's patients."

Schniewind, H. E. and Needle, A. 1978. Group Work: A Component of
   Primary Health Care. Presented at the annual meeting of the American
   Psychiatric Association. 10 May, 1978, p. 10
"Group therapy is an efficient and effective way to care for the vast, often
unrecognized, psychosocial aspects of physical illness."

Nason, Frances and Delbanco, Thomas. 1976. Soft Services: A Major,
   Cost-Effective Component of Primary Medical Care. *Social Work in
   Health Care* 1(3):297.
"An effective program of ambulatory care must eliminate mind-body split in
medicine and integrate the emotional and physical components of its
services."

FIGURE 3-5. *Annotated bibliography used for staff education*

To: Burn unit staff

From: C.C., C.S.W., and B. W., B.S.N., co-leaders

Re: Group meeting for friends and relatives of burn unit patients

This is to inform you that a group for the friends and relatives of the burn patients will begin meeting on Wednesday, May 2, 1979 from 2:30 to 3:30 p.m. on St. Gerard's Hall. The group will continue to meet weekly at the same time and place.

We will be bringing families from the burn unit to St. Gerard's where a space is available for us to hold the group sessions.

The purposes of this group are as follows:

1. To educate friends and family about the problems facing burn patients (we hope to eventually have slides to use as visual aids).
2. To demonstrate staff concern for patients and those close to them.
3. To use professional time in a more efficient way by educating and providing emotional support in a group format. This support is frequently carried out by group members beyond the actual meeting time.
4. To provide a forum for questions and feedback.
5. To provide emotional supports to alleviate fears and feelings of hopelessness among those relatives close to patients (for elaboration, see attached reference).
6. To plan for discharge and the patient's ongoing needs.

We consider these purposes in keeping with the stated philosophy and objectives of the burn unit.

We are eager to have your feedback regarding relatives and friends who attend and we will keep you informed regarding the relatives' participation in the group.

Excerpt from "Adjustment problems of the family of the burn patient," by G. Bròdland and N. Andreasen. In *Coping with Physical Illness*, ed. Rudolf H. Moos, 1977, pp. 167–176.

"A second way of providing communication and understanding among relatives would be the establishment of group-support meetings. A group composed of family members or close friends of patients currently on the burn unit could meet at a regularly scheduled time once or twice weekly. The group would remain in existence, although membership changed as the patient population changed. Ideally, this group would be conducted by

FIGURE 3-6. *Memo to burn unit staff with excerpt included*

41

a pair of group leaders—a psychiatric social worker and a nurse or physician who are members of the burn unit treatment team. A physical therapist, a dietician active on the burn unit, and a psychiatrist familiar with the problems of adjustment to chronic illness would be other potential members or guest visitors.

"The establishment of such a group would serve several purposes. It would demonstrate to the beleaguered relatives the interest and concern of the hospital staff, sometimes prone to leave relatives out of the picture because of their concern for primary patient care; regular group meetings would make efficient use of the professionals' time and experience. The meetings would also serve to educate relatives about problems of burn trauma, particularly when discharge draws near. Family members often take on primary responsibility for the patient at discharge, and they greatly need adequate information about wound care, the need for continuing physical therapy, and the problems of emotional and social adjustment. The group discussions would provide relatives with an open forum for raising questions. . . .They would provide emotional support by strengthening the bonds formed between family members and alleviate some feelings of fear, frustration, futility, and boredom. Such a group would not be designed as therapy, but as a means of sharing strength and information. Limited experience with such group meetings on burn units indicates, however, that often staff members also receive information and support from them."

FIGURE 3-6. (continued)

meetings composed of private and nonprivate patients at St. Vincent's Hospital, only a handful of members expressed concern over confidentiality. Most members wanted their needs conveyed to staff. They saw leaders as representatives of staff and the group as an opportunity to communicate with the people responsible for their medical care. Occasionally, when a hospital group composed of nonprivate patients griped about nursing care, they were afraid of retaliation. They wanted anonymity in that their concerns would be conveyed as a group and not as individuals. Usually, the leader encouraged the members to speak up for themselves. When they refused out of fear, they discussed exactly which concerns the leader should relate to staff.

Some leaders were concerned about sharing detail of patients' participation with certain staff members whom they felt would abuse the communication. The leaders tended to be tactful in how they presented material on the summary sheet, knowing that a number of people would read it. I know of one bad experience where a doctor went in to see his patient and said, "Oh, I heard you were bad in the group today!" in a brazen and offensive manner. This can happen, and group leaders tended to reveal personal data in accordance with their degree of trust of their team members. There is a dilemma here, since good medical care is contingent on a team being open and sharing information about the patient. On the other hand, some team members are more sensitive than others. Articles on primary team care illustrate the problems of a team working together (Beckhard and Kyte, 1974; Delbanco, 1975; Kindig, 1975; Lamberts, 1975). Unfortunately, most medical institutions today do not have this kind of exchange.

It is important for a leader to let staff know the positive results of group intervention, particularly in a medical setting, where a number of staff have never had patients in group treatment or shared patients with a group leader. A private doctor who would not allow any of his patients to attend a group finally let two come and eventually became the group's most avid supporter. When I asked him what made him change his mind, he said, "I'm the kind of doctor who listens to my patients, and they have told me how the group helps them." In other words, in his view the group demonstrated that it was helpful in the most relevant way: His patients were pleased with it.

If groups can help medical staff with such problems as patient compliance, patient management, and health education and help administration with cost containment, the hospital may be quick to sanction the groups. At St. Vincent's Hospital the obstetrics staff was frustrated by Hispanic patients who tended to become hysterical in labor and delivery. They were troubled by the increasing hostility they were feeling toward these patients. When it was suggested that a group might be helpful, the leader had their support. When the group demonstrated that it *did* make a difference in patient management, the leader got even more support (Cooper and Cento, 1977).

It was also demonstrated to medical staff and administration that groups could help with patient compliance and health education, which contributed to the support of the group program. One instance where compliance was demonstrated was with a dialysis patient who had constant weight gain and repeated hospitalizations. After weekly group attendance, his weight problem ceased, and he did not have a hospitalization for three and a half years. He became the longest living dialysis patient among patients seen within a six-year period; the medical chief of the unit attributed this success in large part to group attendance and made his view known to others. An instance where education was demonstrated was in a prenatal group where a patient refused a sonogram because she thought it was a dangerous X ray. After the meeting she arranged to have one. Staff was impressed and pleased by the change in the woman's attitude. In another instance, a member of the Hispanic prenatal group had a stillborn baby and was going to sue the hospital, assuming mistakenly that it was at fault. Because the woman had attended the group, the leader had a relationship with her and was able to clarify the situation and soothe her. She became more amicable and staff was greatly pleased. Since the woman had no outstanding difficulties during pregnancy, she would not have been seen by the social worker if there was no group for her to attend. Staff understood this and was appreciative that the leader included all Hispanic prenatal patients in her group.

Demonstration is especially important in settings where groups are new or referrals are needed from people who are not familiar with the therapeutic potential of group intervention. Demonstration is a slow process, often starting with one, two, or three successful cases. Gradually the word gets around. One must be concerned not with the pace at which one is winning support from staff but with the direction in which the support is moving: positive or negative. If the leader is gaining support, even if it is slow, he should keep going! Each setting has a different pace, and at one point things begin to snowball, either positively or negatively, and the group's ultimate fate becomes clear.

SUMMARY

The supervisor and the group leader must give the hospital system meticulous attention from the moment the group is conceived. The idea for a group should be tested out with members of various levels of staff. Every effort should be made to involve other profssionals in the idea stage of the group and to follow up initial overtures with personal contacts and memos. In order to start a group the leader must have vertical and horizontal sanction. As the group becomes a reality, the leader must demonstrate to other staff the value of the service being offered. If the group is integrated into the ongoing teamwork, the patients will benefit and the treatment team will be continually involved in evaluating the group. Ultimately, the group should be seen as an essential treatment tool for *all* staff in delivering quality patient care.

Chapter 4

Training and Supervising Group Leaders

Leading hospital groups can be considered one of the most difficult areas of group leadership to learn. Hopsital groups can have an infinite variety of unpredictable compositions. Inpatient groups can have a different composition of people every week: the leader often does not know before the meeting who will definitely attend, and only the most apparent "misfits" for the group are weeded out. Thus a group leader has to learn group technique suitable for disturbed, fragile, and emotionally strong people; young and old people; consistent membership and inconsistent membership; homogeneous and heterogeneous groups; and closed and open groups.

Leaders have to have some knowledge of the illness they are working with, and some have to be able to handle such things as aphasics in a group; patient organicity and volatility; management of wheelchairs, intravenous poles, and other equipment, and so forth. Here are two examples of the kinds of difficult situations that come up in medical groups. In both instances the group members were more comfortable with one another than the leaders anticipated.

> One social worker came to supervision and reported that she had a good meeting but wished she was there to enjoy it. The supervisor looked at her inquisitively. She said a man in a group of two other women said he needed a bedpan. She went searching for one. She noticed as she walked by the room that the patients were talking amiably. When she finally returned to the group with the bedpan, the patient had urinated on the floor. The women said, "We understand—we've had such problems," and the three of them kept on talking calmly.

45

A social worker was leading a group of four women, one of whom had vaginal cancer. This patient had told the leader before the group that she was bleeding a lot, and other members might find her repulsive. The worker said that she could leave the group if she was uncomfortable. During the group meeting she ended up standing by a sink in the room, in back of the other patients but where the leader could see her, blotting blood from her vagina, but also listening to the conversation. The other members were actively involved in a group discussion and didn't seem to be aware of or mind what was going on behind them.

There is often a "misfit" in the group—someone out of step with the others. Having an isolated group member is not helpful for the patient or the group. Groups leaders have to be prepared to handle difficult participants such as a monopolizer or an aggressive, hostile person; the leader of the group, not a negative patient leader, must set the tone for the meeting. The group leader has to learn to facilitate group interaction and handle group discussion sensitively, in a manner that enhances patients' self-esteem and group cohesion. This task involves handling similarities and differences among group members. Group leaders can diffuse potentially destructive group conflict by bringing the group together around commonality, while allowing for patient differences. In this way, the group becomes a supportive experience for all the members. When the leader conveys acceptance and comfort with all feelings, patients can begin to feel more comfortable with their own conflicting feelings and not act out their internal conflict with other patients.

Constructive conflict can occur in the group and needs to be recognized and encouraged. Patients can joyously engage in conflict that reflects internal struggles and excitedly continue to do so after the group meeting. Such argument can help to cut through patients' boredom in the hospital.

People attend group with varying levels of pathology. Technique varies with the kind of pathology one is dealing with, so it is important for the leader to be able to diagnose the extent of ego strength in a given patient or group and use technique appropriate to the developmental level involved. For example, leaders have learned that they have to have limited expectations and make repetitive interventions with a group of fragile patients. Sometimes the group varies in composition, and it is a challenge to lead a meeting in a way that meets the emotional needs of both the fragile and the emotionally healthy. Coven (1980) shows how a theoretical analysis of her patient population helped her arrive at suitable group technique.

Knowledge of group leadership is imparted in individual supervision, in consultation with an outsider, in workshop or group supervision where peer exchange and support can take place, and in classroom instruction. The success of these modes of teaching is directly related to how they are incorporated in the hospital system.

JOB-RELATED DIFFICULTIES

Neither the group nor the supervision is isolated from everything else going on in a hospital. How people feel about leading a group will in large part depend upon how they feel about the rest of their job. Every aspect of the leader's job affects group formation. If the leader is part of a cohesive service, is functioning well as a member of the medical team, has a workload that is emotionally and intellectually gratifying and a good relationship with the supervisor, and is not overworked or underworked, he or she has the easiest time forming and maintaining a group. For these reasons it is often necessary to spend supervision time on job-related problems, as we see in these two examples.

> The new social work group leader was having difficulty forming his group in a medical setting. He said he was depressed on his entire job and started to cry. He wondered if he was doing anything of value and if he should look for other employment. He did not feel he was recognized on the team—staff were not responsive to his call for group referrals. His caseload was full of patients who only needed concrete services and were not interested in any kind of counseling—group or individual. He felt trapped in his job because the job market was so tight. He felt angry at the patients for not responding to his overtures.
>
> The supervisor stated that she did not feel the supervisee was trapped on the job, that the job market was tight, but it was not impossible to find employment. This group leader's despondency was short-lived, and within six months he had a successful group and was happier on his job.

One can see by this example how beginning a group and job description are related. When a group leader is despondent and feels negative about his job, the supervisor should listen and take seriously the leader's complaints. She can point out the alternatives available to him so that he will not feel so helpless, and she can instill hope by conveying the feeling that she does not see things as bleakly as the supervisee.

> A nurse and social worker co-leader of a newly formed medical group were angry because the medical director and interdisciplinary team did not acknowledge them for forming and leading the group. Instead, the director took credit for the group's success. The leaders felt that no one had any appreciation for how hard they worked or the role of the group supervisor.

As the supervisor explored the details of the team meeting, it became apparent that the leaders constantly minimized their role and skill with other staff. They never told anyone what they did and conveyed that the group formed itself and ran itself. The supervisor asked them what they *did* do to form the group. They could not answer.

The next supervisory session was spent outlining exactly what the leaders did to form and maintain the group: how they reached out to people who were reluctant to join the group and how they limited criticism in the group to help move the group toward cohesiveness. The supervisor helped them label their technique.

The next task was to present this new-found knowledge to the team. The leaders asked for time in the next team meeting to present their group. The team was responsive. The leaders began their presentation at the staff meeting by saying that they were proud that their hard work had paid off. They explained how they dealt with the defense of denial, poor composition, and the task of creating a supportive environment. They explained how and when they were supervised and the difficult countertransferential feelings with which they dealt. The medical director said, "Gee, there is so much we do not know about handling patients, particularly our own feelings. Maybe we should be talking and learning also. Why don't we talk about the areas we have trouble with emotionally? My area is 'death.' I find I want to protect the patients from it. We could learn by talking like the patients in the group." The team proceeded to schedule meetings to explore their feelings further. It was implicit that the social worker and nurse, given the training they were getting in group supervision, would offer leadership. The group leaders felt as though they had new status on the team and were pleased with themselves.

In this example, the leaders needed help from the supervisor in being assertive and elevating their professional awareness and sense of competence. The social worker was the person on the interdisciplinary team who had knowledge in the psychosocial arena. In order to fulfill her role on the team, she should have been offering leadership in this area. As the group supervisor was helping the leaders get recognition for their group skill, she was influencing their entire job experience and team functioning.

THE EFFECT OF HOSPITAL CULTURE ON SUPERVISION

The culture (a dynamic that is felt on all levels of the system) of the hospital system will often be played out in the consultation session, the supervisory relationship, and the patient groups. The culture can affect how a supervisor feels about his job and, more specifically, how he feels how a supervisor feels about his job and, more specifically, how he feels about encouraging his supervisee in forming a group. Does he feel supported by administration or does his work to form a group seem like an uphill struggle? Is the response to the leader starting a group a demand for more red tape and paperwork? Is the leader expected to lead a group and continue carrying a heavy caseload? If the group is led at night, does the leader get compensation time? Poynter-Berg, in reporting on a survey of groups in maternal and child health in the Northeast, wrote:

> Workers are frequently expected to "do groups" with little real support in terms of systems preparation, intervention, or adequate supervision on groups. One worker explained how this issue was illustrated by departmental statistical forms, which allot little credit for groups, especially short-term ones, which are entered on the bottom of the forms, and which require a phenomenal amount of paperwork. Another staff group described how their setting had had a number of active, successful groups during periods they had access to expert group training and supervision; when that (funding) ceased, so eventually did the groups. (1979, p. 6)

The fact that groups were made possible with the entry of expert supervision does not surprise me. I think that the primary value of the provision of consultation or specialized supervision is that it boosts morale of the staff; it is viewed as a "gift" or as an acknowledgement from administration.

Low morale and "burnout" (where staff lose their energy and interest in dealing with patients or have "negative emotional, psychological, and physical reactions to continuous work-related stress") (Patrick, p. 87, 1979) are frequently problems in a hospital setting. As a consultant, I have often been impressed with the despair, hopelessness, and helplessness a staff might feel. Every suggestion the consultant makes is greeted with "yes but." In other words, nothing can work; everything has been tried before. It is hard to know if this negative response is engendered by personnel above (administrative leadership and supervisory staff) or below (patients).

If we see all parts of the system connected, dynamics of culture will also be played out between staff and consultant. If the consultant explores this relationship, there might be repercussions on other levels of the system. Following are some examples where a staff enacted what was going on in the system—above and below—in the consultation session.

Example 1:   In a drug addiction agency, staff brought case examples to consultation where therapists provided minimal structure for the patients. Patients seemed to "hang around" the clinic all day and were not productive; staff expressed: "At least, they were off the streets." Occasionally, someone mentioned that there might be some selling of drugs around the clinic during these "hanging out" periods. There was concern that somehow this was not right but there was no expectation that the consultant's suggestions would make a difference; i.e., they were not expecting him to assert strong expectations for them. The discussion drifted to the director of the agency and complaints about how she was not giving enough attention to clinical needs. It became apparent that the staff was unstructured; expectations were unclear. Staff members were expected to be supervised, but there were no assigned supervisors. Somehow people were supposed to just get together and supervise each other. The consultant pushed for structure (including clearly delineated expectations) on all levels: during the consultation hour, in the time spent with patients, and in the agency where supervisors and supervisees were matched and time set aside for supervision.

Example 2:   During consultation with staff on a psychiatric unit, it was mentioned that the patients had requested that staff wear name tags which reflected their discipline and rank. The staff group immediately dismissed this idea. The consultant was interested in why they dismissed this idea without any discussion. The staff got furious and upset with the consultant's question and implication. They wanted consultation in order to discuss "deep feelings," not concrete matters. They then revealed that they did not want to be labeled and wanted to be equals—with each other, with the consultant, with administration, and with the patients. Clinically this expressed itself in staff's overpermissiveness with patients and underestimation of patients' pathology. Throughout the system was a desire to perpetuate the fantasy of equality. This illusion in consultation made it possible for staff to avoid dealing with their competitive feelings. The consultant pointed out that "some people were more equal than others" in education, experience, aptitude, skill, mental health, and intelligence. This inequality was true among patients and within the staff group. How did they feel about this fact?

Example 3:   In a drug-addiction agency, a case was presented where the clinic could not meet a patient's needs; he needed a half-way house. It did not occur to the staff to refer the patient: They felt they had to meet all the patient's needs. At the same time, the entire staff had the idea that they were "a family" and often spent time outside work together. There was disappointment when the director was not a good mother or siblings did not "come through" for one another. They perpetuated with the patients one of the parental syndromes common to drug addicts: the parent who loves unconditionally in a relationship where no separation is supposed to take place. The consultant was supposed to be part of this family and supply all of the staff's learning needs. He was idealized. The consultant interpreted all of this after a strong relationship was formed.

Example 4: In a medical setting, it became evident in consultation that there was a matriarchal structure throughout the hierarchal system. Staff had their favorite "mothers," and these mothers were good. The mothers played their role well, giving cards to people on their birthdays and calling staff members into their office to talk when they were feeling blue. The consultant became the "good mother," and there was minimal challenge of her expertise. The consultant started to question this — trying to elicit more conflict and anger—when she wondered if a benevolent, matriarchal structure might not be adaptive in a medical setting. The leaders were caring for their patients as good mothers, being extremely giving and demonstrating much patience under difficult conditions. If they got good mothering from above, perhaps they could be more giving to patients. During a time of severe illness idealization and repression of conflict can be positive for patients (see Chapter 9). The consultant withdrew her tactic of being provocative to engender conflict and expression of anger.

In these examples it is hard to decipher whether role induction comes from above or below. Kernberg (1978) says that staff often play out patients' problems and conflicts in staff meetings. If this is true, in the examples given above, staff would be reenacting the patients' ego deficits in not being able to plan and organize in a committed way in Example 1; patients' grandiosity and faulty reality testing in Example 2; patients' desire for fusion in Example 3; and patients' need to idealize authority and repress conflict in Example 4. Kernberg continues to suggest that staff meetings can regress to Bion's basic-assumption groups: dependence, fight–flight, and pairing (Bion, 1959). This is evident in the examples given above. The regression to the dependency assumption where the group wants a good parent to care for them is apparent in Examples 1, 3, and 4.

It is important to remember that even though regression can take place in a staff group, there is also the staff's ego strength to call upon; there is usually a strong observing ego that the consultant can engage in exploration. I have been impressed with professionals' dedication to growth and learning. In the above examples, the groups were responsive to self-examination. Obviously, this cannot occur before trust in the consultant has been established.

LEARNING NEEDS OF GROUP LEADERS

Given the morale problem that is so prevalent in medical and psychiatric hospital settings, supervision needs to be a source of support; the support takes the form of meeting a supervisee's learning needs. The emotional demands in working with the medically and psychiatrically ill are tremendous. There is often the feeling of being "drained." If a supervisor can give to the supervisee, this is often transmitted to the patient.

Most of the professionals leading or wanting to lead groups in hospitals have had training in individual, not group, treatment (Frey, 1966). Poynter-Berg (1979) reports that a number of those leading groups in maternal and child health felt that they did not have adequate training, and adequate supervision for groups was not available in their setting. Two-thirds felt the need for more training. In the St. Vincent's Hospital group program, only two group leaders had former training and experience in leading groups, and even they felt insecure in their knowledge and skill. The people most reluctant to lead groups were those who had done so in the past, not had good supervision, and found themselves over their heads. They described the experience as frightening.

Providing for a leader's learning needs is the most appropriate and effective way of giving support to a group leader. When I was hired by a university hospital as a beginning social group worker to work with teenage unwed mothers, there was no one on staff knowledgeable in group technique. The department of social work hired experts to supervise me. It more than paid off in the quality of work I was able to perform. In one hospital, staff was constantly complaining. Several confided to their supervisor that they wanted to quit. When they started a group and had their learning needs met, they felt their group experience was the highlight of their week. They no longer wanted to find new employment.

The following can aid in meeting a supervisee's learning needs:

1. The supervisee's learning style must be assessed.
2. A group should be picked that reflects the leader's interests. The formation of the group should be a personal and creative experience for the leader.
3. Every effort should be made to give a leader a good first experience.

ASSESS HOW SUPERVISEE LEARNS BEST

People learn in different ways. Kolb (1974) designed a self-assessment test to distinguish among four learning modes: concrete experience, reflective observation, abstract conceptualization, and active experimentation. Galton (1959) finds learners falling into three broad categories: the intuitive, the intellectual, and the empathetic. Berengarten (1957) identified three learning patterns among social workers: the experiential-empathetic learner, the doer, and the intellectual-empathetic learner.

Before starting a group some leaders want to jump right in and discuss the content afterward; others want to read and do research, feeling that they have a sound knowledge base of the disease and beginning group technique before they enter a new group; and others want to discuss the meaning of the group, such as: "If we bring a patient out of her shell for ten minutes and then she dies, what good is it?" or "If we convince a patient in the group that he has to take his medication and then he is discharged to Skid Row and throws his medication away because he has no place to carry it, what good is it?" or "If I were sick I would want to be left alone. What am I doing telling others to join a group when I wouldn't want to?" Experienced supervisors know that supervision with each person is different.

ENCOURAGE LEADER TO BE CREATIVE

Forming a group should be a creative experience; it should be a way for leaders to "do their own thing." It is just this element that breaks through low morale. Instead of a compulsory group assignment, leaders should form groups voluntarily out of their own curiosity and desire for professional growth. In the group program at St. Vincent's Hospital, groups could be formed outside of one's service if that was where one's interest was. Some people were interested in learning more about a specific disease, and having a group was a good way of proceeding. Several groups were formed around a social worker's desire to get more referrals from or have better team relationships on a particular service. The formation of a group ensured that the leader would be more involved on a service and have more interdisciplinary contact. All of the groups formed around these goals were successful. Changes in caseload or in team relationships resulted and patients benefited from these changes.

The reader may object to the idea of forming groups around a new leader's interest, feeling that the leaders may be self-serving and the leader's ability to deal with unanticipated problems arising in the pre-selected group would be limited. The reader may feel the focus should be on patients' needs, not on leaders' needs. But, as was noted earlier, they are usually very much connected. I have not heard any ideas for new groups where patients would not have benefited. In order for leaders to further their professional skill, they have to have patients to work with who will be responsive to their interventions. One cannot have professional growth without meeting or attempting to meet patients' needs. All groups generate unexplored problems; therefore, given a professional and dedicated leader, the choice of a particular kind of group to work with should neither diminish the leader's opportunity to offer help with a variety of patient difficulties nor lead to narrow specializations and a decrease in the leader's armamentarium.

PROVIDE A GOOD FIRST EXPERIENCE

A new group leader should have a good first experience. This can be most easily achieved if the leader begins to work with the most captive audience and the most motivated population.

If one is trying to start a group program, it is important that the first groups are successful. A "successful" first group does not mean that a leader has to have a well-attended group immediately; it means that it is a positive learning experience and the leader learns from his or her mistakes. Most groups are not well attended the first time around. The supervisor and the leader would be putting undue pressure on themselves to have such an expectation. Kernberg (1978) attributes many organizational problems to the expectation of staff that they do the impossible, such as "curing the patient." Forming a group is usually based on a trial and error process where an attempt is made, problems are identified, and attempts are modified.

Staff attitude toward groups usually snowballs in a positive or negative direction. Eventually, the pervasive staff attitude is either: (1) "Groups cannot work here," or (2) "There is hope—groups are where it is at." For this reason it is crucial to start with the easiest and simplest groups to form—usually these are the captive audiences; they are often inpatient rather than outpatient. Outpatient groups that require people to make a separate trip to the clinic for the group meeting require tremendous motivation and are the hardest to form, unless there is a high degree of anxiety and commonality, such as parents of newly diagnosed cystic fibrosis patients, or a strong relationship between leader and members, such as a group formed from a social worker's caseload.

In starting the group program at St. Vincent's Hospital, I began with the most motivated potential group leaders rather than trying to win over the most reticent. The initial group leaders could tolerate considerable stress in forming their groups because they were the most motivated. When they were successful (which took some time), others decided to try. It was slow going, but I was encouraged that we were moving in a positive direction. In the diary of the program that I kept, one can see the slow pace of the program's development, the frustration, and the rewards when a positive cycle sets in.

September: Everyone seems to be very excited about the potential for groups: workers, supervisors, doctors, nurses, me.

October: Workers have been creative in planning their groups and eager to learn. We're all excited.

November: We're facing the nitty-gritty of getting groups organized and getting people to come. There are a lot of practical difficulties in having groups in this setting. I underestimated resistances and structural difficulties on all fronts. The group that had the best prognosis had attendance of zero. The two most successful groups had two people attending in the first meeting and one person attending in the second. My goal is to keep myself from getting discouraged so I can bolster morale of workers. It is hard!

December: We've had a group of three. Hallelujah. Our goals have to be so limited. As long as things progress, I shouldn't be concerned about pace. More work has to be done in placing groups as part of the delivery system. Staff (including clerical) has to develop a routine where certain patients are automatically referred to group, as they are for lab work and consultations. It is important to get a system developed and a routine outlined and functioning, even if no one uses it for awhile; this approach entails more energy spent orienting staff and less with patients.

January: Top group attendance goes to six. New group will incorporate a nurse as a resource person. Doctors are beginning to request specific new groups. I'm getting a lot of support from the social service supervisory staff and administration. Nursing has been wonderful. My relationship with the workers is deepening; their individual complexities are becoming clearer. I'm getting to know them and like them. Two new workers requested training in group.

February: Groups are beginning to function and several have presented good material for in-service training. I'm bringing leaders together in small groups to share experiences and learn from one another. One group's success should spur another's. Inpatient and outpatient groups should be connected. Inpatients should be able to go to more than one group, if they are eligible. For example, a hospitalized, geriatric, diabetic patient who is going to a nursing home could go to three groups, each on a different day. A diabetic patient could go to the inpatient group and be followed up in the outpatient group. This idea was spurred by one inpatient diabetic coming back to group after her discharge.

Doctors seem to be getting more interested in group. One requested a co-leadership position. Some medical staff have been nervous about "what the patients will say about me" and the potential "for the group causing hostile contagion." Leaders are interpreting to interdisciplinary staff the understanding and treatment of patients' anger and realistic expectations for group.

The groups seem to be facilitating communication between medical and nursing staff and patients. For example, diabetics requested different needles for their insulin shots and Spanish literature, and the staff readily provided these. Many patients have been more assertive in approaching medical staff with their questions after a group meeting.

March: Our first group becomes cohesive. Spanish-speaking prenatal patients are now sitting together in the waiting room, recruiting people for group themselves, not wanting to leave group, lending emotional support to one another in labor and delivery room. Hospital administration and medical staff have seen the value of this group in meeting the health-care needs of the patients. Doctors have observed that group patients are less anxious during labor and delivery and more manageable, despite very difficult deliveries. Some doctors suggested that groups be compulsory. This success has encouraged others working with groups and those who were hesitant to begin. A healthy competition among workers has emerged.

April: Flexibility seems to be a key factor in a worker's success with a group. I also have to remember that I am learning and not invest too heavily in an idea for a group. I have to modify theory and technique constantly to conform with "what works." Several leaders have changed place and time of group, others have broadened eligibility requirements, and others have brought in nurses, doctors, or dieticians as resource people.

I must say, I am amazed at the results of the groups. I find I have a lump in my throat in many of the supervisory sessions as I hear about significant mutual aid among patients. With the breakdown of family and cultural supports in our day and age, many people are socially and emotionally isolated. Groups have begun to meet some of these patients' needs while they're enduring a crisis of chronic illness.

GROUP LEADERS' ANXIETIES

DISCUSS FANTASIES OF FIRST MEETING

Most of the staff workers leading groups in the group program at St. Vincent's Hospital came to the supervisory session before their first group meeting with a high level of anxiety. This session was spent covering the leader's imminent concern: "What do I do?" Most of the workers responded to a direct answer to this question: We discussed what to do if one person came, two people came, a lot came, if everyone was silent, if everyone talked to the leader, and so forth. It seemed as though the more situations we discussed in concrete terms, the less anxious the leaders became. During this session leaders often revealed fears about the group-to-be.

The leaders responded to an individualized teaching approach. Each leader had his or her own fearful fantasies about having a group: one felt patients wouldn't talk in the group no matter what intervention he made; another felt that patients would immediately attack her for not being experienced in group or knowledgeable about the disease or limited in life experience. Some felt uncomfortable in groups themselves but intellectually wanted to master a new modality.

Williams writes about beginning group therapists:

> All saw group psychotherapy as demanding much more of the therapist than individual therapy and as exposing them to the threat of more direct personal and professional evaluation than most other treatment activities . . .anxiety was always high and defensive reactions to it abundant. [They had] fearful fantasies regarding group attitudes and behavior toward the therapist. (1966, p. 151–4)

Fearful fantasies were: (1) members' unmanageable resistance during early group sessions (members don't talk); (2) leader losing control of the group (excessive hostility breaking out); (3) acting out of group members (members dating and dropping out impulsively); (4) members' overwhelming dependency demands; (5) group disintegration (no one showing up at meeting). These kinds of specific fantasies should be elicited by the supervisor and dealt with didactically. New leaders should go into the first meeting knowing what they can do if their worst fantasies are realized (see also Chapter 5).

ATTEND TO LEADER'S ANXIETY

Staff members' reluctance to having a viable group was prevalent but subtle in the St. Vincent's group program. For the first three months no one had more than three people at a meeting. Some leaders were ready to dip their toe in the water but were not ready to immerse themselves in a "real" group. Before starting a group, leaders were able to defend themselves against the patient's catastrophic situation by offering a concrete service. They were surprised that they had tended to see the patients as objects for self-protection. They found that when these patients were in group they had to see them as people, and this became very jarring. The patients took advantage of the opportunity to talk to each other about death and the details of their existence; it was apparent that in individual sessions they had protected the leaders from certain feelings. Patients also talked about their former lives. The leader learned who they were as people, as opposed to patients, and they found themselves more involved and pained by their illness.

I have never supervised anyone who was nonchalant about starting a group. Even the experienced people I know, myself included, are always anxious about beginning a new group. Anxiety before the group is usually transformed proportionately to elation afterward, if the group meeting goes well. Perhaps these strong emotional reactions explain why people are so reticent to start groups and why the rewards are so great when a group succeeds. People both fear and are attracted to basic group processes. Attitude toward groups is also influenced by culture and familial experiences.

It is hard to feel neutral about a group experience. This is testimony to the power of the group, which we know can be positive or negative. Freud and LeBon were concerned with understanding mob behavior (Scheidlinger, 1980). Bion (1959) described how groups regress to unconscious, primitive basic-assumption groups: wanting to depend on the leader, wanting to fight an enemy, wanting to give birth to a messiah. Most of us have been aware of and participated in such group experiences.

I tried an experiment in a group-methods class on a graduate level to see if the power of the group and primitive, unconscious processes could be illustrated. This can happen in groups when the group expects a strong leader and is disappointed (Heath and Bacal, 1972). I pretended to fall asleep during the class. The participants, who were mature people, got very upset and began exhibiting psychoticlike behavior. When the experiment was analyzed, students had the following to say: "I guess we have an idea now how our clients might feel if we are not clear about our role." "If it was hard for *us* to have a passive leader, what would it be like for our clients who have less ego strength?" "I wonder what clients' expectations are of us when they come to a group and if we let them down." With one exception, students felt that they learned an important truth: the group leader is very important, and the role of group leader should be taken seriously. Group intervention is a powerful treatment tool, and it is no wonder that new leaders are timid about its use. But as negative as group process can be, it can be equally as positive.

INDIVIDUAL SUPERVISION

Given all of the justification for new-leader anxiety, the problem of morale in most hospitals (in large part due to real problems of heavy workloads, lack of recognition of all people on all levels, and society's unrealistic expectations for hospitals), and the potential role of groups to change leader's morale, it is clear that the supervisor has to be available and supportive to the supervisee. In a hospital system where negativity can be widespread, someone has to make a change somewhere in order for change to occur. Fortunately, since all parts of the system are connected, a new ingredient, such as a new, well-supervised group, can have repercussions throughout the entire hospital structure.

Table 4-1 presents a group process recording written by a social work student (Attanasia, 1976). It has his analysis of the process and the supervisor's written comments. One can see how the supervisor balances support with suggestions for further analysis. The meeting takes place on a general-medicine floor. It is an open, turnover group devoted to "adjustment to hospitalization."

PEER SUPPORT AND SUPERVISION

New leaders benefit from peer exchange and support for much the same reason that patients do: it is often less threatening to accept new information from peers; and self-esteem can be boosted because one does not feel so alone in facing one's ignorance. In the St. Vincent's Hospital group program, leaders came together for a problem-oriented workshop.

Leaders had the chance to learn from others' experiences and their knowledge of hospital groups expanded. They learned that the groups were very different and yet certain problems were similar. If one leader changed services and was to start another group with a different population, he would have some idea as to the different situations he might encounter. Leading a single group in a hospital is not enough to orient oneself to the myriad possibilities presented by hospital groups.

I wanted to gear the sharing of group experiences in a positive way, because low morale and discouragement with forming and maintaining the groups was an ever-present threat to the leaders' motivation. The format that we became most satisfied with was as follows:

1. Each person presented a problem that he or she had had with a group that was, for the moment, solved.
2. After presentation of the problem, members grappled with solutions to the problem from their own experiences. Members liked the intellectual challenge of this approach.
3. After the group exhausted their own intellectual searching, the group leader shared how the problem, in reality, had been positively dealt with.

The problems discussed in the first year were low group attendance, leader's emotional difficulty inviting seriously ill patients to a "seriously ill" group, superficial group discussion, denial versus confrontation in the group, handling a hostile monopolizer in the group, interference with the group by staff, and handling death in the group. Problems presented the second year were low group attendance, managing a large group (13

TABLE 4-1
Record of a Group Process

Group Process	Leader's Comments	Supervisor's Comments
Mrs. M. remarked, "Gee, there are only three of us here today."		Positive here-and-now focus.
"Well, I've been to groups where there were only three people," said Mrs. C.		
Leader asked, "Well, there are only four of us here. . . . How does that make you feel?"	Reflecting on a group member's concern and focusing it on the group members.	
Mrs. T. said, "It means we have to share things with fewer people."		
"How do you feel about this?"	Sticking with the topic.	
"It's not really the number of people, but just that you miss others," said Mrs. C.	Group member expressed concern.	
Mrs. M. responded, "I was just wondering where the other people were."		
Mrs. T. said, "Well, I saw Mrs. B. earlier. She had a rough night. This new patient in her room was screaming a lot. We could hear her even a few rooms down. So she really didn't get a lot of sleep."	Group member being a source of information.	
Leader remarked, "Yes, when I went to see Mrs. B. she was practically sleeping sitting up in her chair. She said she would like to come to the group, but she was afraid she might fall asleep."	Leader demonstrating that he was attentive to what Mrs. T. had said, had been interested enough to invite Mrs. B. again, and wanted to share with the group what he had learned.	
Here we all laughed.		

TABLE 4-1 (continued)
Record of a Group Process

Group Process	Leader's Comments	Supervisor's Comments
Mrs. C. said, "That would be alright. We would wake her up."		
Mrs. M. said, "I hope she decides to come."		
Leader said, "She may."		
Mrs. M. said, "I saw Mrs. R. earlier this morning."	Group member sharing information.	Yes—they are really using own resources. Somehow you've encouraged and supported their using own strengths and taking responsibility.
Mrs. C. remarked, "Yes, I saw her too; she had a leg bag and they are collecting urine for a period of time, up till noon."		
Leader said that he had spoken with Mrs. R. also, and she wanted to come to the group but found it difficult to sit.		
Mrs. T.: "Yeah, that bag is like a ball and chain."		
Leader says at this point, "You know, we have been talking here about the other people, and what I hear each of you saying is that you miss the other's presence here in the group."	You people are saying that you care about the others—do you what that means?	Good, they are reflecting feelings of self worth. Good.
You do miss them—it's like a space," said Mrs. C.		
Mrs. T. and Mrs. M. agreed.		
Mrs. M. said, "I would like to talk about an experience I had this week; sometimes I feel like I'm always griping."		

61

TABLE 4-1 (continued)
Record of a Group Process

GROUP PROCESS	LEADER'S COMMENTS	SUPERVISOR'S COMMENTS
Leader said, "I think we would like to hear your story."	You don't have to apologize. We are interested in what you have to share.	
Mrs. M. related an experience she had with a person from transportation.		
Mrs. T. spoke about how the night nurses are difficult to deal with.		What are they doing with their anger here? What stage of group are they in?
Mrs. C. replied, "Sometimes it's a lack of communication, and the staff takes it out on the patient."		
Mrs. C. related a story about how the night nurses gave her one set of instructions regarding a urine sample, and then in the morning she was given different instructions and felt as though she was at fault.	Group member relating to a topic presented by Mrs. M.	
Mrs. T. said, "I just gotta laugh. People tell you, go to the hospital for a rest. Ha! Now that is a laugh. Who rests here? You're part of a routine."		
Mrs. M. said, "You know, this week I was waiting for more tests; there was an enlarged vein in my head, and I need further tests, so I was uptight. Having run-ins with certain staff people make you feel worse."		

62

TABLE 4-1 (continued)
Record of a Group Process

Group Process	Leader's Comments	Supervisor's Comments
Leader said, "It's not always just the physical things, but how we are feeling emotionally." Mrs. M. said, "Yeah . . . it just helps to talk about these things here in the group."	Relating to how the people are feeling. Feelings are part of the patient's medical condition.	Yes. Good.
"Yes, I remember you said you thought it was griping, but it seems as though you touched upon an important concern that is shared by the other group members."	We value what you have to share. Leader sending out a message not only to Mrs. M. but to rest of the group as well.	Yes!!
We next discussed how people in the group dealt with such situations.		Wonderful, isn't it?
The members repeated that it helps to talk. Mrs. T. said, "Yesterday when Tina (Mrs. M.) came back from that run-in, we sat and talked about it like we talk about things in the group." Leader said, "Well, it sounds as though you are using your group experiences in places outside the group."		They are really using group. Taking responsibility. You keep turning "griping" into constructive conversation.
Mrs. C. nodded, "Yeah, you would be surprised how we look for one another from the group."	Group member actively displaying how they seek out each other.	You reinforced this behavior.
Mrs. M. looked down the hall and pointed saying, "Look, here comes Elizabeth" (Mrs. B.) Upon sitting down Mrs. B. said, "I made it."		

63

TABLE 4-1 (continued)
Record of a Group Process

Group Process	Leader's Comments	Supervisor's Comments
Mrs. C. said, "We were talking about how much we missed you."		
"Well I was missing the group too. Mr. F. kept coming and telling me that he would be missing me and you would be missing me, so I started thinking, maybe I'm missing something, so here I am."	Group member saying how much she missed the group and how she appreciated leader stressing the importance of her involvement.	Very important—great!
Mrs. T. said, "It's just that you're nosey." Here everyone laughed.	Mrs. T. using one of her assets— her humour is a strength.	
Mrs. B. said, "Oh yeah . . . Barbara is coming too . . . she said she had to take her time."		
Mrs. R. (Barbara) arrived a few minutes later.		Incredible!
The members spoke about their various conditions.	Group members sharing concerns.	
Mrs. R. was greeted by the group.	Group was happy to see her.	
She said, "Oh, I feel 148 years old today."		
We offered Mrs. R. a chair, but she said she could not sit, and if the group did not mind she would stand. Leader noted that Mrs. R. did not stand on the outside of the group but stood close to the other members.	Mrs. R. was sending out a nonverbal message: I want to be part of the group.	Very supportive to every member. They are all getting validation of self-worth.

64

TABLE 4-1 (continued)
Record of a Group Process

Group Process	Leader's Comments	Supervisor's Comments
Mrs. M. spoke of her upcoming tests—head X rays. Mrs. C. was waiting for lung scans, Mrs. B. and Mrs. T. spoke about their diets for diabetes, and Mrs. R. about her 24-hour urine analysis.	Commonality among group members was discussed in relation to individual concerns.	
Leader noted that most of the patients sounded a bit down about their progress. The members agreed.	A tone of voice cued me to this.	
Mrs. T. said, "It's maybe not the progress but the waiting and having to be patient."	Patient clarifying input from leader.	
Mrs. B. laughed, "It's having to be *a* patient."	A very important remark.	Yes!!
Leader noticed Mrs. O. standing off to the side. Leader glanced over and so did Mrs. M. "I was wondering if you would like to join us, Mrs. O."	Leader noting Mrs. O.'s nonverbal behavior.	
"Well . . . I'm just on the outside." Mrs. M.: "You're either in or out, so why don't you pull up a chair."	Message indicating involvement.	
Leader said, "Mrs. O. we would like you to join us."		
Mrs. O. moved closer.		
Mrs. T. said, "Come on, honey, pull up a chair."	Group encouragement.	

TABLE 4-1 (continued)
Record of a Group Process

Group Process	Leader's Comments	Supervisor's Comments
Mrs. O. related how she was at the diabetic group yesterday, and she found it helpful. "I was there with Mrs. T. and Mrs. B." The discussion moved back to how people in the group felt about being patients.	An experience from another group is shared. Identifies with group members with whom she had shared this previous group experience.	
Mrs. M. said, "You know, we are usually talking about other people in the hospital. I wish we could have them hear what we say, you know, in a constructive way."		
Leader said, "What Mrs. M. is saying is important. She is bringing up an idea how we could use our group meetings to better serve patients and staff. How do the rest of you feel about this idea?"	This is important—how do the others feel about this?	Are you skipping over feelings of what it feels like to be a patient? Are they making a move to be more active and assertive?
Mrs. R. said, "It's a good idea. I've always wondered what the nurses think about our group. They seem to tell patients about it." Mrs. B. said, "Yeah, the nursing staff is receptive."	Thinking out loud about involving the nurses.	
Mrs. C. remarked, "Maybe we could get them to come."	Verbalizing the suggestion.	Group feels permission from you to run own meeting.

66

TABLE 4-1 (continued)
Record of a Group Process

GROUP PROCESS	LEADER'S COMMENTS	SUPERVISOR'S COMMENTS
"Well, we could ask them," Leader said. "In fact, Mrs. W. usually stops by the group at 11:30 before lunch to give you your medication; perhaps we could present her with the idea."	Leader making a suggestion.	
	The emphasis was on the group doing the asking.	
Mrs. M. said, "I would like to ask her and whoever else would like to ask, well, let's do it."		
The group members planned what they were going to say to the nurse.	Group planning the agenda. This was unbelievable to see taking place.	I agree. Very impressive.
Mrs. T. and Mrs. B. said, "We'll start breaking the ice by kidding with her, we always swap jokes."		
Mrs. C. said, "I would like to tell Mrs. W., if it's alright with Tina, that there is something we would like to ask her."		
Mrs. M. laughed, "Yeah, like an introduction, and then we could ask her."	Let's work together.	
Leader thought that their planning together was great. They asked the nurse their questions; she was receptive and said the nurses would work on solutions. They told the nurse that they would like her to come to future meetings.	Leader encouraging patient.	Acknowledging them. They are revealing their distrust of staff.

67

TABLE 4-1 (continued)
Record of a Group Process

Group Process	Leader's Comments	Supervisor's Comments
After Mrs. W. left, Leader said, "You were all really working like a group to get your ideas across."	Reflecting on what had taken place.	
Mrs. O. said, "I never thought the nurse would have said yes."		
Mrs. R. said, "Well, I thought she would because she and Mrs. B., the head nurse, seem to like the group idea."		
Mrs. M. said that she found the day staff helpful and that she was glad that they asked.		
Mrs. B. said, "Now we have to keep after the nurses to make sure they come. I wonder if Mr. F. is going to go into his public-relations act."	Let's not stop here. You (to the leader) have to help.	
Here the group laughed.		But they gave you some feedback on your preparation—that was a real gift!
Mrs. B. said, "I'm serious, he kept after me to come."		
Leader said he would do his part and the group would have to build on the work they began.	We are all involved in this work.	

68

TABLE 4-1 (continued)
Record of a Group Process

Group Process	Leader's Comments	Supervisor's Comments
Following this, the patients began to again discuss waiting, and the topic of dying was brought up by Mrs. T. It was raised in connection with her staying on her diet. "I know I cheat sometimes, but then I'm just fooling myself, but who can live forever. I try to remember this." Mrs. M. said, "No one can live forever, but we think we can. I mean we all hope for the best." Mrs. C. said, "Well, I don't know what it's like to be on a diabetes diet, but I am on a low-sodium diet. Sometimes it's like . . . you have to be good and obey the rules of your diet . . . if you want to get better. It makes you feel scared and disgusted because you want to be able to eat what you once could eat without second thoughts." Mrs. O. said, "Yeah, I cheat on my diet a lot . . . but I know I'm cheating on my health. You have no control and you feel helpless."	The conversation about death was quite interesting and displayed the group's strength in discussing related topics and expanding their concerns. It's something we must deal with, but let's hope for the positive, that we'll be getting better.	How was this discussion built on earlier topics in this meeting? How are they feeling about the meeting coming to an end? Want to deny illness and stages of life.
	Sometimes I feel like a child.	
Group members responded to this helpless feeling by each speaking of it in relation to their being so dependent on the doctors and the hospital.		How did you feel here?

69

TABLE 4-1 (continued)
Record of a Group Process

Group Process	Leader's Comments	Supervisor's Comments
Leader said, "But isn't there a lot that depends on the patient's attitude and how each of your are feeling? This gets back to something we mentioned earlier. It's not just the physical aspects but the emotional as well. Perhaps this is one of the things our meetings tap—how each of you are responding to situations and how you are feeling."	Reflecting a prior concern and building on strengths. Reason for the group is emphasized.	
Leader summed up the meeting by making sure each of the members knew one another, discussing follow-up plans to involve the nursing staff, how we could recruit more members, and Leader thanked each of the members for their contributions and their participation especially in letting other patients know about the group and in involving the nursing staff.	(This was really to make sure Mrs. O. knew the others since other members were familiar to each other.)	Their response?

TABLE 4-1 (continued)
Record of a Group Process

GROUP PROCESS	LEADER'S COMMENTS	SUPERVISOR'S COMMENTS
Impressions: This group meeting demonstrated an awareness in group members of their feelings and the feelings of others. There was a great deal of mutual support shown. The people in this group have developed a sense of trust, which is displayed in their willingness to share concerns, respond to topics, and encourage other members. The input of the leader seems to be appreciated by the group. There is a mutual respect that has grown between leader and group, so much that he feels a real part of the group interaction. The group members seem to be patients who can realistically integrate what is discussed in their actions.	*Leader's Roles:* 1. Interpreter— reflecting on what was said. 2. Clarifier—especially important in this meeting. 3. Supporter—in building on group's initiative in encouraging members. *Plan:* Continue to build on group cohesiveness and to encourage group members to engage in planning and making suggestions; involve the nursing staff; reach for new group members in the patient population.	Not "interpreting"—let's discuss.

members), handling a patient in group who attacked the leader verbally, handling a personality conflict between two members in group, identifying with patient's suffering in the group to the point that the leader felt immobilized, handling prejudiced comments by members in groups, and handling a patient's imminent death in the group and then her recovery.

Here are some excerpts from a workshop in which group leaders from medicine and psychiatry came together to share successes with difficult situations. The group leader presents a problematic situation, the staff discusses possible solutions, and then the group leader gives her resolution. In the last example, the workshop leader takes some time to be didactic.

Problem: Mary presented a brief synopsis of a group session she co-led with a male nurse last summer. There were five members present in the group, which was basically focused on discharge plans and reactions to pending discharge.

One member was giving very vague responses around postdischarge plans, and when he was questioned for specifics from the other members, he became furious and walked out of the group. The questions raised by this situation revolved around the leader's responsibility to the individual member and to the group.

Discussion: A general discussion followed during which the following suggestions were made: (1) ask the remaining members what they would like to do; (2) send one of the co-leaders with the patient while the other remains with the group; (3) send one of the remaining four members after the patient. Many felt that a group leader just had to be ready for anything in a group situation and each situation had to be assessed separately.

Resolution: Mary then reported what she actually did in the situation. She waited until the next group meeting when the same situation occurred and the patient walked out again. At that point the leaders were able to discuss the situation with the remaining members. They discussed their reactions and how one can handle anger with the group. It proved to be a helpful experience.

Problem: Tom discussed a PTP (Partial Treatment Program) group which has been set up for patients who were unable to be treated in other groups and needed a group in which expectations were low. The goals of the group are to encourage socialization, help patients understand their illness, and help them formulate some limited expectations from treatment for themselves. It meets once a week for 90 minutes. The patients have been meeting together for about six months.

The group has one patient who always gives a monologue, usually about overeating and vomiting, which she graphically describes. This has a deadening effect on the other members, who are appalled at the severity of these symptoms.

Discussion: Suggestions made by participants were: (1) do not respond to the content of what the patient is saying; (2) bring in the rest of the group by asking how they feel about what the patient is saying; (3) try to stop her before she begins; (4) give her feedback about one's own negative reactions to this; (5) let things go until someone in the group confronts her; (6) talk to her individually about participating differently in the group.

Resolution: Tom found that the patient was doing this sort of thing everywhere and began to work more intensively as her coordinator to set limits. Tom began to understand that the patient could stop herself and reinforced different behavior. He used the group by beginning to ask what had happened to them during the monologue and why they were so silent and unresponsive. They began to let the patient know that they saw the things she talked about as very sick and didn't know what to say to her. It developed that she had seen herself as the healthiest member, because she could reveal things. She became mobilized to try to find other ways to be the "most healthy."

The workshop leader described this behavior as "acting in" using words. The patient almost demonstrates the behavior of overeating and vomiting. The workshop leader continued to talk about the use of such a monologue by a group to avoid intimacy. Such a patient can serve this purpose for all group members. She saw the group as primarily in phase one—the decision about whether or not to trust one another—while they used the patient in this way. In phase two—struggle for power—a group may become angry at such a person, which they were beginning to do when they gave feedback. In doing this, they helped her to move from fantasy to reality. The third phase—intimacy—is difficult for severely disturbed people to reach. However, all groups and all sessions have aspects of all three phases.

At the conclusion of a 20-month period at St. Vincent's, many of the leaders were ready for ongoing group supervision where the focus would be on dealing with current problems rather than those already solved. They began requesting more time with their peers to exchange group experience and needed less individual attention and support. They had achieved a basic competence and confidence in group leadership. Some were ready to assume supervisory roles with beginning group leaders.

An interesting dynamic occurred in group supervision which is reminiscent of the saying "if everyone put their dirty laundry in the wash, they would all pull back their own at the end." Each leader expressed satisfaction leading his or her own group, despite the degree of morbidity, and felt sorry for the other leaders who "had it worse." For example, members felt that working with the oncology group and knowing the patients would die would be the worst. The oncology worker replied: "But I feel working in head-and-neck surgery would be the worst. At least in my group I don't *see* the cancer." The head-and-neck worker responded: "But that is what I like about it. Their illness is out in the open, so it can be dealt with. The patients and relatives cannot use denial so easily, so working with them is gratifying." Others said to the cystic fibrosis worker: "Now I think working with cystics would be the worst. Not only are they going to die, but at young age. And the treatments that they have to do everyday must be awful." The worker replied: "Well, at least the patients are young and vibrant and intelligent. They're a lot of fun; their company is enjoyable." This same phenomenon occurs among patients and is discussed in Chapter 9.

SUMMARY

Both the group leader and the supervisor of the group have to work within the system. Operationalizing this principle means that the supervisor has to be aware that the trainee's total experience in the setting will affect how he forms and maintains a group. Often the transaction in the supervisory or consultation session can only be understood by bringing in "system's" problems. Since most potential group leaders reflect the frustration staff generally feel, it is important that the supervisor support the group leader by being available and meeting the leader's individualized learning needs. The leader should get something from the group: increasing professional growth. Supervisors also have to acknowledge the fear that most people experience in starting a group. Peer supervision or workshops often help leaders feel less fearful and more supported.

Chapter 5

Preparation for Group Leaders

Most new group leaders like to feel prepared before a group meeting, and there are a number of ways to prepare, including reading up on the subject, observing groups, being observed leading a group, and exchanging feelings and ideas with other group leaders.

READING MATERIALS

Reading is not a requirement for beginning a group. In fact some group leaders may not want to read up on the subject until after they have actually begun a group. However, for those who like to prepare for groups in this way, the bibliography at the end of this book provides many valuable books and articles. It is helpful to structure one's reading around certain topics. For example:

1. Group therapy and social group work: articles that provide basic and practical overviews of group therapy theory and technique, such as Northern (1969), Shulman (1979), and Yalom (1970).
2. Beginning groups: articles about processes basic to all beginning groups, such as Cooper (1978), Coven (in press), Fried (1976), and Youcha (1976).
3. Stages of group development: articles that help to improve understanding of how single-session, short or long group therapy should proceed, such as Garland (1965) and Schutz (1966).
4. Relationship between psyche and soma: articles that validate the potential of groups in a medical setting and combined groups of

medical and psychiatric patients, such as Moos (1977), Strain and Grossman (1975), and Usdin (1977).

5. Specific disease entities and related groups: articles that provide information about specific diseases and groups formed around the single-disease or common-situation entity, such as Cooper and Cento (1977) and Israel (1978).

6. Narcissism, separation, and individualization: articles that help to clarify the basic psychodynamics of participants in groups for the severely ill, both medical and psychiatric, such as Blanck and Blanck (1974) and Mahler, Pine, and Bergman (1975). Early developmental dynamics play a part in beginning group process in all groups.

Usually hospital staff do not have time to read books. It is helpful if a supervisor xeroxes part of a book that might be particularly helpful to a group leader, such as Chapter 1, "Curative Factors," in Yalom's book. If a supervisor guides group leaders' reading, they consider it a "gift"; it enhances not only learning but also morale, since the supervisor is responding to leaders' learning needs.

OBSERVE GROUPS IN ACTION

New leaders often request the opportunity to observe a group in action before they begin. Observation can take place by attending a group as a participant-observer or by viewing a group behind a one-way screen. Many hospitals do not have these facilities, but if they are available, they should certainly be exploited. Fortunately, in New York City, a major teaching hospital invites professionals throughout the city to view an ongoing, turnover medical group behind a one-way mirror. One can hope that this hospital's generosity will serve as a model for others.

The turnover groups are usually not bothered by observers. In fact, the opposite may be the case. Having an observer offers the group and the leader the opportunity of getting feedback from another professional. The leader can present the observer in this way: "We thought the observer could learn by viewing this group because it is so special." Members are often flattered by someone wanting to observe a "special group."

Invariably, if the observer does not talk in the group, and the leader opens up discussion of how the group feels about being observed, the members will say, "Well, what did you (observer) think of us?" Some appropriate responses would be: "I've been sitting here listening and thinking how impressed I am with the way you all help each other," or "I'm impressed with the way you cope with such difficult situations," or

"I've learned from you about what it is like to be a patient, and I think it will help me in my work with patients." The group is then rewarded for having the observer, and the observer reinforces the task of the group: to enhance ego strength. This is not to say that the observer should flatter the group dishonestly. Usually, however, an observer can find something positive about the group process or the coping activity of the members.

HAVE OBSERVERS IN YOUR GROUP

Every kind of communication between supervisor and supervisee elicits different learning material: informal conversation, tapes, process recording, or verbal presentation of the meeting, and direct observation. Some new leaders find it helpful if the supervisor or a colleague joins them in the group. This arrangement can be useful if two requirements are met: there is a positive relationship between the observer and the group leader, and the leader has the confidence to experiment with leadership style in the presence of another professional. When a supervisor views the group, he can often give new feedback to the group leader.

Sometimes new leaders request that the supervisor take the primary leadership role in the meeting because they are desperate for a model; without this arrangement, they would not start the group. The danger, of course, is that the new leader's creativity will be squelched. She might idealize the supervisor and want to copy him rather than develop her own style. Some people have to do this before they can work independently. Although I have usually discouraged new leaders from observing me lead their groups, when I have capitulated, new leaders have insisted that it has been of help to them. They were struck by how direct I was, especially in limiting a monopolizer, and by the repetitious nature of my interventions. An alternative arrangement exists where peers demonstrate for one another. Co-therapy arrangements are often made to offer these kinds of learning opportunities.

EXCHANGE IDEAS WITH OTHER GROUP LEADERS

Supervisors can arrange workshops for new group leaders where didactic material on beginning groups is covered, but participants often feel that the material given to them before they start the group is not meaningful. After they have started the group, leaders have high anxiety levels; they never feel they get enough help or attention from the supervisor at this time. Almost universally, participants in a beginning-group workshop say: "I thought I was the only one who was afraid," or "I thought everyone had successful groups. I feel relieved that I don't have to have a perfect group."

Peers can help with the practical aspects of forming a group. The workshop's strength in problem solving is usually impressive, since members' strengths combine; often alternatives for interventions come up in the workshop or group supervision that have not occurred to the supervisor or supervisee.

EXPECT TO BE AFRAID

Milton M. Berger (1958) writes about new group leaders: "Trainees who are not anxious must be sick." I have to say that I have never met a group leader, new or experienced, who was not nervous before starting a new group. One leader described her first meetings as being like "wading through mud." Another said it was like "playing blind man's bluff." These are strong images depicting the frustration of not being able to understand a new and complex situation. In the first instance the person is trudging along persistently; in the second instance the person feels helpless because of lack of knowledge. These were conscious associations to how the leaders were feeling about having a group. The intensity of feeling was often unconscious.

Many leaders reported nightmares immediately before their first group meeting.

Dream 1:   The leader had to be hospitalized for a knee operation. There was a lot of detail about what was wrong with her and how she should be treated.
Dreamer's associations: The leader remembered that the day before she had the first group meeting she said to her co-leader, "The only thing that would stop me from coming to the group would be if I had to have an operation." She was sure that the operation she had to have in the dream was meant to keep her from the group, because she was so scared.

Dream 2:   The group convened around the conference table, and there were about 40 people. She (the group leader) was shocked. She counted each one to make sure. She had expected four. She then found out that most of them were waiting for clinic and not really in the group.
Dreamer's associations: The leader had been discouraged with the low attendance of her new group (one to three people attending). In the workshop, peers confronted her with her negative and depressed attitude. Others did not feel as hopeless about her group as she did. They made an impression on her; the dream had some optimism and hope in it.

One can see in the dream how the leader is resistant to having a large group. She has 40 people and is overwhelmed. She then scales the group down to four. It is not uncommon to see small groups result from the leader's resistance. Some people need to start with a few people and gradually increase the numbers.

Dream 3: Patients had a big fight in the group. The leader (dreamer) was very upset.

Dreamer's associations: Leader said he was very afraid of conflict in the group. He did not know how to handle fights if they occurred. This is a commonly expressed fear of group process.

Dream 4: Co-leader did not show up in the group.

Dreamer's associations: The leader was ambivalent about having the group because of his heavy work load and agreed to it only if she could share the responsibility. He was still not sure he had made the right decision.

The following two dreams are from a sophisticated clinical social worker psychotherapist who was beginning a group for schizophrenics.

Dream 5: I was seeing a private neurotic patient who complains a lot. A psychotic patient came into the room. I didn't know what to do, who to see, or how to contain the psychotic patient. I was thinking: I have to get her on medication; I have to call Dr. M.; maybe she needs to be hospitalized.

Dreamer's associations: Since I had not worked with schizophrenics directly for five years, I was nervous about beginning the group. I was afraid of the responsibility of knowing when a patient needs medication and needs to be hospitalized, that is, of properly assessing the pathology. I was afraid of being overwhelmed by their neediness, especially when added to the demands I already had. Could my needs be met if I added this group to my work load? Most important is my fear that the patients' craziness would intrude into my own private space, which ultimately would mean invading my own psychic boundaries, and I would become crazy too. The theme of containment is present. The psychotic patient represents my own impulses; containing the patient's pathology becomes as important as containing my own impulses.

Dream 6: I was working within an agency setting, and I had to pick a leader for one of the groups. I chose Bill (one of the schizophrenic group patients). As the time came closer for him to lead the group, I became increasingly uncomfortable. The agency had a great deal of trust in me. Could Bill really lead the group well? Would he not be able to do it and would my reputation be ruined? As the time approached for him to lead the group, I got more and more anxious. I finally decided to have someone else lead the group.

Dreamer's associations: My struggle with Bill is underestimating his pathology and not wanting to see him as sick as he is. If I saw Bill's severe pathology, I would have to see that of my family's. I don't want to see my family members or Bill as sicker than me. Seeing that would make me feel guilt and pain.

These dreams present anxiety about groups and group members on varying levels:

1. The work level: How is this group going to affect my work situation? (Dream 4)
2. The group level: Will the group be rejecting or hard to control, thus making me feel helpless? (Dream 3)
3. The intrapsychic level: What about this group is going to force me to look at painful feelings within myself? (Dream 5)

It takes courage and strength to analyze one's fear of and ambivalence toward starting a group. But when a leader can do this, it is rewarding. One woman realized as she was starting a geriatric group that she would feel at the members' mercy. She would feel guilt at saying no to any of their requests because they might die the next day. She also imagined that they would hate her for being young and beautiful. It was only after the leader faced these feelings and worked them through that she was able to lead the group effectively. Similarly, in Dream 5, the therapist had to work through fears of fusion with the patients.

There are reasons for being afraid of leading groups other than those mentioned here. The most important point to remember is that it is alright to be afraid. If you are afraid to lead a group, you have a lot of company.

LEADING THE DIFFICULT GROUP MEETING

Group leaders' fear of leading groups often centers around managing the difficult meeting. Leaders' most dreaded fantasies about a first group meeting include: the silent group, the hostile group, the depressed group, and the group with the difficult members, such as a monopolizer or a disoriented patient.

THE SILENT GROUP

The silent group is often a dependent, passive group. Since it is the interaction among people that ultimately becomes the treatment tool, the leader does what he can to get people to talk to one another. The leader can facilitate interaction by: (1) using good discussion-leading technique, (2) using eye contact, (3) acting as a "translator," (4) allowing the group to be leader-centered, and (5) using the "go-around" technique.

Discussion-Leading Technique

When communication occurs in the silent group, it is usually leader-directed. The leader tries to deflect comments to other members. For example, the leader might say: "Does anyone else have that concern?," or "Does anyone else have the answer to that question?" The leader might even call on a specific member: "Don, perhaps you can help Harold."

Eye Contact

When a patient looks at the leader, the leader can look at the group as he is listening. In this way the leader is including the group in the conversation, whereas if the leader and the patient only look at each other, the rest of the group would be excluded. Often the member talking to the leader will pick up the leader's cue and begin darting quick looks at the group. On the other hand, if someone is reticent to talk and needs to be encouraged, the leader's direct and steady gaze can be a strong reinforcement.

The Role of Translator

Sometimes a person will talk in the group, but he will be unintelligible to the others. He may mumble or ramble. If the leader doesn't intervene, the member is ignored and the value of his communication is lost. The leader can extract the main point from what he is saying, state it clearly, and then ask others to respond. A leader might spend an entire meeting translating for members so that communication takes place. In hospital groups, many of the participants have poor communicative skills, which perpetuates their isolation.

The Leader-Centered Group

What if the preceding suggestions do not work? Members simply do not respond to leader's interventions, but they are willing to talk to the leader. Some hospital groups need to be leader-focused for a long period of time. It is often the way medical and psychiatric patients make the group fit into their personal narcissistic needs. These needs revolve around the leader: idealizing or being dependent on him or her. The leader needs to recognize and respect this way of relating. Focusing on the leader in the group can be viewed as one step beyond focusing on the leader in a one-to-one relationship.

For example, in an ongoing schizophrenic group, one member always talked to me. I suggested he look at the other members. He got angry, "You're the one I come here for. You're the therapist." The group defended him: "We understand. It's easier to talk if you look at the therapist." They were telling me that just because he looks at me does not mean that he doesn't know they are listening, and just because he doesn't look at them doesn't mean they don't know that he knows they're listening.

The Go-Around Technique

But what if the members don't talk to the leader and don't follow the leader's leads? The last resort is the "go-around." The leader says, "Now, we will go around, and everyone can give their name." The leader expects everyone to contribute. Members give their name. Then what? The leader gives another subject for a "go-around." The entire meeting can be spent having go-arounds.

The leader has to be careful in choosing subjects for the go-around. They have to be superficial and nonthreatening, such as: "What do you think about the hospital?" not "What disease do you have?" These groups are in the beginning stage, where it is most appropriate to indulge in superficial, nonthreatening "cocktail" talk. Any talk at all, no matter what the content, is going to give people a chance to get used to one another and test each other.

It is important to keep in mind that the purpose of the go-around is to stimulate interaction. If interaction occurs (someone saying to another, "Oh, I live there too!") the leader should not cut the interaction off and persist with the go-around. Usually, the go-around does spark some interaction. The leader should let it go, see how far it gets, and just before it totally dies, continue with the next person. If a go-around is not completed in the meeting, there may be disappointment among the members who were left out. An effort should be made to give everyone a chance before the meeting ends.

THE HOSTILE GROUP

A beginning group cannot tolerate intragroup hostility. In order for a group to develop, members have to feel that the group is a safe place. If the group is a place where attacks and judgments are made, the members may feel that it is a replica of other bad group experiences (including early family experiences).

Because group process cannot develop without trust and because attack threatens the development of trust, the group leader *must* intervene when attacks occur. Interventions should be made at the first hint of conflict. For example, if someone says to another, "You shouldn't cry. It is wrong to cry. It will only make you worse." The leader should immediately intervene and say: "Everyone is different here. One of the reasons we have the group is so that people can meet others different from themselves. It is what makes the group interesting. What is right for one person, may not be for another." If the attacking member does not respond, the leader will have to make stronger interventions. If nothing else works, the member will have to be taken out of the group.

Externalize Hostility

Hostility needs to be externalized in the beginning group. If all the "bad guys" are outside the group and all the "good guys" are in the group, it makes for a safe and trustworthy situation. Externalized hostility—on a group level—is a big help in moving a group toward cohesiveness.

Sometimes staff becomes nervous if hostility is externalized onto hospital administration or team members not in the group. It is easy to miss the fact that often the purpose of this hostility is to help members feel safe with one another (because all bad is outside the group); the content and target of the attack is of secondary importance.

Some leaders are afraid that if members are hostile toward staff or administration, the leaders might secretly agree with the patients and subtly encourage them. They know this would not be helpful, but at the same time they know that patients have complaints with which they can identify. Leaders in a hospital have to remember that patients are heavily dependent on staff; this is especially true for the acutely ill patient. To agree with such patients that the people who are caring for them are inadequate or the system is faulty is to foster anxiety, since one is confirming that they are in an unsafe place at a time that they are helpless to change it. The purpose of most hospital groups is to give the severely ill support and to minimize anxiety, not to escalate it.

The need to feel safe in the hospital can be so great that some patients use the defense of denial when there is *real* question about the care they are getting. For example, one medical patient was awaiting an operation for removal of some bits of sponge that were left in her from a former operation at a different hospital. She had exhibited low anxiety in facing the current operation and described the accident that had occurred matter-of-factly. Whereas the group leader was horrified at the story, the patient remained calm.

The more blame is removed from the group and the institution that patients are dependent upon, the more secure patients will feel and the lower their anxiety will be. Some of patients' complaints are global enough that they could as easily be directed toward society as toward the hospital administration. The patients feel frustrated about their total situation, and they need a target for blame. Usually the reasons for the problems are a complex set of factors which *do* include such things as the world's economic situation. For example, on one inpatient floor there

were complaints about the nurses not giving the patients enough attention. In fact, the floor was short-staffed because the hospital was in an
economic crisis—a dilemma most hospitals were facing. This crisis was the
result of a complex combination of factors, including the political and
economic state of the country. Sometimes it helps for a leader to ask,
"Whose fault do you think it is?" Usually one member will allude to
sources of blame other than immediate staff, because there are so many
from which to choose.

Acknowledge the Reality Base of Anger

This does not mean that leaders should encourage group members to
be passive and not try to change things in their immediate environment
when this is possible. Leaders can help the group sort out complaints that
the leader feels can be acted upon constructively and changed. This
approach deals with the helpless feelings that people have underneath
the anger they are expressing. The anger can be a mask for feelings of
helplessness.

Some patients who are not acutely ill respond to the leader's acknowledgment that there is a reality to their complaints. They find such an
acknowledgment supportive because the validity of their perceptions is
being recognized. People who need this kind of validation are those who
are questioning their reality testing. The solution to the problem can be
less important than the verification that they are not crazy.

THE DEPRESSED GROUP

The group composed of depressed people has the reputation of being
one of the worst. It is hard for the leader not to be sucked into the group
depression, which can seem so much more powerful when it is coming
from a number of persons. This is especially true when there is a reality to
the members' woes. Sometimes it is less overwhelming if the leader thinks
of the depressed group as one person. Techniques that a therapist would
use with a depressed individual may be useful in dealing with the group as
a whole. For example, the leader can elicit differences of opinion among
members or the anger behind the depression; or the leader can offer her
own positive viewpoint as an alternative to the group's negativity.

Elicit Differences of Opinion among Members

Very often one person in the group can see another (positive) perspective with the encouragement from the leader. The leader can reinforce
any positive note in the group, with comments such as: "I'm glad you

brought that point in," or "It is good when a group has differences of opinion," or "I agree that there is more than one way of looking at things."

Elicit Anger behind Depression

The leader can try to elicit the anger behind the depression. If anger emerges in the group, the group may become more active and assertive and less dependent, passive, and helpless. With conflict emerging in the group, there is a more dynamic process for the leader to work with, in contrast to uniform depression, which the leader may experience as a massive wall.

Oppose Group Negativity with Positive Viewpoint

Something that the leader needs to do in any depressed group is to let the group know that she does not see things as negatively as the members do. She understands and hears the reality of their unhappiness but feels that there are some positives—there is hope. The leader does not have to convince the group that there is some hope; she simply has to state her view strongly, so that she symbolizes an alternative to the members' way of perceiving the situation. She should periodically repeat her statements throughout the group, at the same time that she reflects what she is seeing in the group. For example, the leader might say: "You all seem to feel there is no hope for improvement. I agree that there are big problems here, but I don't see things quite so bleakly. I don't see it as you do—that it is all hopeless." More does not need to be said.

Sometimes it takes many periodic repetitions before a member in the group catches on and begins repeating the leader's viewpoint as though it were his thought in the first place. We might call such a process "identification;" it is a subtle process but usually happens in groups with time. Many hospital groups are too short for this identification to be accomplished. If a leader handles a group in the ways suggested, she will have done all she can do. She will stand for a hopeful frame of reference that some of the patients may be able to use privately.

THE DIFFICULT GROUP MEMBER

There are many different kinds of difficult group members. Yalom (1970) writes about the monopolist, the help-rejecting complainer, the self-righteous moralist, the doctor's assistant, the schizoid patient, the silent patient, the psychotic patient, and the homosexual. Each group leader and each group will find different patients difficult. The attacker, monopolizer, and disoriented members have been a source of concern to me and to the leaders with whom I have worked. The attacker was alluded to in the section on the hostile group and is discussed further in Chapter 9. Limiting the monopolizer—the member who talks incessantly—has been a challenge for a number of group leaders. The disoriented patient was not as big a problem in the open turnover group as one might anticipate.

The Monopolizer

The monopolizer is as destructive in the group as the attacker. The monopolizer is often very self-involved and perceives the group as a place to talk and have an audience rather than a place where listening is as important as talking. He may talk out of anxiety, with the flow of words being an attempt to lower anxiety. It can work in the opposite direction: anxiety increases as he senses his isolation from others.

A beginning group cannot be expected to challenge the attacker or monopolizer. They are not a group yet and will not develop into a group if trust is not established. The leader must help the group establish an atmosphere that is safe: a place where there is room for each person to express himself free from fear of being hurt and attacked. The leader has to stop the monopolizer if the group is to progress. It is important to set limits in groups of disturbed patients (Rabiner, Wells, and Yager, 1973; Viviano, 1969).

Members may encourage monopolizers so that they will not have to expose their own feelings. This is a convenient mechanism when members are not sure of one another. In a first meeting this dynamic is secondary to the intrusiveness of the monopolizer on each person's "space" in the group. If the members use the monopolizer to avoid exposing themselves in any way, they will never test the group to find out how safe it is. They leave the group unsatisfied, not believing that there is room in the group for their own needs to be met.

Once I did some role playing with a staff working with posthospitalized mental patients. Many dramatic things happened in the group. At the end of the session I asked the members and observers what stood out for them. To my surprise, they all said, "The way you stopped the monopolizer." Members said my behavior with the monopolizer was the strongest communication to them that I cared and was genuinely interested in what they had to say. I was actively working to make space for them in the group. The leader can do the following to stop a monopolizer: (1) intervene early in the session, (2) educate the monopolizer about group membership, and (3) actively try to stop the member from talking.

In the first few minutes of the group, when the leader has an inkling that someone might be monopolizing, he can extract something superficial from what the monopolizer is saying and intervene with a statement such as: "Wait a minute, you just said something very important (for example, about how you could not sleep at night) and I want to hear what others have to say about that. One of the things we want to do in the group is hear everyone's ideas about a subject." In this way the monopolizer, who usually is in desperate need of support, is not cut off and excluded from the group. Instead, the leader helps her make a contribution to the group at the same time that he limits her talking.

The leader can explain to the monopolizer that everyone who comes to the group has to be able to listen. Does she think she can listen? If not, she cannot be in the group. The ability to listen is an absolute requirement for group membership. Most often, the monopolizer will say that she thinks she can listen, but when she tries, she can only listen for a few minutes. When the leader and patient agree on the fact that the patient needs to listen, the patient usually accepts and appreciates help from the leader. There is an implicit contract that both patient and leader will try to help the patient listen.

The leader can help a patient stop talking by using a number of techniques. For example, the leader can use eye contact and facial expression to reward (encourage) or punish (limit) behavior. Direct, quick, reproachful looks from the therapist can stop a patient from talking. The leader can put a hand up to signal the person. The leader can even put his hand in front of the patient's mouth to stop her from talking. If the contract is clear, the group and patient will take these overtures with a sense of humor. *The monopolizer often does not understand subtle communication!* I have been as blunt as to say: "You can't talk now." "You have to wait." "One more minute and then you can talk." Most important, the leader, not the monopolizer, has to be in control of the group.

If the leader is effective in limiting the monopolizer so that she can stay in the group, the monopolizer often feels a sense of accomplishment. As the monopolizer is able to control herself, her anxiety lessens, and she becomes more open to the supportive mechanisms in the group. However, if all else fails, the leader must remove the monopolizer from the group. (This is discussed in Chapter 7.)

The Mildly Disoriented Patient

People usually assume that the disoriented patient cannot participate in a group. In a medical setting, it is not uncommon for the patient with organic brain syndrome to automatically be excluded from many activities. Yet patients have different degrees of organicity, and many of them *can* participate in a group. There are at least two reports in the literature where groups were composed solely for these patients, with positive results (Allen, 1976; Monaster, 1972). Open turnover groups can often absorb the mildly disoriented patient. At St. Vincent's Hospital such patients were included in adjustment-to-hospitalization groups and they usually contributed. Staff was frequently surprised at how lucid they appeared in the group.

If a mistake is made and a patient is too disoriented to participate in the group, he can stay in the group if he is not disruptive. Sometimes just the social stimulation of being in other peoples' presence in a structured setting is comforting, and the other members are comforted by an additional body attending the meeting (beginning groups like numbers). If the disoriented patient is disruptive, he has to be gently ushered out of the group.

AN ACTIVE, STRUCTURED APPROACH
TO GROUP LEADERSHIP

All of the suggestions mentioned above point in the direction of the structured hospital group with an active leader. Many professionals' training does not prepare them for the short-term hospital group or the groups composed of medically ill and severely disturbed patients. Reports in the literature concur that the supportive, structured approach is necessary with severely disturbed patient groups (Youcha, 1976), the turnover group (Shulman, 1979), and medical groups (Cooper Lonergan, 1980).

The first group meeting, as well as meetings to follow, should have structure. Bednar and Melnick, write that structure makes it possible for people to modulate the degree of risk and exposure they take in a group. They found that group members engaged more quickly in "therapeutically prescribed behaviors" when the leader provided structure in the beginning meetings (Bednar and Melnick, 1972, p. 33). How should the first meeting be structured? Knowledge of stages of group development is a big help in answering this question.

STAGES OF GROUP DEVELOPMENT

Most models of group development suggest that groups go through trust, power, and intimacy phases (Garland, Jones, and Kolodny, 1965). This can occur in one meeting. The implication is that a group cannot be intimate unless it has positively resolved trust and power issues. A number of group leaders expect group members to immediately interact and share their inner feelings. At times, this happens because people are in a crisis and quickly pass through the trust and power phases of group development. Despite this occurence, the leader should be wary and not encourage immediate exposure. He should expect that members will need a warm-up phase, where they will talk superficially as they get used to one another.

Often the leader is deceived in the group, assuming that the first thing members talk about is the most difficult, when in fact it may be the easiest. For example, a group of disturbed patients may talk about their morbid histories with facility but have a much harder time talking about where they are going to live when they leave the hospital. A group of medical patients may talk about their illness with facility but not be able to talk about their recent loss of jobs or friendships because of the progression of the illness. Thus what might appear as counterphobic exposure in the beginning of the meeting might not be.

In the following example, a patient truly overexposes herself in the beginning of the meeting.

> The leader recruited a single-session group from an in-patient psychiatric unit. One member immediately exposed her feelings of despair over her illness and recent death of her daughter. She felt totally alone. She started to cry and gave details of her situation. The other members ignored her. The group leader was upset by the insensitivity of the other members and tried to facilitate a response from them. "Does anyone else have a similar situation?" "What would you do if you were in Mrs. P.'s shoes?" No response. The leader became inwardly angry with the selfishness and self-involvement of the group members. She felt they were very insensitive. She finally reached out to the despairing patient and tried to comfort her.

This kind of situation is not uncommon. The leader misses the fact that it is the rest of the group that is responding appropriately (not wanting to get into highly charged emotional material), not the patient who is over-exposing. The leader is not being helpful to the despairing patient because she is encouraging her alienation from her peers (the more she talks, the more the members want to flee from her) and she is also discouraging reality testing (slowly testing the waters of the group). As the patient becomes alienated from the group, she is being cut off from a major source of support.

The leader can extract something nonthreatening from what the upset patient is saying and elicit feedback from others. For example, in the above situation the leader might intervene with: "Wait a minute, Mrs. P., there is something you said that I would like to get more feedback about. The purpose of our group today is to discuss how people are feeling on the floor. You said that you have been in the hospital three days and no one has helped you. Is this true for others? Have you felt that your needs are being met here?" The leader here assumes that a gripe session or a praise session is a much more common and appropriate way for a new group to begin.

THE BEGINNING OF THE MEETING

At the beginning of the meeting the leader can introduce himself and state the purpose of the session. He can mention that he has met each person individually and everyone has agreed to come and share regarding the meeting's topic. For example: "I am Mrs. Lonergan, the social worker on the floor. We're here today to discuss your reactions to being hospitalized on this floor. I've met you all individually, and you've all agreed that you want to talk about this."

The leader can then open the meeting up to discussion and reactions. The group may immediately begin to interact. If not, the leader will have to call upon the techniques mentioned in the section on silent groups. The leader must always remember that in a beginning meeting, the content of what people say is not as important as the process of interaction that occurs. It is the interaction that helps the leader make therapeutic interventions. Once interaction occurs, the leader can get an idea of where these patients are psychologically and what they need. People can expose themselves more by the way they relate to others than by what they say.

THE MIDDLE OF THE MEETING

If trust is developing, the leader can expect that about two-thirds of the way through a group meeting, members will be quite genuine with one another. It is at this point that someone might say, "This sure is not what I expected. I really didn't want to come today but now I'm glad I did." If the leader wants an honest response to a question, this is the time to ask, *not* at the beginning of the meeting. This is a good time for the leader to ask for an evaluation of the group meeting: "What *did* you think of the meeting today? This is the first time we've had a group like this. Do you think it is a good idea? Should we continue it? Should it be different in some way? Your opinions are very valuable to us." (If a leader asks, "How did you feel coming to the group today?" at the beginning of the meeting, he will probably get a superficial response.)

THE END OF THE MEETING

As the meeting gets closer to the end, the leader might tell the group that it has five or ten more minutes left. He can help them summarize the content of the meeting and reach a resolution to problematic material that has come up. For example: "Many of you voiced unhappiness with the way you have been treated here, but a few of you found that if you spoke up and were assertive, it helped a lot." Or, "Despite the physical pain many of you have, most of you have said that it is the loneliness that is the most painful. You've given examples of how you have helped each other on the floor. Now that you know each other better, you can continue to socialize. You seem to be able to give something to one another that staff cannot give." In the conclusion, the leader takes the opportunity to reinforce the part of the meeting where strengths such as assertiveness and mutual aid, are shown.

Another reason for informing members of the meeting's approaching end is to help members pace themselves. Leaders who let the meeting run on because members are involved in meaningful conversation are not allowing members to limit their exposure. It is important to have an ending so that "doorknob therapy" (people blurting out significant information at the door) *can* occur. When people blurt things out as they are leaving, they often do not intend to have the subject fully explored at that moment. It is helpful to confront them with their action: "You are telling us something important as you walk out the door. Maybe next week you can bring this up earlier so that we can have time to discuss it." Or in a single-session group: "Would you like to meet with me later today to discuss this further?" The member may say "no" and that is alright. Just verbalizing his or her thoughts and letting some people know what is going on may be enough support for the moment. Chapter 9 explores further how people protect themselves in crises and how important it is to understand and respect the ways in which people cope.

STRUCTURE AND GOALS

Structuring the meeting and having a goal for the group are intimately connected. Grobman (1978) writes that the major task of a group of disturbed patients is for them to be comfortable. The leader should not comment on here-and-now interaction or make interpretations. Shulman writes that one can expect to achieve the following in the first meeting:

(a) To introduce members to each other.

(b) To make a brief, simple opening statement which tries to clarify the agency's or institution's stake in providing the group service as well as the potential issues and concerns that group members feel urgent about.

(c) To obtain feedback from the group members on their sense of the fit (the contract) between their ideas of their needs and the agency's view of the service.

(d) To clarify the job of the group worker, the worker's task, and method of attempting to help the group members' work.

(e) To deal directly with any specific obstacles which may be involved in this particular group's effort to function effectively. For example, dealing with stereotypes group members may bring of either group work, helping people in authority, or dealing with their feelings of anger if the group is involuntary.

(f) To begin to encourage intermember interaction rather than discussion only between the group leader and the group members.

(g) To begin to develop a supportive culture in the group in which members can feel safe.

(h) To help group members develop a tentative agenda for future work.

(i) To clarify the mutual expectations of the agency and the group members. For example, what can group members expect from the worker? In addition, what expectations for their involvement does the worker have for the members (e.g., regular attendance, meeting starting on time)? Such rules and regulations concerning structure are part of the working contract.

(j) To gain some consensus on the part of group members as to the specific next steps. For example, are these central themes or issues with which they wish to begin the following week's discussion?

(k) To start to encourage honest feedback and evaluation of the effectiveness of the group. (Shulman, 1979, pp. 139–140)

The reader may agree that this is an ambitious list, and it is unlikely that this will all be accomplished in one meeting.

Universalization and Differentiation

One goal for any group meeting is to move the group toward cohesiveness. Yalom (1970) cites studies that indicate that the more cohesive the group, the more members' self-esteem is elevated. Since cohesive groups can be negative as well as positive, we must assume that the norms that develop in the group are those of mututal acceptance among members. The leader can help to move a group toward positive cohesiveness through the use of universalization and differentiation. The leader needs to underscore the commonality in the group, so that members can identify with one another, and at the same time allow for individual differences in the group, so that diversity and lively discussion can emerge. At the beginning of an open-heart surgery group, for example, the leader might say: "You are all here because you have had open-heart surgery, but you have not all had the same operation." The open-heart surgery group at St. Vincent's was a turnover group: people came one or two times. Most meetings evolved into cohesive sessions. There was high commonality because the trauma of surgery which they all readily shared. But the group consisted of patients who had both by-pass and valve operations: the procedure of surgery and the length of recovery period for these operations are quite different. Some patients felt immediate relief after surgery and were euphoric, while others felt no such magic. Without a clarification by the leader, patients were confused as they shared experiences. The group could easily split in two without the leader's interventions to prevent this. In a relatives' group of patients who are hospitalized on the acute-care unit, the leader may foster cohesiveness by saying: "You all have in common a relative who is hospitalized on the unit. At the same time, we all know that each of your situations is different."

Kellerman (1979) writes that "the tension level of the group...depends upon a desire...to establish boundaries and a simultaneous fear of losing individuality in the gradual coalescing of the group as a whole." (p. 127) The leader's use of universalization and differentiation helps to mediate members' basic wishes (to be united with others) and fears (losing one's identity) in joining a group.

Lowering Anxiety and Tension

Structure is one way to lower tension and anxiety in the group. Regulation of tension and anxiety is one of the primary tasks of the leader, and in supportive groups, tension and anxiety need to be as low as possible. Kellerman (1979) states that in order to stabilize tension, the group needs unambiguous leadership, clearly defined rules, open communication channels, a well-established dominance hierarchy, good reality testing, and low narcissism. None of this can be readily accomplished without a structured approach to group leadership. The leader must help mediate conflict and be active enough to be viewed as (1) consistent, (2) a reinforcer and clarifier of rules, (3) a facilitator of communication, (4) a reinforcer of members assuming roles in the group (including the leader actively accepting his role as leader), (5) a helper of members' reality testing by the encouragement of sharing of information, and (6) a reinforcer of interpersonal sensitivity. This leadership approach is in contrast to that recommended for psychoanalytic or interactional group therapy, where it is often useful for the therapist to generate anxiety and tension in the group by being a withdrawn, provocative, or confrontational group leader.

SUMMARY

Group leaders often feel better about beginning a group if they are prepared. Potential leaders can prepare by reading relevant literature, observing groups, and exchanging feelings and ideas with other new group leaders. Most new group leaders are frightened before leading their first meeting; such fears seem to be universal. Often anxiety centers around the leader's fantasy of the "worst" group meeting (the silent group, the hostile group, the depressed group) or the management of the difficult group member (the monopolizer, the disoriented patient, the hostile patient). It is helpful if the leader has an idea of how to handle such groups and patients before he begins to lead his first group. In general, handling these difficult groups and members requires an active, structured approach.

Chapter 6

Interdisciplinary Teamwork

Groups in hospital settings should be formed and structured so that they are integrated into the ongoing teamwork and aid in interdisciplinary communication. Knowledge in the fields of psychiatry and medicine grows constantly. It is impossible for one person to master his or her own discipline and all the others as well. Doctors are using computers to aid mastery because there is so much information to be learned. There is some truth to the saying that general practitioners are doctors who know less and less and about more and more until they know practically nothing about everything, and specialists are doctors who know more and more about less and less until they know practically everything about nothing.

The same can be said for all professions: whether people specialize or generalize, something is lost. Each representative of a discipline has a special contribution to make in understanding the patient, but the separation of the human being into distinct parts is only useful for the purpose of study and mastery. It is a *theoretical* and not a *real* reflection of the parts of the human being. Popper writes the following about categorization of disciplines:

 We are not students of some subject matter but students of problems. And problems may cut right across the borders of any subject matter or discipline . . . and theories, as opposed to subject matter, may constitute a discipline (which might be described as a somewhat loose cluster of theories undergoing challenge, change, and growth). But this does not affect my point that the classification into disciplines is comparatively unimportant, and that we are students not of disciplines but of problems. (Popper, 1962, p. 67)

THE IMPORTANCE OF TEAMWORK

The problem of providing good treatment can best be approached by consistent and unhampered communication among members of the treatment team representing different disciplines.

Sometimes team members can be of help to one another in surprising ways. A very sophisticated social worker was discussing the location for a group with a doctor who had a reputation for being quite insensitive to patients' emotional needs. The leader was asking about one of the few available rooms on the patient floor for a group of relatives of neurology and neurosurgery patients. The doctor said hesitantly, "But wouldn't the relatives be bothered by the brains in the room (pictures, models, and some in formaldehyde)?" The leader hadn't thought of this and was surprised at himself. He found another location.

The main value of groups cannot be realized unless the information obtained about patients in the group is integrated into the medical treatment plan. Frey (1966) found that the groups had many purposes and objectives, including education, treatment, orientation, and socialization. A few were designed to "counteract potentially destructive emotional reactions to illness and institutionalization such as dependency, isolation, depression, and anxiety." (p. 11) Most groups were reality oriented: personal and social problems encountered by the patient were faced. Intervention was directed toward issues which were, or might become, obstacles to recovery and social functioning. But of all the groups surveyed, only one group had the direct input of a social worker and a staff member of another discipline. Most groups were viewed as an extension of a particular worker's special interest; when the worker left the job, the group ended.

Groups can be used as a tool to bring everyone together in communication, including the patient. They should be viewed as a focal treatment and diagnostic tool for the interdisciplinary team. Groups can foster and enhance the interdisciplinary approach, adding to the crucial self-critical element of each discipline—an element that has been sorely lacking in the traditional approach to patient care.

The integration of the group into the team can be accomplished either by using a medical co-leader (nurse, doctor, physical therapist, rehabilitation counselor) and a psychosocial co-leader (social worker, psychiatrist, psychologist, psychiatric nurse) or by having the group leader report the contents of the meetings regularly to the interdisciplinary team. An example of the former is Payn's (1974) medication group for chronic schizophrenics. He is the expert on medication and his co-leader, a social worker, is the expert on social resources. As they lead the group together, they collaborate. An example of the latter is Schniewind and Needle's (1978) primary-care group where the social work group leader presented the content of the group meetings at rounds each week. Referrals were elicited for the groups when the social worker on each team discussed the indications for group therapy at team meetings.

PROBLEMS INVOLVED IN TEAMWORK

There are many problems when people from varying disciplines try to work together. There are a number of articles from primary care units where the problems of teamwork are discussed. (Delbanco, 1975; Kane, 1975; Kindig, 1975; Lamberts, 1975; Petersen, 1975; Wise, 1972; Wise, Beckhard, and Kyte, 1974). Sometimes competitiveness and distrust among staff prevents a coalition from occurring. Weiner (1958) writes that after a staff meeting, it is common to hear such comments as: "The doctor is too controlling," or "The nurse is too defensive." Howell outlined the best ways that team members could alienate one another:

1. Always be aloof, satisfied of your own complete understanding of the problem, dogmatic, and patronizing—then you are certain not be asked twice to assist in a group discussion.
2. Always find a place to work where the top man has the same attitudes—then you can be certain your organization will not find time to do any community planning or collaborate with any other organization.
3. Never complete any assignment that unavoidably you get, but by getting a reputation for procrastination and nondelivery of assignments undertaken you can generally avoid collaboration.
4. Always put second things first. Be continuously too busy to cooperate with other busier people.
5. A few good excuses are a help—"They do nothing but talk, just debating societies."
6. Avoid your professional societies as much as you can. You may run into someone who believes in collaboration and who tries to indoctrinate you.
7. Be unfaithful in little things. When you get a prepared history of a case from some earnest and busy person, don't read it till he gets there.
8. Don't answer telephones. Have them blocked by a chain of at least four to six people. If messages are left to call back, ignore them. If you really must go to a meeting, have your secretary

phone after it has begun to say something urgent has turned up
and you can't be there. Or if you are driven to make an appearance, get there very late, and then ask for a summary of everything that has happened in your absence.

9. If you see some dim reason for collaboration and attend the
necessary meeting, you can always be helpful by (a) contributing
nothing, sitting silently throughout, (b) harping on one point
which is completely off the subject, (c) talking all the time in long
sentences of Latin structure so that everyone else present is
cowed, (d) go for the purpose of getting your own way and be
entirely blind to everyone else's point of view.

10. If you've agreed to be chairman—don't do anything about
calling the meeting till the secretary pushes you to do it. Don't
prepare for the meeting—come in cold. But if you have a few
ideas, talk all the time. If you are interrupted, talk more loudly.
If someone manages to bring up a pertinent or controversial
point, tell him it will be dealt with later on the agenda—but
somehow never get to that item. In other words, prevent participation. Collaboration can be discouraged by these methods.
(1953, pp. 56–57)

I have heard nurses and social workers complain that doctors were not
sufficiently involved in patients' total treatment. Yet when doctors were
willing to rotate through the groups, some of these same people wanted to
reject their participation because "it is too hard to train one person after
another." There is some reality to the difficulty of orienting different
people to group leadership. The longer the new co-leader stays in the
group, the better, because it is less taxing on the stable leadership. However, often the stable leaders are reluctant to share the group. Some
leaders say, "The group is the best part of my job. I want to keep it for
myself."

GROUP DYNAMICS OF THE TEAM

By definition, if the team members do form a task group, a complex
organization develops. Often an understanding of group dynamics is
necessary to uncover obstacles that stand in the way of a team becoming
an effective task group. Weiner (1958) suggests that the team be viewed as
a system, with attention given to status, ranking order, and vested interests. The team should also be viewed within the context of the bureau-
cratic structure of the hospital; it will probably reflect a similar structure.

Wise (1972) thinks that the subject of how to work within the team group should be a crucial part of medical, nursing, and social work training.

The obvious factors to look at when analyzing the interdisciplinary team are the status of the doctor compared to the nurse and social worker and the sex composition and roles of the team. A number of primary-care units are trying to counter the status system where the doctor is always perceived as the "boss" by having members of varying disciplines alternate team leadership (Brickner, 1977; Wise, 1972). Gender composition in the team can be very important.

> One interdisciplinary clinic team could not work together. At team meetings, no one risked exposure of feeling and little was accomplished. There was a definite lack of communication, and patient care was not well coordinated. Team members complained about one another. Many felt that the medical director did not give them enough attention.
>
> The male member of the team left the service. The team was now all women, and the dynamics quickly changed. People became warm, friendly, open, and communicative. Feelings about patients were freely discussed, and treatment was coordinated. Team members became empathetic toward one another, and complaints were at a minimum.
>
> When the team discussed the sudden change in the way they related to one another, they attributed it to the fact that there was no man around. The female medical doctors said that they were always insecure around the male doctor because they had to prove themselves. It was a relief for them not to have to be "on guard" and try to impress the man. (Although this was probably true, a crucial dynamic may have been that the women no longer had to compete for the man.)

Sherman writes about the sexual politics in a hospital:

> Unfortunately, many physicians remain threatened by the multicolleagial treatment approach toward patients. . . . The field of medicine continues to be male-dominated, and the hospital social work staff continues to be predominantely female. The sexual politics in hospitals has enough substantive content for a separate institute. . . . Another form of competition can be seen when the nurse and the social worker vie for the love of the doctor. (1979, p. 22)

HOSPITAL GROUP LEADERSHIP

One of the major questions staff has with regard to leadership of hospital groups is: "Who is qualified to lead a group?" Sherman's frustration comes through as she states that "social workers . . . sometimes find themselves objects of sabotaging nurses . . . the nurse without any prior access to supervision wants to co-lead a group" (Ibid., p. 23). Some professionals think that an R.N. or M.D. title is sufficient qualification to lead a group, even if no prior training in group leadership and no available supervision exists. Others have trouble recognizing members of another profession who *do* have training in group leadership. An example of this lack of acceptance is the social worker not accepting the qualifications of the psychiatric nurse who has had training in group leadership. In general, it is true that any professional can run a group, but the quality and scope of the group will be limited by the skills of the leader. For example, a nurse or a doctor can lead a question-and-answer group and much will be accomplished. But if a psychosocial co-leader is present who is familiar with group dynamics, the potential of the group will be more fully realized.

Group leaders may or may not have had training in the medical aspects of illness, psychosocial assessment, and group methods. All of these areas of knowledge are important for the leader to maintain a high-quality hospital group. Most professionals are trained in one area or another; few have had training in all three areas. Co-leadership solves the problem of bridging the medical–psychosocial split, but what about training in group methods?

Any professional in the health field can be trained in group methods. It is usually a part of social work training, occasionally a part of nursing training, and rarely a part of medical training. The solution to optimum group leadership when a leader has not had such training is either supervision or co-therapy with an experienced group leader. Usually the department of psychiatry or social work is most prepared to offer supervision in group methods. Occasionally a psychiatric nurse can offer this service. Schniewind and Needle (1978) introduced primary-care residents to ongoing groups as guest observers for four to six weeks. This eliminated problems of competition for leadership and the expectation that "a doctor should know everything," including how to lead a group. In the primary-care program at St. Vincent's Hospital, where groups were abundant and led by interdisciplinary staff, the medical director made it a requirement that all groups be supervised by the social worker, who was a trained group therapist. For example, a medical doctor led an adolescent group at a neighborhood school and was supervised by the social worker. If the nurse or doctor co-leader attended supervision and also began to learn about group methods, group leadership evolved into a shared responsibility. Sometimes primary leadership of the group alternated so that each person could get experience and training.

ROLES OF THE TEAM MEMBERS

In a survey of maternal and child health groups, 73 percent of the groups were led by social workers, and 44 percent had co-leaders. Leaders complained about lack of clarity of roles (Poynter-Berg, 1979). This is, no doubt, a common concern when two people of different disciplines lead a group.

MAINTAIN ROLE SPECIFICITY, BUT LEARN FROM COLLEAGUES

Shared group leadership does not mean homogenation of roles. Borriello (1976) voices his concern in psychiatry where professionals' roles merge and specificity is lost: "Everyone does everything!" It is possible for two people to lead a group, with each contributing in his or her area of expertise. However, when people of different disciplines lead a group, they do learn a great deal about their colleague's work. For example, when a psychiatric nurse clinician and a cardiac nurse clinician worked together leading a group, the cardiac specialist became more interested in and knowledgeable about patients' unconscious feelings and the psychiatric specialist learned a great deal about the procedure of open-heart surgery. Similarly, the consistent reaction of doctors, nurses, and physical therapists to observing groups at St. Vincent's was: "Gee, we rarely get a chance to sit down and really talk to patients about who they are and what they feel." They were exhilarated by the experience, although at times they were nervous about the nature of the social worker's "probing" questions. They were comforted by the patients' responses to these questions and the adeptness with which the leader handled the material. They learned as they observed the social worker in action and as a result were able to elicit and handle more of the patents' feelings. When there is co-leadership, a social worker can learn to skillfully handle repetitive medical questions and the nurse, doctor, or rehabilitation counselor can learn how to elicit feelings behind questions.

The group format has something to offer members of each discipline in order to facilitate the performing of their task. The group process focuses on patient problems and as mentioned earlier, these problems run across discipline lines.

THE ROLE OF THE PHYSICIAN

Doctors need to have an orientation about groups so that they can make the best use of them. One physician, revealing his lack of familiarity with the group concept, wrote in the medical chart: "Patient very cheerful today. In good spirits. Attended group without any adverse reaction."

At. St. Vincent's there were numerous instances where information was revealed in the course of group interaction that was crucial in influencing medical orders:

> A patient reported in the post–myocardial-infarction group that he was very nauseated. He did not feel it was important to tell anyone. It was a side effect from the medication, and his orders were changed.

> In the relatives' group for patients hospitalized on neurology and neuro-surgery, a wife reported that the patient was in so much pain that he told her he wanted to die. The patient had been telling staff that he was "just fine." After this meeting, he was given regular medication for pain, and his morale improved.

> Members of a prenatal group complained of nausea from iron pills, and medical staff talked of trying to get a different brand of medication.

The example of the patient who needed more pain medication but didn't "speak up" is especially interesting, since it has been reported in the literature that many doctors and nurses have no idea how much medicine their patients require to control pain (Marks and Sachar, 1973).

Most important, however, is the potential for doctors to use the group to get a view of the total patient—emotionally, socially, and physically. Grinnel et al. writes, "In recent decades, medical educators have expressed a growing concern that too little attention has been given to the concept of providing comprehensive health care for the 'total person in his total situation'" (1976, p. 317). Doctors are usually trained as technicians of the body, and yet they are often expected to encompass total knowledge of the person in formulating their diagnosis and treatment plan. Strain and Grossman write that "it is unrealistic to assume that any teaching program can guarantee that all physicians will be competent to provide adequate psychological care for all their patients" (1975, p. 8). When doctors participate in group they can observe the social worker who deals with emotional material and at the same time advance their knowledge of the patient. Interestingly, Grinnel et al. (1976) report that in an opinion survey, 30 deans of medical schools said that they would like social workers to teach more in their schools.

Doctors are beginning to participate in groups as a learning experience. One resident said, "Now that I've learned about the patient as a person. I feel that I need to spend 45 minutes talking to each patient, but how can I do that when I have so many patients to see? It is so frustrating, now that I know how important listening is!" The response was, of course, "Have a group with your patients. It is an economical use of your time." One experienced doctor observed a group and said afterward, "I still have so much to learn. I wish I could come all the time." One resident attended group after working all night in the intensive-care unit and before he went home to sleep. It is not surprising that this doctor would sacrifice his comfort in order to obtain increased understanding, control, and emotional security in the face of what was formerly overwhelming and threatening to him: treatment of the "total patient," including the patient's emotional life.

THE ROLE OF THE NURSE

Groups have the potential of helping nurses use floor events constructively. Often during the meetings it is the nurse that understands best what is going on between two patients. The nurse on the floor is the member of the team who knows all the patients in the group and how they have been interacting on the floor, as well as significant floor events that have occurred. The nurse is also the person who observes visiting hours and the effect of families on patients.

Nurses that participated in the groups on a regular basis expressed that the group was the highlight of their week. The group added a dimension to their job that they found gratifying; they were dealing with the patients as total people rather than concentrating on their concrete physical needs. In one instance, a nurse was having difficulty relating to two young women on the general-medicine floor; they had made a mutual alliance and were quite hostile toward her. The nurse found these two women easier to relate to in the group and felt she would have less trouble gaining their cooperation after group participation.

A head nurse of one floor co-led a group. She had an excellent reputation and knew her patients well. She felt the group was a help to her in running a good floor. The group was the highlight of her week. For three months we charted every patient in group and looked at whether this nurse learned something new about each as she interacted with them in group. With few exceptions, she learned something new about each patient. Often it was sociological or biographical information that helped her empathize with the patient. Sometimes it was information crucial for the prescribed medical care.

THE ROLE OF THE SOCIAL WORKER

Groups can help social workers perform their tasks of providing concrete services, counseling, and screening of patients who need special

services. Generally, the provision of concrete services is the least important aspect of hospital groups; but sometimes such services are paramount, as in the case of a member of the Hispanic prenatal group.

> The patient approached the social worker before the group and said that
> she needed a homemaker when she went to the hospital, because she knew
> no one to care for the children. The social worker would have seen her
> individually to discuss this issue, but there was no time before the group.
> The leader then suggested to the patient that she bring up the problem in
> group.
>   D. said to the 12 members present that she did not know who to leave her
> 2-year-old with when she came to the hospital. The group said, "You mean,
> you don't know anyone?" She said there was a neighbor who offered, but
> she didn't trust her. The group explored the reasons, and they felt the
> neighbor sounded fine, as did the group leader. The group said, "You have
> to start trusting sometime." Members encouraged her to test out her neigh-
> bor a bit further.

> A discharge problem was immediately picked up by the social worker when
> one patient was on the coronary intensive-care unit because his relative
> spoke of the problem of the discharge plan in the relatives' group.

Concrete services that involve utilizing community resources can often
be facilitated by group sharing. Some patients are more skilled in utilizing
resources than others, and serve as good teachers. In a group for Hispanic parents of chronically ill children, one woman told another about a
day-care center in their neighborhood, and she proceeded to go there
and make provisions for her child so that she could go to school.

All of the social work group leaders at St. Vincent's Hospital felt that the
group helped them with the counseling aspect of their job. Aside from
learning new things about their patients in groups, they found that they
were able to tolerate some of the more difficult (provocative, repetitive, or
dull) patients more easily in group. They were able to give patients more
time and attention with group attendance. For example, a number of
people in the outpatient dialysis and medical groups would have been
followed by the social worker in a routine manner: they would have been
contacted when they came to clinic (sometimes every one to three
months), or they would have had interviews on an "as needed" or crisis
basis. Social workers found that seeing these patients in group once a
week helped them get to know the patients better (and vice versa), which
made therapeutic interventions more effective.

Ideally, casework should deepen the worker's experience with the
patient in group and having a person in group should deepen individual
work. All the social workers felt that having their own patients in group

(those they had seen individually prior to group attendance) deepened their understanding and work with the patient. Sometimes leader and patient sharing the life experience of the group made them feel closer, and a mutual identification was aided.

As members are screened for a group (a designated population) or as members (unknown to the social worker prior to the group) participate in the group, people who reveal special needs can be picked up as cases; these are cases that would be missed by the ongoing method of referral to the social worker. Members that interact in a somewhat bizarre way in the group can be seen individually for further evaluation. Use of group was especially appreciated by Maria's social worker.

> Maria, pregnant with her first baby, attended the Hispanic prenatal group as part of her clinic routine. She presented no problems, so there would have been no other reason for the social worker to be very involved with her. Maria was a leader in the group. She attended regularly and was verbal, and she interacted sensitively with other group members. During her seventh month of pregnancy, complications arose and Maria lost her first baby. The social worker and medical staff were glad that they had a relationship with her. Because of the group, the leader was able to make more effective interventions at a time of crisis for the patient.

Had Maria not been in group, no one on the staff would have had a relationship with her. She did not speak English and there were few Spanish-speaking staff members. It is likely that Maria and her husband would not have cooperated with medical recommendations, since they tended to blame the hospital for the death. However, after their feelings were handled sensitively by the group leader, and after staff used the leader's recommendation on dealing with the patient, the couple's anger was replaced by appreciation for sensitive care. (In this case the group leader became the head of the interdisciplinary team.)

A number of social workers seem to have problems with their self-image in the medical setting. They tend to underestimate their role and the contribution they make to the patient and the team. Strain and Grossman write that medical staff tend to undervalue and underutilize the skills of the social worker.

> . . .the social worker is trained to evaluate the patient's psychological functioning, the quality of his family relationships, and his psychological environment outside the hospital . . . .She is in a unique position to detect adverse psychological reactions, and to make important recommendations as to how the patient's psychological and social needs can best be met while he is in the hospital and after

he is dicharged. . . . In fact, however, the social worker is rarely given an opportunity to demonstrate her considerable expertise in this area. Instead, she is expected to perform what might be described as a housekeeping function . . . social workers have come to accept their professional fate. (1975, p. 181)

One social worker at St. Vincent's expressed these feelings. "I felt uncomfortable with medical staff. I didn't want to speak to the doctors. They always seemed in a rush, and I felt they had more important things to do than speak to me."

But group leaders were expected to interpret the group to team members and educate staff about the group's potential importance. Social workers' confidence rose as they got increasing support and recognition from medical staff for their group work. Some social workers who were more assertive than others, served as models.

Phyllis, a social worker, was leading a pediatric group. Anne, another social worker, was observing. Children with wheelchairs and intravenous poles crammed into a room for their meeting. Dr. E. interrupted the meeting and said he had to take blood from one of the children in the room. Phyllis did not have a relationship with Dr. E., but she said, "If you could wait until after our group meeting, we would appreciate it." He said, "Sure," awkwardly and walked out. After the meeting, Anne was asked what she had learned from observing the meeting. To her supervisor's surprise she said, "The way Phyllis talked to the doctor, and the way he responded."

In a number of other instances at St. Vincent's Hospital, a doctor would come by to see a patient who was in the group meeting, and when he realized that the group was in progress, he would quickly excuse himself and say he would be back later. The group leaders and the patients were impressed by how important the doctor felt the group was—that he would alter his schedule for it. Once I was leading a group for private patients on the medical inpatient floor, and a nurse interrupted the meeting saying that a doctor wanted to see Ms. W. I asked the nurse how important the matter was and if it could wait until after the group meeting. She left and came back ten minutes later to say that it was important. My co-leader went out to confirm this information and found ten doctors waiting to see the patient: an attending, a specialist, residents, and interns. The physicians must have worked quickly because the patient came back to the group ten minutes later and talked about the examination. These examples were demonstrations to staff that patients' group attendance can have high priority in the treatment sequence; this is the case even if the group is led by a social worker; group attendance can take precedence over seeing the physician for an unscheduled appointment.

MISPERCEPTIONS OF TEAM MEMBERS

Sharing group leadership is one means by which interdisciplinary problems can be solved. Colleagues can be exposed to each other's direct work with patients; as a result, roles and areas of expertise become clearer. Misunderstandings of function are often cleared up and knowledge about other's fields expands.

A social worker observing a nurse lead a group was impressed by the directness of the nurse's comments and questions and learned by observing patients' reactions to this different approach. Her appreciation of the nurse was enhanced.

In a stroke group, social workers gained an appreciation for how the physical and speech therapists worked. With the speech therapist's participation, aphasics were able to participate in the group process more fully. The physical therapist's presence in one meeting made it possible for a partially paralyzed person to get in a more comfortable position, much to the group's relief. Some rehabilitation therapists expected the group to have exercises or be highly didactic. The social worker used the opportunity to explain to the therapists that she used the group to elicit patients' feelings, and sometimes these feelings are rather morbid and depressing (in order to prepare the therapist, who had shown some discomfort with the these feelings). The rehabilitation therapist had the chance to hear such feelings in the group and also see how the social worker handled them positively. Her comfort with the social worker's approach increased.

The doctor's view of the social worker as one who only delivers concrete services (for example, discharge planning) is a common source of friction. At St. Vincent's there were a number of instances where this misconception was dealt with as groups progressed and communication continued between doctor and social worker. For example, social workers only saw private patients by physician referral. Most of these referrals were for discharge planning. At the same time, nurses and social workers often felt certain patients who were not referred would benefit by speaking to a social worker. With support from the director of the department of medicine, private physicians agreed to send their patients to group meetings led by social workers. Patients got some services from social workers and some attention to their feelings by other staff members. Social workers also had a positive format from which to communicate with the private physicians and mutual appreciation and understanding developed.

CONFLICT AND RESOLUTION

USE THE GROUP EXPERIENCE

Working together in the group gives colleagues the opportunity to directly conflict and immediately work on a resolution. Sometimes there is a problem when two psychosocial leaders or two medical leaders run a group together. I have noticed competition and antagonism between the psychiatric consultant and the social worker. The social worker may wonder, "Will the consultant respect and acknowledge my expertise or push me out?" The consultant has the task of impressing an ongoing group—the interdisciplinary team—because he is the outsider. In one instance a doctor and nurse tried to lead a group together, had difficulty, and ultimately found a resolution.

> The post–myocardial-infarction group had a nurse, doctor, and social worker leading the group. It took the team a while to define their respective roles. At first, the doctor and nurse allowed the social worker to provide group leadership, while they remained passive. Finally, they alternated leadership so each would have the experience of leading the group and become an active participant. When the doctor was not present, the nurse would answer medical questions; when the doctor was present, the nurse turned to him for the answers. The doctor wasn't happy with this behavior, and they finally decided they should both be equally considered as medical resource people.

SELF-CRITICISM

Howell (1953) specifies the personal qualities that she thinks are necessary for a professional to practice the art of collaboration:

1. Goodwill.
2. Knowledge of method of collaboration.
3. Integrity (willingness to admit error and accept its consequences).
4. Respect for colleagues in other disciplines.
5. Flexibility (a willingness and capacity to change and modify pre-judged opinions).
6. Imagination (being able to put self in other's places).
7. Communication (continually share frustrations, get brief, informative memos out, telephone people back).

8. Nondefensiveness (accept own weaknesses and other's criticism).

Howell is referring to a person of high ego strength who has good self-esteem. Such a person can risk flexibility and reflection. Thus we come to the second path for resolving interdisciplinary conflict: self-criticism.

There is a dilemma in making a plea for self-criticism: those people who read Howell's list and reflect on their own behavior already have the needed attributes; those who read the list and see the other team members (externalizing) do not. Usually the team members who are the most disturbed are those that are most criticized by team members.

Since it is unrealistic to expect someone to participate in the process of self-criticism who has not already begun it, supervisors have to take a different tact: "What will get you what you want?" Usually the group leader wants and needs the cooperation from the team; in order to get this cooperation he or she has to win over other staff, instead of alienating them. It is hard to do this without the leader having some empathy for the people with whom he or she is working and developing the skills of collaboration.

Members of all the disciplines in the health field should heed the criticism Hirsch and Lurie make of their fellow social workers:

> Too much of the psychic energy of social workers has in the past been drained in a struggle to define the areas the profession serves. Social work has a proud history in humanitariam service to the community. However, it does not have sole claim to this role; other disciplines are allied with social work in the service of man. . . . The fact is that a long-range idealistic goal for social work, as well as other helping professions, is to make its services unnecessary. (1969, p. 78)

With all of the conflict among team members and with the hospital system and the energy needed to make for resolution, it is often very difficult to keep in mind that the sole purpose of this struggle is to improve patient care.

INSTITUTIONALIZATION OF THE GROUP

Ultimately, groups should be institutionalized on particular services and viewed as a necessary part of hospital routine. This has been accomplished in many mental-health settings, but it is rare in medicine. This goal was realized at St. Vincent's in a few instances.

During oncology clinic the patients knew that they went to lab, went to group, and then saw the doctor for their examination. This was their clinic routine. The oncology specialist nurse and the social worker lead the group. Immediately after the group, while the patients were preparing to see the doctors, the group leaders met with the doctors and briefed them as to the content of the group. The doctors then saw the patients and were prepared to deal with specific concerns or problems that certain patients had.

Leading the post–myocarial-infarction group was the head nurse of the inpatient service, the social worker assigned to the floor, and a resident interested in heart disease. The supervisor met with the leaders after the group and discussed each patient, as well as the group process which reflected the process occurring on the unit. Information elicited was quickly translated into changes in nursing, medical, or social work care. Consultations were ordered, discharge plans changed, or medication reviewed. One doctor asked the group leader to assess his patient. He knew the patient was anxious but wanted to know how he compared to others. A doctor could find out if his patient appeared more fragile, depressed, or anxious than the average group member. The answer to this question often determined whether tranquilizers would be considered, dosages changed, or psychiatric consults ordered.

When a group is institutionalized in a hospital, staff considers it an integral part of delivery of service. If the group were to disband, staff would protest because the group would be seen as a *necessary* treatment tool. It became most apparent that two groups were institutionalized in the general hospital at St. Vincent's Hospital when the social work group leaders terminated employment and no replacements were hired because of a job freeze. In both instances, the medical directors made a strong and supporting plea for the workers to be replaced and the groups to continue. Their pleas were heard, and the workers were replaced. All levels of the system were involved in this move: patients, group leaders, department heads, and administration.

SUMMARY

It is crucial that the group be integrated into the teamwork taking place to deliver quality care. Since it is impossible for one person to master the knowledge and skill involved in treating the total patient, teamwork is a necessity. The traditional psyche–soma split can be bridged if medical and psychosocial group leaders work together. If this is not possible, they should communicate afterward and use the information that has evolved from the group to better diagnose and treat the patient. But such a prescription is not easy to fulfill. The professions are rivalrous and competitive with each other.

If professionals of two disciplines co-lead a group, misunderstandings and misperceptions can often be resolved. Seeing one's colleague in action helps one understand his or her role with the patient. Leaders share a mutual experience and often find themselves together in the struggle or faced with open conflict that they are compelled to resolve. Of course, such progress as a result of increasing familiarity requires mature professionals who are able to be introspective, flexible, and willing to change former attitudes with new experiences.

Chapter 7

Setting Up a Group

People generally approach the idea of group therapy with the basic assumption that "groups are good" or "groups are bad"; they bring to group therapy a basic trust or basic mistrust of group process. It seems to be the exception that a patient requests group therapy as his first choice of treatment. At one large city hospital, there were a lot of groups and patients had no choice; they were automatically put in a group if they wanted outpatient care in the mental-health clinic. This contrasted with a private mental-health clinic, where only a small percentage of new intakes were referred to the group therapy department. Most private patients are cajoled into groups by their individual therapist. This leads to the questions: Why such resistance to joining groups? Why do most new patients automatically assume that their needs will be better met by an individual therapist than a group? Why don't people have the basic assumption that something good will happen when people come together? Why don't people think, "There are many people to help me and not just one"? Perhaps the answer is societal, cultural, or familial. It would be interesting to know if individuals raised in a community which provided emotional support and continuity are less reluctant to choose group therapy.

Fortunately groups are becoming more popular and acceptable as a source of pleasure and learning. Self-help groups are proliferating. This change may be a reflection of the increasing freedom in our culture to explore new avenues of problem solving. Prominent people publicizing their personal struggles have facilitated the process. Although fear of exposure to strangers and doubts about peer helpfulness still exist, they are often put aside when countered by an authority figure's encouragement.

COMPOSITION OF THE GROUP

There are three things to look for in composing a group: the balance between homogeneity and heterogeneity, the potential isolate, and the potentially destructive or inappropriate group member. The latter are often visible to staff and stand out because they are too sick or disoriented, or because they are in a stage of accepting their illness where their withdrawal needs to be respected. More often than not, however, people are excluded from the hospital group who need not be.

As was mentioned earlier, one of the striking characteristics of hospital groups composed of people in a crisis situation is that they can tolerate very heterogeneous groupings. In working with families with genetic disorders (cystic fibrosis), Tannebaum (1978) suggests that groups be homogeneous in disease, prognosis, and stage of illness. Frank (1952) writes that it is obvious that medical patients would be adversely affected by seeing others sicker than themselves. However, we did not find this to be true in the general hospital groups at St. Vincent's Hospital. Groups composed of disturbed psychiatric patients can also be very tolerant. In one cohesive, outpatient group, for example, members listened with perfect equanimity to a woman speaking about her compulsion to look at men's flies and a man talking about his homosexuality. In another cohesive group, members shared their homicidal and suicidal fantasies. One member graphically described how she had spontaneous orgasms at work. The members did not flinch or withdraw.

In a long-term group for the aged, no one who applied for the group was excluded, since I did not know enough to predict success or failure. In retrospect I could say, "Yes, I should have known that this person would drop out." In fact, someone who appeared psychopathic in the intake interview *was* psychopathic. He influenced the group process both positively and negatively. Another very deprived member dropped out of the group, as could have been predicted, but I was still touched by what she gained in the meetings she attended. However, there were two people whose behavior could not have been predicted: one dropped out and one stayed, thus confirming my feeling that we simply do not know enough yet to compose the "perfect" group or to be sure who will do well in the group and who will not. Yalom writes that diagnostic interviews or psychological testing have not been shown to adequately predict a person's group behavior.

I have had the opportunity to study closely the conception, birth, and development of approximately fifty therapy groups—my own and others—and have been struck repeatedly by the fact that some groups seem to "jell" immediately, some more slowly, while other groups flounder painfully, spinning off members, and only emerge as working groups after several cycles of attrition and addition of members. . . .In large part the critical variable is some, as yet unclear, blending of the members. . . .No rigorous study exists which investigates the relationship between group composition and the ultimate criterion-therapy outcome. (1970, pp. 192–193)

There are constant surprises for the group leaders: those group meetings that become cohesive that we least expect and those members who surprise us with their social facility. This is one of the reasons why leading a group can be such a good learning experience; we still have so much to learn about people and group process! Taking chances in composition when we are not sure of the outcome helps us learn because we can then look at the results and analyze them.

There have been times when leaders have said a member did not get anything out of the group because he or she was so withdrawn in the meeting. I accepted this fact but suggested that the leaders ask such patients what they thought of the group after the meeting. Usually leaders were surprised by the responses they got. A common answer was, "I was listening but too tired to talk. Don't forget to ask me to come next week." If a patient says the meeting was "good" or "bad," it is important to ask specifically, "How?" so the leader and supervisor can learn from the patient.

There are times that the leader is concerned about a member's impact on the other members. In such a case, the leader can ask the other members, after the meeting, how they felt about the meeting. The leader can acknowledge with the other members that it was a difficult meeting and express that it would be understandable if they were displeased. In the post–myocardial-infarction group, which was a turnover inpatient group, a man was very anxious and monopolized the group. We were afraid he was making everyone else anxious. On top of his anxiety, he was judgmental toward others, which threatened the atmosphere of acceptance that the leaders were trying to establish. The leaders said after the meeting that they were sorry they included him. When they spoke to the two other members, both of whom had been attacked, the members said, "Oh, we knew he was off the wall and didn't take him seriously. He's that way all the time. It was still nice having the group and breaking up our routine." Before the leaders questioned these members, they had not realized that these three patients were all together on the floor and had already become desensitized to one another. In the meeting, they probably sensed the leaders' support.

Do a Face Sheet

Very often when we think of composing a group, we have a subjective view of the population with which we want to work. Mistaken perceptions or gaps in knowledge of population often lead to dead-end groups. One way leaders can check their perceptions is to design a face sheet. One can look at the face sheet and see how a group balances out in terms of homogeneity and heterogeneity; one can also spot potential isolates. Sometimes our perceptions are clouded by one or a few individuals who stand out for us but are not representative of the total population.

Table 7-1 is an example of a face sheet that we made for a male, inpatient, general-medicine group. The worth of a face sheet is dependent on the category headings. This face sheet includes "organicity," "alcoholism," and "social isolation" which are important variables for this particular population. For each population different data will have special importance. This face sheet has question marks on it, which would be common for an inpatient turnover group, where the leader does not know all the patients before the group begins.

One can see from the face sheet that there is a balance of heterogeneity and homogeneity. The group might be quite homogeneous in that most of the members are alcoholics. There is an age range of 42 years, but it seems to be balanced nicely at both ends of the range. The group is primarily White and Catholic, but there is more than one Protestant and more than one Black to prevent isolation. Most are ambulatory and receive financial assistance. They have a variety of diseases and a variety of discharge placements. A potential isolate would be the one Jewish man. Possible management problems might be the men who have some organicity and the agitated schizophrenic.

In doing a face sheet for a long-term geriatric group, I learned that all but one member of this potential group was Jewish. I had conducted intake interviews for everyone but had not realized this fact. The person who was not Jewish had a strong personality, so my subjective feeling was that the group was more balanced than it was. Also I did not take much note of religion when I was interviewing, and I was struck by this representation on the face sheet. As it turned out, religion was a crucial dynamic. The fact that most of these aged people were Jewish meant that they had lived through the European holocaust, which had greatly affected their character development. Most of them came from large families where there were traumatic separations. There was sexual repression among the women and repression of hostility in both men and women. Absorbing the one non-Jewish member—the potential isolate—was a major struggle for the group. The situation was resolved when he ultimately became the peer group leader.

TABLE 7-1

Face Sheet for Male, Inpatient, General-Medicine Group

Name	Age	Religion	Race	Socioeconomic Situation	Ambulatory	Diagnosis	Affect	Discharge Plan	Organic/(O) Alcoholic (A)	Isolated
P. S.	75	Catholic	White	Social security	Yes	Hypertension, malnutrition	Depressed	Placement	O, A	Yes
S. M.	54	Catholic	White	$800 per mo.	Yes	Fourth heart attack	Pleasant	Nursing home	No	Yes
T. L.	52	Protestant	Black	No assistance	Yes	Sickle cell anemia	Withdrawn	Placement	O, A	Yes
C. A.	33	Catholic	White	No assistance	?	Anemia	Withdrawn, cooperative	Nursing home	A	Yes
G. H.	57	Catholic	Black	Welfare	Yes	Anemia, tuberculosis, schizophrenia	Agitated	State hospital	Not determined	Yes
S. B.	36	Baptist	White	Unemployed	?	Hypertension	?	Not determined	A	No
M. P.	42	Catholic	White	Unemployed	?	Liver disease	?	Not determined	A	Brother
V. C.	43	Catholic	White	Social security	Yes	Blind, tuberculosis	Withdrawn, depressed	Nursing home	A	Yes
F. H.	63	Catholic	White	SSI (supplemental social security)	?	Asthma	Pleasant, cooperative	Nursing home	Not determined	Friend
F. D.	44	?	White	Men's shelter for homeless	?	Cellulitis	Withdrawn, cooperative	Not determined	O, A	Father
B. N.	66	Catholic	White	SSI	No	Orthopedic problem	Pleasant	Single-occupancy hotel	No	Friend
D. O.	72	Jewish	White	?	?	Artereosclerotic cardiovascular disease	Disoriented	Single-occupancy hotel	A	Not determined
J. W.	45	Protestant	Black	Unemployed	?	Edema	?	Not determined	A	Sister

Source: Joyce Laudon, St. Vincent's Hospital, Department of Social Work, 1977.

The Potential Isolate

Yalom would suggest not putting a potential isolate in a group, and I think, for the most part, his prescription is sound. However, I have found that in groups where there is high anxiety because of crisis, the wish and need to belong to a group is greater than the discomfort of not having a "buddy" (Gitterman, 1970) or a "Noah's Ark mate" (Yalom, 1970) in the group.

In the program at St. Vincent's, it was not unusual for a potential isolate to be spotted as a group was being formed. For example, on an inpatient medical floor where a hospital-adjustment group is being formed, there might be eight women over 60 years old available for the group, and one 21-year-old; or in forming a group for relatives of seriously ill patients, there might be five people whose relatives had had heart attacks and were on the coronary-care unit and one person who was coping with a dying relative on the intensive-care unit. Rather than automatically excluding such people, I encourage leaders to explain the situation to them and ask them if they want to attend the group. For example, the leader would say: "You would be the only young person in the group today. If you would like to come we would love to have you." Or, "Other people in the group today have a relative who has had a heart attack. You would be the only person whose relative is critically ill and on the intensive care unit. But all of you are in a state of crisis. Would you like to come?" A number of potential isolates accept such an invitation and integrate well into the group. Again, this successful inclusion may be because of the high stress factor in the medical group.

The Destructive Group Member

It is very common for group leaders to underestimate the tolerance of group members in a crisis and the healing value of group attendance. On the other hand, when a member in the group is blatantly destructive—attacking or monopolizing, not stopping, and threatening the accepting atmosphere of the group—group leaders seem to have a terrible time asking the person to leave the group. There are times when one may have to take someone out of the group or else sacrifice the group experience for everyone. In both medical and psychiatric settings, I have seen leaders' denial of even the possibility of removing a member! If a member has to be removed, it can become a painful experience for the leader. Leaders are afraid of being the "bad guy" and of other members feeling threatened, thinking that if one member can be removed, so can they. Leaders feel in a bind: whether the member is kept in the group or expelled, the group is lost.

PROPERTY OF WASHINGTON
SCHOOL OF PSYCHIATRY
LIBRARY

However, if a member is out of control in the group, it is no better for him to remain than it is for the group. In order for the group to work, each member has to give something to the group, and the group has to give something to him. If this is not operative, group treatment cannot take place. Therefore, one can say to the patient honestly that group is not the treatment for him. The leader can offer to see the patient individually to discuss what treatment would be most suitable.

The leader must remember that he is helping an unsuitable group member by taking him out of the group. The leader can also assure the other members that they are different from the dismissed member (if this is true) in that group treatment *is* the treatment of choice for them. The leader can assure the rest of the group that no one else will be asked to leave for the duration of the group meeting. Usually there is relief in the group.

In one long-term outpatient group for chronically disturbed patients, a long-term member was removed who had monopolized. The members continued to talk about the terminated member, so that she continued to dominate the group even though she was not present. The group was using her to avoid talking about themselves, even in her absence. The leader interpreted this behavior, and the group painfully and slowly began developing, with each person having to take some responsibility. Even though the group was using the monopolizer to avoid personal exposure, it was not to the group's benefit to continue this behavior.

RECRUITING FOR THE GROUP

PLAY THE NUMBERS GAME

Forming a successful group is contingent on being practical and using common sense—one cannot have a group without numbers! The less motivated a population and the less captive the audience, the larger the population needs to be from which to draw group members. Leaders often have wonderful ideas for a group, but there may simply not be enough people to make a group available. In many instances this can cause a negative first-group experience for the leader, particularly if the lack of population is not recognized until the leader has already put in great effort to form the group (for example, by circulating memos and holding preparatory meetings with staff). The leader can be spared disappointment if more thorough preparation is done in testing the availability of population.

The leader can carry out a survey among potential group members to find out what they think of the idea. There may be some surprises in store for the group leader, as is often the case when guesses are tested out. One leader was quite sure that her multiple sclerosis patients would not want to be in a group, but when she asked them directly, they all expressed an interest. Other factors, such as timing, also need to be considered. For example, when a group was planned for relatives of a group of inpatients, a preliminary survey was done to find out when and how many relatives visited the patients. The group was then planned for the appropriate day and time. I have been told that out-patient day groups should not be planned during soap opera television times.

In one instance a successful prenatal group that had been running for a year suddenly dropped in attendance. This was not initially perceived as a problem—ongoing groups in a hospital often have seasonal cycles. For instance, Schniewind and Needle (1978) report greater attendance of primary-care groups in the summer than in the winter. But the problem persisted, and in exasperation the leader decided to do a face sheet.

As one can see, the leader did not have some of the information that was pertinent, such as what day people came to clinic and whether they worked. The leader filled in the missing spaces. What she found was that approximately 40 percent of the women were in their first trimester and only coming to the clinic once a month. They were also coming on different days: the women simply were not in clinic as they had been before. Each week there were one or two suitable people; but even if a small group was held the leader felt rejected and disappointed with the attendance.

Now that the leader knew what the problem was and why, she could search for a solution. The leader decided to have the group once a month and gradually increase the frequency of meetings as the majority of the women proceeded in their pregnancy. She arranged with the medical staff and office staff to have the women come to clinic the same day of the week and the month. More specifically, there were two "group days" in the month. When a person with "group" written on her chart came for an appointment, the clerk would schedule her for one of the two days. Medical staff indicated whether the patient should come in "earlier" or "later" if there was a discrepancy between their order and group date. A number of other groups at St. Vincent's became possible by using this method of organization. Obviously, it required much support and cooperation from interdisciplinary staff.

BROADEN ELIGIBILITY

The other way of increasing numbers so that prognosis for group improves is to broaden eligibility requirements. The group just described

TABLE 7-2
Face Sheet of Prenatal Group Members

Candidates	Age	Marital Status	Lives Near Hospital	Work or School	Day of Appointment	Month of Pregnancy	Primaparous or Multiparous
C. R.	17	M	Yes	No	?	5	P
A. C.	19	S	No	?	?	2	P
M. B.	19	M	No	?	?	6	P
R. R.	15	S	Yes	?	Wed.	4	P
Z. A.	19	S	Yes	?	?	3	P
A. S.	19	S	Yes	?	?	5	P
W. M.	19	S	?	?	?	?	P
Y. C.	29	S	?	Yes	?	7	P
C. O.	17	S	Yes	?	?	6	P
Y. B.	19	S	No	?	?	2	P
A. M.	16	S	No	Yes	Wed.	3	P
C. R.	20	S	Yes	No	Fri.	3	P
J. P.	19	S	?	Yes	?	6	P
C. Mc.	19	S	Yes	No	?	8	M
L. K.	22	?	No	No	?	4	P
C. W.	21	S	No	No	?	2	P
B. C.	20	S	No	No	?	7	P

was originally set up for women who were adolescents expecting their first baby. Eligibility was broadened to include married teenagers, then to any woman who appeared not prepared for motherhood, then to multiparous women, and finally to any prenatal patient who exhibited a good prognosis for benefiting and contributing to the group. As the eligibility changed, so did the goal of the group. Goals have to be broader and become more general as the heterogeneity in the group increases.

NURSES: SCREENING AND RECRUITING

Usually the nurses have the greatest contact with the most number of patients, so that in a turnover group such as an inpatient adjustment-to-hospitalization group where large numbers of people rotate through a service, the nurses are the most logical people to be involved in screening. They are the ones who have an overview and know the patients who are ambulatory, disoriented, etc. They also know the doctors of the patients and can identify the doctors who need to be solicited to for permission for group attendance and those who generally trust the judgment of the interdisciplinary staff. One can see that nurse co-leaders in a group are not only valuable as medical resource people, but also as people with an overview of the floor and acquaintance with the doctors.

The social work leader working without a medical co-leader is often dependent on nursing staff for selection and recruitment. Sometimes social workers are intimidated by how busy the nurses are and do not want to bother them by asking for help. At St. Vincent's Hospital, nurses were almost universally supportive of the groups, but they had little free time to participate in them. If the leader came up to the floor unannounced, the nurse might appear too busy to talk, and the leader would feel uncomfortable at pushing. If the group leader asked the nurses when was the best time to talk, they were responsive and would arrange a time at their convenience. When their participation was necessary for recruitment, a time was made for the nurse and group leader to go through the cardex and select suitable group candidates. Periodically, meeting times were set up where the group leader discussed the content of meetings with the nurses so that they were rewarded for participating. They benefited by the group meetings in that they got more information about their patients which helped them perform their task. Supervision was often arranged to take place on the floor, so that nurses could more easily participate.

ADVERTISE THE GROUP

Recruiting is sometimes enhanced by advertising the group. This is particularly appropriate for turnover groups where the leader would like to work with a large sample of the target population. The leader can advertise by distributing leaflets, putting a sign up on the floor or in the clinic, or distributing invitation cards. Through these means, large numbers of people can be made aware of the group without much time and effort on the part of the leader. Sometimes people show interest in the group who otherwise would be missed.

Invitations that are printed in bulk on three-by-five-inch index cards can be particularly helpful in recruiting for inpatient relatives' groups. At St. Vincent's on several medical services, when a patient is admitted to the hospital, the relative is given an invitation to the relatives' group by the floor nurse. Also a sign posted opposite the elevator or at the nurses' station alerts people to the group. The sign and cards are followed by nurses' reminders that the group exists, and finally by personal invitation from the group leader.

Plan as Many Meetings as Possible

Most inpatient groups in medical settings do not meet more than once a week for one hour. In psychiatric settings where groups are well established, group meetings can take place every day. Youcha (1976) writes that inpatient groups for psychiatric patients require at least three to five meetings a week. He feels once-a-week meetings during a one-to-four-week hospitalization are almost valueless.

Given the powerful rationale for groups in a medical setting, it is regrettable that more frequent meetings are not held, particularly on the inpatient service where patients have such a need for structured activity. Because general hospitals have not institutionalized groups in their delivery of care, groups have not been supported by the provision of staff time for group leadership. Most of our inpatient groups at St. Vincent's did not meet more frequently because staff was too burdened to devote more time to them. As it was, staff members could hardly fit in time for one group meeting plus supervision.

In medicine, frequency of outpatient groups is often contingent upon how often a person comes to the clinic. It takes a great deal of patient motivation to make an additional trip to the hospital for group attendance. Groups have an easier time of succeeding if they can be built into the clinic schedule. For example, in the prenatal group, patients received a note giving them their clinic schedule: (1) see the doctor, (2) go to group, and (3) have laboratory work. In the oncology group the patients: (1) went to laboratory, (2) had a group meeting while they were waiting for lab results, and (3) saw the doctor. The group leader personally accompanied the patients from the laboratory to the group, so she would not lose anyone along the way. Bennett (1979) and Bloom and Lynch (1979) give excellent examples of groups that are integrated into a clinic schedule and an inpatient service.

In some of the outpatient clinic groups at St. Vincent's the leader encouraged attendance during weeks when patients did not have a clinic appointment through the use of positive reinforcement (see Chapter 10). Each week the leader would ask who was present without an appointment and reiterate that she hoped they would attend. Every week that someone attended without an appointment, the leader brought it to the group's attention and showed her pleasure. It worked; attendance in the group increased. It is said that group therapists get what they want from a group; in this instance it happened.

GOALS FOR THE GROUP

One reason group leaders in hospital settings feel so frustrated is that they do not have realistic expectations for the ill patients they are working with and they do not appreciate what the limited group has to offer. For example, it is hard for a group leader to empathize with the value of having a brief social experience when the leader is personally looking for a long-term, in-depth group therapy experience. When goals are unrealistic and not achieved, the leader is often angry at himself and the patient.

It is important that goals be limited and short-term. If a severely disturbed, narcissistic patient hears what another person is saying to him and is able to respond, this is a wonderful achievement for the patient, the therapist, and the group. If a person looks up at the sky for the first time in ten years (or in any way expands her universe), treatment benefits have occurred. Experiencing any form of success with people increases the patient's confidence and ability to negotiate in the real world. But these kinds of successes are often shared only by the therapist, the patient, and the group; they are often not visible to society or to hospital administrators. From their point of view, the patient is often still seen as sick and not functioning. It is similar to the situation in which a patient has a fever of 106° and medical treatment helps bring it down to 102°. For the patient, this change is a great relief, even though he is still sick, still in the hospital, still not functioning, and a burden to others and himself. It is often hard for a leader to feel good about reaching goals that are not applauded by others.

SET REALISTIC GOALS

Kibel (1978) feels the following are appropriate goals for a short-term inpatient group of psychiatric patients: (1) limit-setting, (2) corrective emotional experience, (3) support, and (4) relief from outside pressures. In a similar setting, Youcha (1976) has groups at different levels and group goals appropriate to each level. For the group where the psychotic process dominates, his goals are to: (1) reduce the acute psychotic manifestation and (2) help the patient seal over the eruption of unbearable psychic pain and anxiety.

In a medical setting goals have to be related to medical care and physical recovery because that is where the person has stated a need. Goals need to be flexible, and the group leader has to listen to what the patients are stating as their needs. For example, in medical groups, people often ask a multitude of medical questions, sometimes over and over again. Leaders often want to lead a group to discussion of feelings and try to change the subject. The patients don't respond to the leader's interventions but continue to ask questions. Leaders of maternal and child health-care groups reported that issues of concern to members that frequently took precedence over physical and emotional health-care problems were housing, finances, and child care (Poynter-Berg 1979). In an outpatient medication group in a psychiatric setting, patients just came for their medication. In another outpatient group for posthospitalized schizophrenics they wanted to talk about budgeting and nutrition. Group leaders should incorporate these kinds of concerns into their goals and use them as a springboard to get more interaction, which ultimately is the therapeutic tool. With many of these groups the content is not as important as the critical process of interaction that results. It is the contact with others that is curative.

Respond to Questions

Frequently, following the patients' agenda means listening to questions and providing answers to questions. An example is the medication group Payn (1974) described where he spent group time writing prescriptions and discussing medication. He encouraged patients to ask questions about their medication and to compare medication. When the patients did this, they made contact with each other; the resulting interaction was part of the healing process. Tannenbaum (1978), leading a group of parents of cystic fibrosis children, had success when beginning the group "intellectually" with speakers being invited. Discussion about the practical problems of caring for children took place before "feelings" were elicited.

In a medical group, questions should be answered, but in such a way that every opportunity is given to facilitate interaction. The leader should never answer a question immediately but say, "I am happy to answer that, but first I would like to hear what others think the answer is." "Has anyone else had such a problem?" "Has anyone asked their doctor?" "What did he say?" The leader can confirm or question the answers members give.

Most often the leader has to say, "You will have to ask your doctor, because everyone is different," or "No one knows the answer to that." These are the kinds of answers the patients do not want to hear and one reason why they ask the questions repetitively (each time hoping they will get a different answer). It is at this point feelings can be dealt with. "How does it feel that no one can tell you why you had a heart attack?" "How does it feel that no one can tell you how to prevent another heart attack?" Patients can then share feelings of rage and helplessness in the face of uncertainty.

RUN A TRIAL GROUP

Goals need to be made at the beginning of the group, tested out in the trial group, and then modified. A trial group can be from 4 to 12 sessions—at the leader's discretion. At the end of the trial group, the experience is evaluated by patients, leader, and the interdisciplinary team.

In the survey of maternal and child health-care groups, only 38½ percent of the groups had established the number of sessions in the first meeting (Poynter-Berg, 1979). Leaders expressed discomfort over this vagueness of commitment. The time-limited short-term group can be helpful to both patients and leader. Often the new leader and group members do not know if they will like the group. The members' commitment is short-term, and they can discontinue at that point if they choose. The evaluation gives the leader and members a chance to make changes if they want to continue with the group.

Some leaders need to rest between trial groups, integrating the experience, reevaluating their own commitment, and deciding whether the energy expended is worth it in terms of their own learning needs. Others will not want to take a break, feeling that they would have to start all over again and lose momentum. Leaders of maternal and child health-care groups felt that with long-term groups, natural breaks such as vacations, end of school year, etc., were important in preventing burn-out among leaders (ibid.). Such breaks can also be used for evaluation of the group.

Groups should have formal and informal evaluations built in. Informal evaluations would take place during casual conversation with group members and the interdisciplinary team. Formal evaluations should be written up as a follow-up memo, which should go to the same people in the hospital system who received the original memo. It is a way of keeping levels of staff in the hospital system informed about, and therefore participating in, the group.

Figures 7-1, 7-2, and 7-3 are examples of a leader's original memo regarding a group of Hispanic parents of chronically ill children, the written evaluation, and the follow-up memo that was extracted from it and distributed among various levels of staff (Manley, 1976).

To: Attendings, residents, nurses, dietition, pediatrics clinics

From: M. M., Department of Social Services

I am starting a trial group for Spanish-speaking parents of chronically ill children who are followed in the pediatrics outpatient department. The purpose of this group is to provide supportive help to these concerned, frequently anxious parents.

Many parents of chronically ill children spend much time attending to their children's medical needs. Often, despite their efforts, these children continue to present medical problems. The group is an attempt to involve these parents in discussing some of their concerns as they relate to management of their sick children. The group might also be helpful in facilitating more effective use of medical services by these families.

I would appreciate any referrals from the pediatrics clinics or any inpatients who will be followed in our clinics. I can be reached at extension 1581. I hope that staff will reinforce the potential of the group with any parents involved. I will use notes and personal communication to inform staff of members' progress in the group.

The trial group will be meeting for six consecutive weeks, beginning Friday, January 30th, from 9:45 to 10:45 A.M. in the social service department, third floor, Lowenstein Building. Members are expected to attend whether they have a clinic appointment or not. Children under care of the clinic will have their clinic appointments scheduled for Fridays, the day of the group. Patients will check into clinic at 9:00 A.M. and then proceed to the social service department for group. They will see the doctor after group at 10:45 A.M. Provisions will be made for child care during the group meetings.

I look forward to sharing with you the content of the group and eliciting your feedback in evaluating its helpfulness to Spanish-speaking parents.

FIGURE 7-1. *Memo regarding formation of a trial group for Hispanic parents of chronically ill children*

Group: Hispanic parents' group

Group leader: M. M., Department of Social Services

Number of Meetings: 21

Dates Covered: January 30–July 2, 1976

Summary of group experience: Five of the six members attended group meetings regularly. Members ranged in age from 25 to 31 years old. They were all married, except for one widow. They came from Puerto Rico, Peru, and the Dominican Republic. They were in the United States for varying amounts of time. All were from working-class families. All had children who were repeatedly ill with croupe, pneumonia, gastroenteritis, and respiratory infections. All had more than one child. Members attended an average of 12 sessions. Most sessions consisted of three members.

Goal evaluation: The primary goal of this group was to provide supportive help to parents of chronically ill children. Secondary goals included facilitating more effective management of illness and more efficient use of medical services. These goals were accomplished in the group. Members provided emotional support to each other. They shared alternative ways of coping, clarified misconceptions, discussed child-rearing techniques, and engaged in problem solving. The group gave these mothers additional knowledge and confidence: two factors which lead to more effective use of medical services. Parents were later observed to make less frequent use of the emergency room. They began to implement ideas offered in the group at home.

Team evaluation: The Department of Social Services enlisted the support of medical and nursing staff for establishing group as a central part of the delivery of medical care. Doctors and nurses made referrals to the group. Doctors reinforced importance of group to parents. Clinic nurses were helpful in coordinating children's clinic appointments with group. Dr. I. came to one session and answered questions and discussed problems. He felt the group was a vital means of communication and was willing to participate again in the future. Other doctors felt that the group was an important way of increasing their awareness of patients' problems and questions concerning management..

FIGURE 7-2. *Written evaluation of trial group for Hispanic parents of chronically ill children*

Leader's role: Leader reached out to interdisciplinary team for referrals and support. She provided ongoing feedback to staff through verbal communication and notes on chart. Leader arranged for child care with hospital volunteer. She communicated regularly with volunteer and by doing this enlisted her support. Leader provided an open, supportive, accepting atmosphere, which greatly fostered group interaction and cohesiveness. Leader communicated belief in group and importance of group to members and staff. Leader took an active role in limiting one member who monopolized and brought frightening subject matter into the group. She rewarded this member when her behavior was appropriate. She was sensitive to other members' discomfort with this member and dealt with this by structuring the group meeting. She reached out to individual members when they failed to attend the group and enlisted support from member's family. She encouraged use of group's strengths for problem solving. She facilitated members' expression of feelings about termination and separation.

Plans and recommendation: The group is ending because the leader is leaving the agency. As group came to an end, each member identified a goal for herself and began working on it. This was an effort to prevent members from returning to social isolation. One member investigated sewing classes and Head Start programs. Another began English classes and obtained child care. Another planned to continue craft courses and began to consider employment. The disturbed member agreed to pursue psychiatric treatment.

This was a trial group done on a small-scale basis. Members responded to the group. Group was presented as part of medical treatment and was seen by members as such. Future groups seem to be an important means of serving the outpatient population in pediatric clinics.

FIGURE 7-2. (continued)

PATIENT RELUCTANCE TO JOIN A GROUP

Although group treatment can be a powerful treatment tool, patients are often reluctant to join a group. Yalom (1970) specifies some common misperceptions people have about groups that contribute to this reluctance: group is second-rate therapy; group is diluted therapy because it is shared time; group is cheaper, which is why they are being asked to join.

Of those who attended the group program at St. Vincent's, few staff or patients reported a negative experience. Almost all of those who attended

To: Staff, Department of Pediatrics

From: M. M., Department of Social Services

The purpose of this memo is to give you feedback on the trial group for Spanish-speaking parents. This group met weekly for a total of 21 weeks from January 30 to July 2, 1976. This group consisted of six mothers, five of whom attended group regularly. Members were all parents of chronically ill children. The children's diagnosis included croupe, pneumonia, asthma, repeated gastroenteritis and chronic respiratory problems. The mothers ranged in age from 25 to 31 years and were all married except for one widowed woman. They came from Puerto Rico, Peru, and the Dominican Republic. Members had been in the United States for varying amounts of time, however, and all seemed to be in some phase of adjustment to city life. Members attended an average of 12 sessions each. Most group sessions consisted of three or four members.

The primary goal of this group was for members to provide supportive help to other parents of chronically ill children. Secondary goals included facilitating more effective management of the child and his or her illness and encouraging more efficient use of medical services. Members did provide emotional support to each other. They shared alternative ways of coping with illness, clarified misconceptions, discussed child-rearing techniques, and engaged in problem solving. The group gave these mothers additional knowledge and confidence—two factors which led to more effective management of their sick children and more efficient use of medical services. Members showed behavior changes in coping with their own lives, in caring for their children, and in relating to staff.

I enlisted the support of doctors and nursing staff for obtaining referrals and in establishing the group as part of the medical treatment plan. Medical staff responded positively. They provided referrals and reinforced the importance of group with individual members. Clinic staff was extremely helpful in coordinating the children's clinic appointments with group sessions. Dr. I.'s participation in the group and availability to these mothers for questions provided an important means to clarify their misconceptions.

The team effort contributed greatly to the success of this group for Spanish-speaking parents. I am very grateful to all of you for your cooperation. I especially want to thank Mrs. K. of the Volunteer Deparment for her excellent and greatly appreciated child care.

FIGURE 7-3. *Follow-up memo on trial group for Hispanic parents of chronically ill children*

This group was conducted on a small-scale basis. It ended because I am leaving the hospital to continue my education in social work. Group work appears to be an important modality for treatment within our pediatric clinics. I hope it will be expanded in the future so that the needs of this population will be most adequately met.

FIGURE 7-3. (continued)

groups stated voluntarily that they enjoyed the group experience. Given the benefits of group for so many patients and staff, one wonders why it is often difficult to get patients to come to group and staff to participate. We tried a number of groups that didn't get off the ground, and others that took a year to function optimally.

There are certainly patients and staff that are not suited to the group modality. Some patients are withdrawn and despondent; this is an important and constructive phase of adjusting to illness that should be respected. Some people have enough internal and external supports that they have nothing to gain from the group. Others respond negatively to the group idea out of a long-standing personality pattern that they especially cling to in time of crisis, and it is not helpful or appropriate to ask them to break that pattern.

But, most interestingly, there are a number of patients for whom group would be helpful, and yet they resist attendance. And there are the patients who know themselves that they need it and resist. Many who do come to the group verbalize how helpful the meeting was, and staff note patients' positive behavioral change after the meeting; yet the patient finds excuses for not coming back to group. One such patient locked herself in the bathroom during her second group session. Another patient said spontaneously, a few days after her group meeting, "I'm only happy when I go to group." She also never came back.

RESISTANCE

The psychoanalytic concept of resistance is helpful in understanding patients' reluctance to join groups, especially in those instances where we know it is a positive experience for patients and staff. It refers to people's resistance to any change, whether it be positive or negative. Freud wrote about "the 'resistance' with which the patient clings to his disease and thus even fights against his own recovery ... it is this phenomenon of resistance which alone makes it possible to understand his behavior in daily life" (1953, pp. 261–262).

Although the term "resistance" was used to refer to the psychoanalytic treatment situation, the concept is helpful in better understanding why patients fight any kind of medical or psychiatric treatment that might be of help to them. Groups for these patients are designed to foster change in their maladaptive ways of coping with illness. Change inevitably leads to disequilibrium and hence calls upon one's capacity to face the unknown. Many patterns of coping evolve from childhood experiences, and fears become second nature. Accordingly, in times of stress people protect themselves in ways that are familiar to them.

> If one probes what lies behind the painful affect, one will discover some dangerous instinctual impulse and eventually some link to a relatively traumatic event in the patient's history .... The clinging to old gratifications ... is an underlying fear of the new or mature satisfactions which make the old gratification intractable. (Greenson 1967, pp. 81–82)

Most important about what Greenson is describing, is that when people cling to old patterns, even if they are viewed as harmful from an outsider's point of view, they do so because they are afraid, and they are afraid for a reason. The group leader must appreciate that a patient's reluctance to attend a group may spring from a complex and deeply ingrained rationale. If people are going to change, they may need support and sophisticated understanding from staff.

Some patients and staff resist group because they have no idea of what coming to a group means. They may feel that therapy—any therapy or intervention that is "good for them"—must, perforce, involve discomfort; they may look at group as just another request to take their medicine. Most patients have never been in a hospital group, and they only have a fantasy to visualize. It is often helpful if the leader explores this fantasy with the patient by asking, "What do you think the group will be like?" When they attend the first group, the leader can ask, "Was the group what you expected it to be?" Invariably, the answer is, "No! It is much nicer than I expected!" Garland, Jones, and Kolodny (1965) say that people come to a new group experience with a reference point from societal exposure such as boy scouts, clubs, etc., unless someone has had a former group-therapy or group-work experience. Gombrich (1956) agrees that the perception of any new situation is in part determined by previous models and experience. Patients who resist groups may have had negative group experiences. One need only to look back at adolescence and the pain of not being included in the "in" group or at the frequently cruel latency-age groups where children are judged by arbitrary and rigid standards.

FEAR OF CONTAGION

Yalom (1970) reports that some patients say that they drop out of groups because they have been adversely affected by hearing others' problems. Some patients are afraid that they will be contaminated by other people in the group. (Staff members have also expressed this concern.) It is not uncommon for people to respond to an invitation to group with: "What do I need to hear other people's problems for? I have enough of my own," or "Talking to sick people will make me feel worse," or "I take people's problems too hard." These people somehow feel that if someone else in the group is sick emotionally or physically, it will make them sick. One group of geriatric patients literally insisted on sitting in different corners of the room because they were afraid of "the germs."

Fear of contagion is a common expression of reluctance to join a group. I have been encouraged by the results of having such patients in group and have been struck by their ability to protect themselves with their ongoing ego defenses. There is also a self-selection in group attendance. I do not believe in forcing someone to attend a group or to stay in the group. But sometimes the tendency toward contagion in the group may enhance patients' self-esteem; that is, it may work in the opposite direction. Someone may come to group and be surprised at how good someone looks who has the same illness and leave the group feeling better about himself.

TECHNIQUES TO ENCOURAGE ATTENDANCE

With the severely disturbed patient—both medical and psychiatric—the leader has to recognize technique appropriate to the pathology when inviting someone to join the group. Techniques may include: use of the individual relationship; appealing to the patients' sense of importance; using "leverage"; taking seriously patients' reasons for not wanting to attend the group; and reaching out.

USE THE INDIVIDUAL RELATIONSHIP

Patients who are narcissistically involved are generally reluctant to join a group and frequently perceive such a suggestion by the therapist as a

rejection. Yet they often develop relationships with the individual therapist. In forming a group it is important to capitalize on this relationship;
sometimes it is the only way to get the patient to come to group. Thus, for
example, the therapist may motivate the patient by saying: "Having you in
the group will give me more time to get to know you." Success in forming a
group is most likely to occur when therapists work with their own patients,
with whom they have developed individual relationships and have some
personal investment. Blanck and Blanck (1974) feel that the treatment of
the severely disturbed patient involves the use of the therapist as a real
object for the purpose of building object relations.

APPEAL TO PATIENTS' SENSE OF IMPORTANCE

Some authors are afraid that patients' self-esteem would be wounded
by an invitation to a therapy group. In approaching parents of children
with cystic fibrosis, Tannenbaum (1978) invited them to a "workshop,"
feeling that an invitation to "group therapy" would be too threatening.
Frank (1952) went further, saying that a psychiatrist should never lead a
group with medical patients because it is too powerful a message that the
patients are emotionally sick.

Kernberg points out that there exists in the narcissistic personality a
"curious apparent contradiction between a very inflated concept of themselves and an inordinate need for tribute from others" (1970, p. 52). The
leader must appeal to the patient's sense of importance and in some way
communicate that he is being asked to join a special group because he is
special. The invitation to join a group must be personalized and connected with the leader's unique understanding of the individual's personal goals. The group should not be presented as "another therapy
group" but as a group with a special structure or focus. For example,
"I am starting a new kind of group, which is an assertiveness training
group. I felt that you would be especially suited for this group because
I've seen you successfully advise your friend on how to get his disability
benefits. Also, you have told me how distressed you are about not being
able to say no to your mother, and I think this group could help you with
that."

Approaching the individual and group as special should not be confused with indulging the patient unnecessarily or being seductive and
manipulative. The leader must appeal to the patient's sense of importance to a degree that facilitates his participation in group treatment. One
cannot treat a patient without his presence!

Use Leverage

A leader rarely can get a patient who is narcissistically involved to come to a long-term group or stay in the group without using leverage. It is often difficult to find something that the patient is concerned enough about for him to become engaged in making a treatment contract. The leader must search for something meaningful and personal to the patient. Moffet, Bruce, and Horvitz (1974) looked at professionals' and drug addicts' goals in the treatment relationship and found they differed greatly. Leaders' goals can be unrealistic if they do not recognize the motivation of patients.

Leverage is obtained where there is an area of anxiety in the patient. This area may, for example, derive from family or pressure from the courts. Such pressure can be useful in helping the patient engage in treatment and should not be discredited by the group leader. A therapeutic contract may be made around something totally insignificant to the leader. The patient must be reminded frequently that coming to the group regularly will move him toward his established personal goal. For example, a posthospitalized schizophrenic said that all he wanted was to get married. The leader said, "Fine. Join the group, and it will help you get married." This could be said honestly because the group would help him develop his social skills, which would help him meet women. Resnick et al. (1974) used medication (methadone and naltrexone) as a way of engaging the drug addict. Coven (1980) used medical patients' attachment to the physician to get attendance. In these instances, the leaders utilized the areas of heaviest emotional investment in order to elicit the patients' cooperation.

Take Patients' Reluctance Seriously

The following are excerpts from a process recording of a male, inpatient, general medicine group whose leader persistently recruited for one group and concretely dealt with a member's reluctance to attend the group. The leader took the reasons the patient gives for not wanting to attend the group seriously.

> When Mr. L. was invited to attend, he said he would like to come but he would probably make the others angry because most likely they would not like to hear what he had to say. I told him that I was sure that he had something to offer, that everyone had a right to his opinion, and that we really cannot expect everyone to agree with everything we say. He decided to come to the meeting.

In the next meeting, the same leader continues to facilitate group attendance by dealing with the patients' reluctance. The patients are responsive. The leader respects the concerns they voice, which elevates their self-esteem.

> Recruiting for participants had been quite difficult prior to the meeting. We were finally able to find four men who said that they would attend; however, three of them expressed doubts as to whether or not they should attend because they were concerned about other things. Mr. T. began to back out, asking how long it would last, and how far he had to go to attend, but he was convinced that he should attend. Mr. N., who was scheduled to be released later that day, said that he might miss the doctor and the results of his report if he were not around when he was called. I convinced him to come by walking with him to the nurse's station and having a nurse promise to look for him across the hall, if necessary; he then attended. Mr. L. was about to refuse to attend, by saying that he might miss a very important telephone call. I pointed out the fact that the room where we were meeting is quite near the telephone booth, and that if he asked, one of the men who were sitting there watching television would probably come to get him when he was called. He relented and attended the meeting.

If the reader is uncomfortable with the leader putting this kind of pressure on group members, it should be noted that at the end of the meeting, these members spontaneously thanked the leader for a good experience.

Another example where potential group members' reasons for not wanting to attend the group were taken seriously had this result.

> In forming a relatives' group for patients hospitalized on neurology and neurosurgery, potential members said that they did not want to take time away from visiting their relatives who were severely ill. The nurses arranged for the group members to have earlier visiting times so they could attend the group and have the same amount of time with their relatives. Attendance in the group was expedited, and the alteration seemed to help.

Taking a patient's reasons seriously and responding to them concretely can also be useful after a patient joins a group.

> On an inpatient service for severely ill patients, there was a woman who believed she had cancer. Tests were given and they were negative. The doctor, nurse, and social worker all told her repeatedly that she did not have cancer. She was getting more agitated every day. In the weekly group meeting she said, "If I could just see my chart with the test results, I would believe I don't have cancer." After the group, the leaders arranged for her to look at her chart. She was elated and thoroughly convinced that she did not have cancer.

This is an example of how professionals can make solutions much more complicated than they need be.

REACH OUT

Grobman (1978) describes the first stage of group life with chronically disturbed patients as one of irregular attendance. He suggests the leader make phone calls, write letters, and make home visits to help this situation. In working with psychiatric inpatient and outpatient groups, Youcha (1976) cut the rehospitalization rate considerably. In describing how he did it, he spoke of constant phone calls to people after they were discharged, and if there were no phones he went to their homes. He felt he had to impress upon members that they were missed and they were important. They seemed to assume that their absence would go unnoticed. This has been corroborated by my experience with medical and psychiatric patients.

In a group of posthospitalized mental patients, a member was absent. I asked the others if she was missed. One man said, "It is like a finger on my hand missing." Another member said, "Gee, I want to be absent so I will be missed." We talked about how important each member was. I spoke with one patient concretely about her belief that she was invisible. Others felt similarly and always showed surprise when I called if they were absent.

Coven (1980) gave a dramatic example of patients' isolation from a group of emotionally disturbed outpatients. There was a death in the group, and discussion of feelings around death led to the members opening up and revealing more of themselves. They cared for and missed the dead member. As she was spoken about, members seemed to compete for attention with the dead member by sharing their own self-destructive escapades. They wanted to die so they would be missed and eulogized. The leader skillfully moved the group to a more positive reality; since they were members of the group, they would be missed if they died, whereas before group membership they felt no one would miss them if they died, so they were now valued members of a society. They could be valued and get recognition by living in the group and continuing to give and take from one another in a meaningful way. The group took on the task of monitoring each other's self-destructive behavior and openly sharing how important each one was to the other. Similarly, a suicidal outpatient said to her group: "I wanted to commit suicide but then realized I would not be able to go to the funeral. It would be like only going to the first act of a show." The other group members understood. The fantasy of being missed was wonderful.

Schizophrenic patients are known to be overly dependent and this can be draining on a therapist. For this reason, many of us feel hesitant to tell patients that they can call us at home or even at our office. I gave my phone number out reluctantly to members of a posthospitalized group of schizophrenics. Some said they needed to call me between sessions. I agreed but said the calls would have to be very brief. The calls seemed to serve as a contact with reality; just hearing my voice—making the contact—seemed to be enough. The phone calls rarely went beond three minutes and fell into one of the following three categories:

1. The member told me something positive and I shared their pleasure and thanked them for telling me.
2. The member shared a problem, and I said, "I'm glad you called to tell me how that disturbs you. I want you to bring it up in the group."
3. The member shared a problem, and I gave a one-sentence response; he then immediately said, "Oh, I feel so much better. Thank you!"

Sometimes members would ask for a time to call and never call; just having the number was enough. It is difficult for the severely disturbed to keep the group as a frame of reference over a week's time; they require more frequent meetings. The phone call can help. Some of our group discussions centered around how to remember what the group says.

EXPECT PEOPLE TO ATTEND

Leaders' reluctance to have a group is often subtly expressed when they are inviting someone to join. With the severely ill, leaders need to convey an expectation that members will attend the group. When a nurse sees a depressed patient lying in bed all day, she usually does not hesitate to say, "Hey, get out of bed already! Time to exercise." In contrast, the psychosocial group leader sometimes subtly communicates to patients that the group is not recommended as part of their treatment by saying meekly, "You can come if you want to," instead of, "Doctor, nurse, and social worker have decided group attendance will help you get better!" The principle of self-determination and voluntary attendance is often confused with giving a mixed message to patients regarding the value and importance of their group attendance. Leaders often expect a degree of motivation, enthusiasm, and capacity for decision making that is unrealistic, given the disturbance of the patient.

Both medical and psychiatric patients come to a hospital for help. The hospital contracts to provide medical or psychiatric care if patients cooperate with their treatment plan. This plan may include group treatment. One shouldn't go through a series of discussions about patients' willingness to attend group any more than one would discuss someone getting a blood test or an X ray. Patients have already declared their intentions by coming to the hospital for help. It is the professional that makes the treatment plan and only enters into a debate if patients object. The leader should spend time with the few people who have strong objections to attending the group, for the same reason that a professional would spend time with any person who did not understand or was resistant to any recommended treatment.

In a medical setting with an open group, one can ask resistant patients to come to the group for a short time, with the idea that they can leave if they are uncomfortable. If the leader asks patients why they do not want to attend, they will often say, "I don't want to talk." The leader can respond, "You don't have to talk; you can just listen." Someone may say, "I don't have any problems." The leader can say, "I know you are doing very well. I thought you could be of some help to others," thus boosting self-esteem.

CONSIDER MANDATORY ATTENDANCE

Sometimes it is appropriate to be explicit about mandatory attendance; conveying the expectation for attendance is not enough. Program policy can be: "If you want to be in this program, you must attend the group regularly." This is true in at least one New York City day-hospitalization program. Similarly, in one medical hospital there is a policy that if attendings want admitting privileges they have to agree to their patients going to the postsurgery group.

Mandatory attendance for patients is usually necessary when there is a major ego deficit, as with some drug addicts. For the self-medicating drug addict, addiction is an extreme attempt at solving problems of self-care and self-regulation (Resnick et al., 1975). Khantzian and Kates describe the drug addict that has ego impairment and is desperately needy, disorganized, and out of control. Such patients are notorious for not following through on treatment; there is "an over-determined need to fend off help as well as the tendency of these individuals to be insufficiently anxious, concerned, and responsive about many aspects of their life" (1978, p. 93).

Khantzian and Kates studied the effect of mandatory group attendance for drug addicts. If one wanted to join the methadone program and receive supportive services one had to agree not only to attend the group but to come on time and not miss more than three meetings. To the staff's surprise, the results were positive. Fewer people dropped out of the program, and staff morale was elevated. Prior to the mandatory attendance policy, group attendance was sporadic, tardiness common, attrition high, and within seven months the group was disbanded. They attributed the addicts' initial unwillingness to come to the groups to: "ritual" protest; defense against acknowledging problems as internal; and defense against wishes for and fear of closeness. Patients with character disorders often need greater anxiety, and a push to attend a group when these reasons are operative is indicated if they are to grow and change. This would not be true for schizophrenics and the severely ill medical patient, where anxiety needs to be assuaged. In all of these populations, I am most concerned about those who make a superficial ritual protest and are taken too seriously by the professional who may have his or her own reasons for not wanting to lead a group.

HAVE A POSITIVE ATTITUDE

The group leader's attitude toward starting a group clearly affects outcome. Truax and Wargo (1966) present research confirming that the most successful therapists are those that are warm, genuine, and authentic and do not focus on pathology. O'Brien (1975), among others, observed that new leaders formed groups more easily with psychiatric patients than did others because they were so enthusiastic. Students can be almost naively positive and get good results.

Coven examined her role in group formation. The frustration that many group leaders feel is evident in the following excerpts:

Originally, I wrote memos and spoke to doctors and nurses explaining the group, and asked them for referrals on a regular, daily basis. When this was unsuccessful—referrals did not come through—I stood in clinic each day, reviewing charts of diabetic patients, interviewing these patients, telling them about the idea of forming a group, and asking them if they were interested in attending. They responded positively to the idea but never came. I began looking through my own caseload, hoping the rapport I had with certain diabetic patients might provide motivation for group attendance. But these people, too, said it was a nice idea and then never came.

I became more discouraged the more I attempted to form a group in this way. Since returns on my efforts were minimal, I felt less willing to expend energy in what seemed a hopeless situation. I contacted fewer doctors, didn't press the nurses for referrals as insistently as I had before, and spoke too freely with the medical staff and the patients about the difficulties of group formation. I wanted a group, I told myself, but if patients weren't going to come, I wasn't going to push . . . . I was now working on group formation half-heartedly, with a deep sense that my efforts were worthless, and with a deeper feeling that I did not have the skill and commitment to follow through and in fact establish the group. My emotional involvement in group formation became minimal; my investment in proving that a group could not be formed was major. I needed immediate gratification for my efforts, and the gratification was not forthcoming. (1978, pp. 4–5)

When she realized her negative attitude, she called upon "the phantom group" to help her.

Essential to the process of forming the group was concretizing the *idea* of a group. I needed, for myself, a fantasy group—actually an extension of the idea that one day a clinic-patients' group would exist—in order to maintain my own morale, in view of what often seemed to be overwhelming obstacles of this particular clinic . . . . Of course, the group did not exist yet, but I spoke to patients about it as if it already did. "We have a group," I would say, and then continue to talk with them. (Ibid., pp. 1 and 6)

The leader met with two women individually around group issues. They understood that this was "group time." Coincidentally, the two never came to group at the same time. Coven continues:

Again, it was most significant to me that I *felt*—I fantasized—I had a group. For the third meeting only Laura came again . . . . In this meeting, and in the fourth (at which Anna also made no appearance) Laura requested discussion of some "private" financial matters; I set up individual sessions for discussion of these things and refused to spend "group" time discussing other than "group" issues . . . .

During the week, between the third and fourth meetings, Laura called me to discuss her problems with Disability, and asked me to set up an individual session.

"By the way," she said, "I would like this to remain just between us."

"Oh," I said, remaining calm-voiced, but wondering what in the world she meant. "Of course it will, Laura. Why would I tell anyone else?"

"*You* know," she said (Did I?) "I mean I don't want to discuss it in front of other people." (*What* other people? I thought.) "*You* know," she continued, "the other people in the group!"

The phantom group did exist! Laura had defined the essence of my work towards group formation by letting me know that now, in her mind, too, was the fantasy of group—the "phantom group." A group existed for her; there were many things she did not want to share with the phantom members. Finally I had concrete proof that the essential step between the invitation to group and the beginning of treatment—a step I could no longer take for granted—was the step that makes the idea of group real.

The idea—the phantom—was now something with which Laura and Anna, and other prospective members of group, could connect. By using a fantasy I had maintained my belief that eventually a group would exist, and now it did—for myself and the patients. Therefore, treatment could only begin when: (1) the idea of group was real for leader and patients, and (2) patients used the reality of the idea of group to motivate themselves towards group attendance. (Ibid., pp. 9-11)

The concept of the phantom group was a way of acknowledging internal frame of references as part of the total system. Systems-group therapists refer to this as the "member" system. The phantom group is also a way of concretizing the expectation that a group will form and a trust that the group exists.

Anthony (1973) writes that it is the attitude of the therapist and participants that make a group. A group of two is possible if the two bring other people in their heads and share them. If a leader is talking to five people individually about the phantom group and it is real to five people, then a "frame of reference group" does exist and is real to the people involved. In this case Coven succeeded in making the phantom group a reality and it continued to meet for three years.

The reader may be critical of the phantom group, feeling that its use is a way of deceiving or duping the patient. I think it is another example of how technique needs to be modified for the hard-to-reach populations. Let us not lose sight of the fact that it worked. The phantom group did eventually evolve into a long-term group where members attended regularly. The leader called upon the phantom group in desperation, and it was a help to both leader and patients in coming together. The result was a positive therapeutic experience for patients who were formerly socially isolated. Patients dramatically changed self-destructive behavior, and the quality of their lives improved as they participated in the group.

The patients who appear unreachable, unmotivated, and unavailable are often those who are enveloped in the protective withdrawal that characterizes medical and psychiatric patients who are severely ill. If patients are convinced that the leader is providing a crucial piece of treatment, they will usually participate. Borriello, in working with chronic schizophrenics, writes: "Patients have to realize that group therapy can help make their life easier in the long run" (1976, p. 102). But the leader has to believe in what he or she is offering in order to convey this to a patient. This is why it is so important that the leader's existential questions be dealt with.

SUMMARY

In forming a hospital group the leader has to be very practical. Few hospital groups are formed under ideal conditions where composition, time, place, etc., can be given careful attention. More common is the open turnover group, where the leader may only have a vague idea who is going to attend. Many patients will only attend one time. In order to lead a group under such circumstances, the leader must be able to handle the misfit in the group and have realistic goals.

A practical approach is important for recruitment, since many group leaders complain of low attendance. Groups usually have to be formed from large, available populations. The way a leader approaches potential participants is crucial. The leader must convey an expectation that patients will attend the group because it is part of their hospital treatment. The leader must have a positive attitude and truly anticipate a positive experience for both patients and leader.

Leaders often expect an unrealistic degree of motivation and sophistication on the part of patients. Leaders have to meet the patients on a level that is meaningful to them, and often this involves appealing to patients' sense of importance or acknowledging their anxiety in order to engage them in the group process. Leaders must recognize that often fear of group is an expression of self-protectiveness. Patients often need support and reassurance in order to risk the unknown: the group experience.

Part III

HOW TO MAINTAIN GROUPS IN MEDICAL AND PSYCHIATRIC SETTINGS

Chapter 8

Treating Wounded Self-Esteem

Self-esteem and recovery from psychiatric or physical illness are intimately connected: as people interact positively with others, self-esteem and prognosis improve; conversely, as people withdraw from contact with others, their ability to test reality diminishes. Davis et al. (1961) illustrate how mental aberrations occur with extreme social isolation. Detre, Kessler, and Jarecki (1963) voice concern over the isolation of the medical patient. Grobman (1978) states that it is the social-club aspect of the group for disturbed patients that leads to external change. Fidler (1965) describes psychiatric patients in a day hospital who spent most of a 30-hour week together and did not know each other's names. He feels the major goal with such patients is to increase the rate of communication and cooperation among members.

Group participation is a powerful treatment tool. Freud describes how group participation alters self-involvement:

> This self-love works for the preservation of the individual, and behaves as though the occurrence of any divergence from his own particular lines of development involved a criticism of them . . . . We do not know why such sensitiveness should have been directed to just these details of differentition . . . . But when a group is formed the whole of this intolerance vanishes . . . within the group. (1921, pp. 42–3)

In order to understand this profundity more fully, I will detail the narcissistic phase of individual development, which characterizes the state at which many withdrawn patients are fixated, and the narcissistic phase of

147

of group development—the pregroup—which characterizes the group composed of members who are extremely narcissistic. The reader should remember Stolorow and Lachmann's (1980) description of narcissism: it is the piece of psychic structure that is designed to protect, restore, repair, and stabilize self-esteem. Self-esteem is necessary for survival: when self-esteem is threatened, people enter a narcissistic state in order to heal the wound to basic psychic structure. The initial stages of development are characterized by narcissistic activity because self-esteem is not yet firmly established, but in a state of formation. It is, consequently, quite fragile and must be nurtured with care by internal and external forces.

THE NARCISSISTIC PHASE OF DEVELOPMENT

Groups will go through phases at different time intervals, partially reflecting the stage of psychosexual development of the majority of the members of the group. A treatment group composed of neurotic members will move quickly through the trust and power phases and soon be grappling with Oedipal issues of intimacy. Groups tend to spend more time in the group that parallels the development phase at which most of the group members are fixated.

In order to see the dynamics of the pregroup clearly, the therapist must be familiar with the characteristics of the narcissistic phase of individual development. Severely disturbed patients' difficulties date back to the first few years of life. Freud (1949) refers to the earliest time as the stage of autoeroticism, a period which predates the development of the ego and where gratification is obtained without any external love object. Blanck and Blanck clarify this: "The first stage of life in the neonate has been variously termed autoeroticism, primary narcissism, nondifferentiation, undifferentiation, the objectless stage, autism. Whatever the term, it is agreed that this is the stage of life when there is no awareness of the outside" (1974, p. 81). Kohut (1971) explains that as the ego develops and objects are differentiated (secondary narcissistic phase), two prominent healthy narcissistic configurations designed to cope with narcissistic blows emerge: the "grandiose self" and the "idealized parent imago." In those cases in which narcissistic blows are traumatic and psychotic processes are involved, these structures persist pathologically into adult life: the "grandiose self" becomes delusional grandiosity and the "idealized parent imago" becomes a fixation on an omnipotent object. Freud describes megalomaniacal, grandiose narcissists who manifest "an over-estimation of the power of [their] wishes . . . omnipotence of thoughts . . . the art of magic" (p. 32). He also describes the anaclitic narcissist who, in contrast and complementarily, overestimates the object. "Whoever possesses an excellence which the ego lacks for the attainment of this ideal becomes loved" (1914, p. 58).

Few disturbed patients are in a primary narcissistic state where there is *no* awareness of an object; most relate to others narcissistically—the object attachment fulfills a narcissistic need (the need to bolster self-esteem). Severely disturbed patients carry the more pathologic narcissistic defenses into later life in order to maintain a sense of well-being. All of their social interactions and personal activity are geared to helping their psyches achieve a sense of self-esteem and maintaining an inner stability. Such a person may have object relations, but these relationships must serve to enhance his or her intrapsychic cohesiveness. There is a lack of mutuality in such relationships; the disturbed person is essentially self-involved, to the detriment of mature object relations.

Since most of the narcissist's psychic energy is invested in maintaining inner balance, there is not much left over for empathy with other people. Object relations serve as extensions or representations of inner needs. In working with such patients, the leader must always keep in mind the patients' major emotional task: to do everything possible to help themselves feel worthwhile and to maintain a psychic homeostasis.

THE PREGROUP

Severely disturbed patients (chronic schizophrenics, borderline personalities, narcissistic character disorders with overt borderline characteristics, and self-medicating drug addicts) are usually self-involved and have a tenuous capacity for object relationships. For these reasons, they are often not considered for group treatment; supportive group intervention is the treatment of choice for many of these patients.

When patients with severe narcissistic conflicts and excessive pathology come together in a group, they spend considerable time in the narcissistic phase of group development: the pregroup. The pregroup has two stages—a stage of "parallel" talk which is concluded by members recognizing each other's existence, and a stage where members use each other and the group for a narcissistic purpose. The group members cannot move easily into the normal beginning phase of group development, where people face and recognize the strangers around them and wonder if they are trustworthy. In order to enter the trust phase, members face the fact that fellow members are strangers and could be hurtful, as opposed to fellow members being an extension of themselves and present in order to fulfill their narcissistic needs—that is, an extension of one's grandiosity or an object for one to idealize.

The pregroup is a collection of individuals whose thought and actions are primarily motivated by narcissistic needs. Initially, their talk is parallel; their verbalizations are not in response to what another person has said. We see this initial pregroup stage in young children when they play in parallel fashion. A child may grab another's toy because it suits his or her needs. The intention is not to deprive the other child but to meet one's own needs.

Severely disturbed adults usually show little interest in joining a group. They have an image of group which is a projection of their own fantasy of what their family (primary-group experience) was like. When they do get together, their own sick family is recreated: a family in which all the members are narcissistically involved and no one helps each other fulfill his or her narcissistic needs.

The task of the group leader is to help patients use the group for their own narcissistic needs, so that group will be useful and meaningful for each patient. The leader must understand how the group can help the patient achieve and maintain self-esteem and psychic stability. Stolorow says: "Narcissism is literally in the service of the psychic survival of self" (1975, p. 184). It is possible to break through parallel involvements when the patient can experience how the "grandiose self" or the "idealized parent imago" manifests itself in group. When these defenses begin to operate in the group—on a group or individual level—the group becomes a meaningful, helpful tool for the patient.

Grandiosity or idealizing the parent can take many forms. A member may openly express grandiosity by saying, "This group is too sick for me." The drug addict may say, "This group is made up of street junkies, but I'm not like them; I just got into a bit of trouble." The group may become an extension of the patient in which he or she feels greater by virtue of being part of the group: "We're all mental patients and you know that we're more sensitive and intelligent than most people." With self-medicating drug addicts, it is important for the group to move from "we're all junkies" to "we know what the world is about because we know how to hustle and con people; if you can make it on the streets you can make it anywhere."

Those who maintain their own grandiosity in a group have a much harder time staying in the group. They can do so, however, by identifying with the leader and feeling, "I am a co-therapist, and since I can help you (the group) as the leader does, and I have one equal in the group, I will stay with you." Groups seem to tolerate this form of grandiosity in their initial phases (the group is more threatened by members leaving then by their condescension). It is in the second, power, phase that these members have to face the hostility of the group members. Burstein (1975) labels and describes two kinds of narcissistic group members: the "inadequate" narcissistic patient who tends to be quiet in the group and idealizes the therapist, and the "grandiose" narcissist who is noisy and tends to demand a lot of attention. The latter is difficult to manage and usually drops out of the group prematurely. Burstein feels that the "inadequate" narcissist has a better prognosis in group therapy, because his or her passivity is an important factor in staying in treatment.

Groups of mentally and physically ill patients typically idealize the leaders and attribute magical powers to them. Many leaders report such group members as having strong, infantile, dependent transferences on the leader (Bloomingfeld, 1970). Group members will call a social work therapist "Doctor" for years, even though it is frequently brought to their attention that the leader is a social worker.

Group members can become addicted to a group or leader in the same way as they can become addicted to drugs. When the parent image (group or leader or drug) is idealized, Kohut explains, "all bliss and power reside in the idealized object, the child [patient] feels empty and powerless when he is separated from it and he attempts, therefore, to maintain a continuous union with it" (p. 37). Kohut goes on to say that the aspect of the archaic object focused on is "not as a substitute for loved or loving objects, or for a relationship with them, *but as a replacement for a defect in the psychological structure*" [author's emphasis] (1971, p. 46). For this reason, idealization of the group or leader and grandiosity should be respected and dealt with carefully by the leader. Leaders should recognize and support these essential narcissistic defenses and also understand that if the group is used by the patient to enhance his or her self-esteem, any break in the continuity of the group will probably cause some regression in the patients. For this reason, it is useful to have co-leaders in such a group.

Use of denial is common in the pregroup; it seems to cultivate the notion that "we're all the same; there are no differences between us." In one pregroup, two lonely women with uncontrolled diabetes were told that a blind man would be joining the group. One of the women came to the next meeting wearing a new wig and bright red lipstick. The second time the three met, another women took out pictures to show the new male member. He proceeded to "look" at the pictures and say how nice they were. Everyone left the group happily (Berger, 1975).

Severely disturbed patients with narcissistic disorders require a long time in the pregroup phase. Theory and technique called upon by the leader must be appropriate to the developmental level of the patient. For this reason, these patients do poorly in healthier groups—often to the dismay of both group and leader. But if patients experience a pregroup with a mature leader, they can progress. After considerable parallel talk, they begin to notice one another and respond to each other narcissistically. At a certain point, group members begin to feel that they are in a safe place (all bad is outside the group; all good is inside the group); they look around and begin to think, "Who are these people? Can I trust them?" The first trust phase of group development has begun; the pregroup is now a group. Freud wrote:

> Love for oneself knows only one barrier—love for others, love for objects . . . . And in the development of mankind as a whole, just as in individuals, love alone acts as the civilizing factor in the sense that it brings a change from egoism to altruism . . . . If therefore in groups narcissistic self-love is subject to limitations which do not operate outside them, that is cogent evidence that the essence of a group formation consists in new kinds of libidinal ties among members of the group. (1921, pp. 43–44)

DEGREES OF WOUNDED SELF-ESTEEM

People with wounded self-esteem in need of supportive group interaction fall along a continuum in terms of psychiatric pathology. Although technique in leading the supportive group is somewhat constant, the pregroup composed of the severely disturbed medical or psychiatric patient requires more specialized technique. Table 8-1 shows this continuum.

People's capacity to regulate self-esteem can be retarded in infancy or early childhood, resulting in a forever fragile ego; this weak and limited ego has the immense task of compensating for crucial missing links in psychic structure. Although long-term group participation helps treat such deep damage to self-esteem, the progress is slow and a group leader can be easily discouraged. One member of an inpatient turnover geriatric group for medical patients came to three meetings before he stopped reading his newspaper. Monaster (1972) describes the slow pace of cutting through senile group members' self-involvement but he does eventually succeed. Grobman (1978) writes that it is important for the group leader not to demonstrate too much enthusiasm when walls between severely disturbed people start to break down. It is more important for the leader to appreciate the anxiety members have in the beginning of this process.

The leader has to recognize that minimal gains are really giant gains when one faces the magnitude of the problem. Even when progress is

TABLE 8-1
Degrees of Wounded Self-Esteem

MOST DAMAGED SELF-ESTEEM				LEAST DAMAGED SELF-ESTEEM
Severely disturbed psychiatric or medical patients; a number of these people together compose a pregroup and show no interest in their environment.	Medical patients who function well when not under stress regress to narcissistic states when traumatized by physical illness.	The majority of medical and psychiatric patients show a mixture of psychiatric and physical pathology, respond readily to group leader's guidance to interact positively.	The acutely ill psychiatric patients who recover rapidly and quickly show genuine interest in others.	The emotionally healthy medical patients self-esteem is wounded from physical illness. Patients show genuine interest in others, require a supportive group experience when traumatized by illness.

achieved, the leader has to face the fact that a break in narcissistic withdrawal is often temporary, and the patient's relief from internal struggle may be momentary and short-lived. It is not unusual to see such patients in a medical setting. Often they have never officially been given a psychiatric diagnosis because they have always refused psychiatric care. They have not been threatening to others, so hospitalization has never been a forced issue. No one is close enough to them to know they are suicidal. Such patients may be induced to join a turnover group and may respond to others, with affect and mood improving. However, after the meeting, they retreat again. The leader can only be comforted by the fact that the quality of life improved for the patient, even for a short time.

> Ms. C., a 63-year-old single woman, alternated between living on the streets and in a shelter for undomiciled women. Her social worker felt that she may never have had a single friendship. She never worked. A relative commented, "She should have been institutionalized a long time ago; she's paranoid and a shrew." She refused psychiatric help and only accepted limited medical help. During her last hospitalization she signed out against medical orders. She had cancer of the uterus and accepted this hospitalization because of profuse vaginal bleeding. On the floor she was nonverbal with patients and staff. The only time she talked was to say no to medical

treatment. She came to group because of the persistence of her social worker, the group leader, and perhaps because she did not want to say no.

She came to the meeting with matted hair and an intravenous pole and sat with her head between her knees. When others said they didn't want to come to the hospital, she lifted her head and said she also didn't want to come. She shook her head, agreeing with others that it was hard to be dependent. When the subject of alcoholism came up, Ms. C. said that her family drank (it was the first time the social worker heard this information). She stayed in the group for the whole meeting, although she was free to leave.

Ms. C., who was almost totally withdrawn prior to entering the group, spontaneously related to her peers within the group. This was a great surprise to her social worker and perhaps even to herself. This brief puncturing of narcissistic preoccupation and withdrawal and relating to the world outside can be helpful in alleviating feelings of low self-esteem. Fried writes that "genuine contact keeps narcissistic self-involvement at bay. Creating interest in and understanding of the needs and mental make-up of others, authentic contact reduces the danger of falling back upon an image of a world where wishes and magical thought rather than facts rule" (1970, p. 15). Even in the terminal phase of illness, these patients can be afforded an opportunity to have a growth experience as they participate in group. Granted, it is a short-lived connection but a meaningful one nevertheless. I might note that these patients are very hard to get into a group. They usually come as a result of their relationship with the group leader or because they are simply passively following hospital routine (Cooper, 1976, 1978).

At the other extreme is the emotionally healthy person, whose self-esteem is wounded because of the blow of illness. These patients may, under normal circumstances, be candidates for long-term in-depth group therapy where anxiety might be utilized to further growth so that the person's full potential can be achieved. However, with the occurrence of physical illness, such patients are in need of a supportive approach. They may use primitive defense mechanisms adaptively in order to cope optimally with trauma.

Many members will fall in the middle of the continuum presented. For example, low self-esteem was illustrated by two members attending a long-term group for posthospitalized mental patients. They both arrived at the group early and separately. They saw a note on the door of the group room. The secretary had put up the note, notifying the members that she would not be present that evening but to come in and make themselves comfortable. Neither member read the note to the end. After reading the first line, they assumed the group would not be meeting and went home. This pessimism was a result of their low self-image (who would want to meet with *them?*). These people were not at the extreme of self-involvement. They recognized and cared about their fellow group members but still were in need of self-esteem boosting because of past trauma.

All of the people who fall on the above continuum require self-esteem reparation technique, which includes the leader helping patients see that they are unique, not alone, helpers, and have strengths. Since narcissistic withdrawal is evident in all the groups along the continuum, even though the degree may vary markedly, the leader must recognize, respect, and at times encourage narcissistic defenses such as "grandiosity" and "idealization" and strongly encourage relatedness to external reality. The latter two techniques are crucial for the pregroup.

The pregroup is the usual kind of group in a psychiatric setting where one is solely working with the severely disturbed patient. However, it is not uncommon to find them in a medical setting since many psychiatric patients are hospitalized for medical illness and many functional people regress under the stress of illness. In an open, turnover group on an inpatient service, one will find that there are often clusters of narcissistically involved people who make up most of the group membership. They talk in parallel fashion and do not respond to one another. This happened frequently in the heart-attack and geriatric groups at St. Vincent's Hospital. In one long-term outpatient group for patients with chronic medical illness, everyone talked at once. No one listened to anyone else, but all seemed pleased that they were talking and had an audience. The leader felt like taking out a baton and conducting the orchestration of voices. The same tone was evident in a long-term geriatric group whose members came to treatment for emotional adjustment problems. Both groups had a tone of excitement, and it was deemed best to let them verbalize a while before intervening.

PREGROUP TECHNIQUE

RECOGNIZE AND RESPECT NARCISSISTIC DEFENSES

Two men from a group for seriously ill medical patients were functional under normal circumstances, but their narcissism was wounded by the onset of severe physical illness. They benefited from the mobilization of basic narcissistic defenses.

Mr. N. found Mr. C. as an object to idealize in the group to be described. At the same time, Mr. C. clung to a grandiose overindependence and appeared to be fighting for a sense of autonomy, despite his severe illness.

(He died about two months after this meeting, soon after his doctor told him he would not be able to walk again and would have to think of getting some custodial help.) Mr. C. seemed to need to take the "giver" role to boost his self-esteem.

> Mr. N., a 61-year-old man with cancer of the kidney, told Mr. C., a 60-year-old man with lung cancer, that he could tell Mr. C. was more intelligent and educated than himself and that he was impressed at the way he expressed himself. Ms. O., a 28-year-old woman with chronic renal disease, agreed. Mr. C. acknowledged their praise factually and then magnanimously told them, "Underneath we're all the same." The leader said that in a hospital people are equal in a way that they are not outside, namely dressing the same and not having their occupations visible. Also, hospitalization can be seen as an opportunity to meet people that one ordinarily might not meet. Mr. N. said that he was ashamed of the work he did. He never advanced on the job or took opportunities to be educated. Finally, reluctantly and ashamedly told the group he was a bus driver. Mr. C. said that being a bus driver was wonderful; "What would society do without bus drivers?" Ms. O. said, "I think any work is alright, if you're happy with it." Mr. N. said, "I always was happy on my job. Others griped and were miserable, but not me." The leader said, "So being contented on a job is a challenge unto itself." Ms. O. said that she was a secretary and liked her work. Mr. C. said that being a secretary was wonderful too; his office would be paralyzed without the help of a secretary. "What would a businessman do, if he couldn't get a letter typed?" The leaders observed that these three members were beaming.

If patients with self-esteem problems project an idealized transference onto the leader, they are making a narcissistic effort to help themselves. Members with damaged self-esteem often come to the group to comply, depend, please, or help the leader. These motivations succeed in getting patients to stay in the group, where they can get treatment for their illness. The leader needs to appreciate the value of idealization and not try to get patients to change their motivation for coming to and staying in the group.

As the group relieves patients of some of the emotional work load by mobilizing and supporting narcissistic defenses, emotional energy is freed. At this point, the leader (and eventually the group) can begin to make work demands on the members to break through parallel involvements and face one another directly. The pregroup helps the patient make the first step in mature object relations: recognizing that there is an object to be noticed and dealt with.

DEMAND RECOGNITION OF EXTERNAL REALITY

The severely disturbed patient needs help in seeing and hearing another person. Once I had a pregroup for six months, until I realized that everyone seemed to be looking at the floor or into space. At one meeting I asked all the members to close their eyes and tell me what they observed in the room in which they had spent one hour a week for six months. The revelations consisted of one person's noticing a tiny detail, another a mass of color, etc. When the patients opened their eyes, they were anxious to look at the room. Later members reported being taught in childhood not to look at people, and they had extended this admonition to all objects. They began to realize that when they walked down the street they looked at the sidewalk. When they looked up for the first time, they were frightened but exhilarated at the expansion of their world. The following week I repeated the exercise, but asked them if they had noticed anything about any other member in the group. They experienced the exercise as a game and seemed to enjoy looking at each other afterward and checking their perceptions.

The severely disturbed can often talk in the group but it is very difficult for them to learn to listen. They have to be taught that listening is as important as talking, and they need to be reinforced when listening occurs. The leader needs to be specific and concrete: "It is very good that you hear what Paul says to you. Did you hear what he said?" "No." "Paul, would you repeat what you said?" A dramatic example of a narcissistically withdrawn man who responded to pregroup treatment resulted in greater compliance with medical prescription.

Mr. H. was a 58-year-old man who had been on renal dialysis for two years. He had never been married and had no family or friends in New York City. He lived in a welfare hotel, dividing his week into dialysis days and no-dialysis days. The worker at the dialysis center which he had attended for 18 months did not know who he was. He was hospitalized repeatedly as a consequence of not following his diet, and he was considered a "vegetable." The hospital social worker who saw him regularly for disposition planning once sent a replacement for herself, and he did not know the difference. Mr. H. and Mr. I., another group member, had been dialyzed next to each other numerous times and never spoke. Mr. H. came to the pregroup because the leader explained it was part of his medical treatment. He came out of compliance but suggested members be exactly like himself. Mr. I., also socially isolated but with more ego strength, came to the group to "help" the leader and show his gratefulness to her for doing him a favor. After the first meeting, the two members went down on the elevator together and exchanged a good-bye. After two meetings, Mr. H. said to a nurse that he belonged to a group and recognized and recalled by name his group leader. During the third meeting, he told the leader he saw Mr. I. was sick. The leader said, "It is nice you noticed." In the fourth meeting, Mr. H. arrived with his usual 14-pound weight gain. Mr. I. said, "What happened to you? You're huge!" Mr. H.: "Well, how much did you gain?" (Leader notes that this is the first time Mr. H. has asked Mr. I. a question about himself.) Mr. I. answered: "Two pounds." Leader said, "It's very good that you could compare yourself with Mr. I. and ask him a question." The following weekend, Mr. H. only gained 7 pounds.

The leader should help patients make connections between their inner world and external stimuli; these connections need to be presented in a concrete and simple way. If someone leaves the group, the leader might ask, "Did anyone notice what just happened in the group?" Such questions help to cultivate an interest in the here-and-now.

All five senses can be worked with in order to help patients relate to their surroundings. Program media may be very useful in working with the tactile and olfactory senses. Textures such as clay, fur, and fabric can be felt and compared. Cooking can be used to awaken the pleasure of smell. One schizophrenic patient told me that she did not want to get well because she hallucinated a wonderful perfume which she loved. Patients can be helped to find such pleasures in external reality.

The importance of good discussion-leading technique should not be underestimated. Grand (1973) describes a group of ambulatory schizophrenics in which patients typically began the group by talking directly to the leader about their last hospitalization. The leader encouraged others to tell him about their own experience, which enforced their self-esteem. Leader and patient began to see connections between different people's experiences and interpersonal curiosity was sparked. The leader can accelerate the process with such interventions as: "Did you feel the same way about ECT as Jim did?" "Kathy, you were on the same ward as Bill. Can you tell him about your experience?" The leader begins by appealing to the patients' sense of importance as a preliminary tool in engaging them to work on development of more mature object relations.

Principles and techniques of the pregroup can be used in certain forms of marital therapy:

Mr. A. was a 50-year-old married man who had been addicted to Darvon and other pills for 15 years. He came to the clinic for detoxification. He tried individual treatment numerous times but found it not helpful. Individual sessions revealed severe narcissistic involvement, which expressed itself in rumination about pills and hypochondriacal symptoms. No therapist had involved his wife in the treatment. Mrs. A. was a masochistic woman. She strength than her husband. I saw Mr. A. once a week individually, enhancing his self-esteem by giving him attention and allowing him to talk about pills. I saw Mr. and Mrs. A. together once a week, focusing on helping him develop an elementary awareness of his wife (the object). He said his wife was the only reason he was living, but he demonstrated in the session that he had no notion of her feelings or actions. He really had not "seen" her, almost literally, for at least ten years, except as an extension of himself. At the conclusion of the first marital session, I gave Mr. A. a homework assignment: to notice something about his wife that he had not noticed before. Because both patients idealized me, they took my directions seriously. Mrs. A. could accept attention from her husband because it was "doctor's orders" and "for my husband's treatment." My next assignment was to ask Mr. A. to take an action related to anything he noticed regarding his wife. He noticed that his wife did not like doing dishes, and so he did them one day. I rewarded him, as did his wife, and his self-esteem improved. Subsequent sessions were devoted to helping Mr. A. become more aware of his surroundings. Sometimes, I felt the reality issues they both had to face were painful and I reflected this. They would respond, "You're the doctor—whatever you say." (I am not a doctor, and they had been told this at the beginning of treatment.) Mr. A. showed steady improvement. After six months, his use of Darvon dropped from 15 to 1 a day and he appeared more angry than depressed. When I asked him what he got out of seeing me, he said, "You stop me from taking pills."

These interventions are reminiscent in some ways of those of a nursery school teacher or of a parent with young children. The leader must relate on a level appropriate to the patient's developmental level at the point of treatment. It is possible for the leader to intervene in this way without being condescending. In illustration, a summary from a process recording follows (Coven, 1976). One can see the arduous task a leader may have in breaking through parallel discussion in the pregroup.

Meeting began with Sally relating anxiety regarding her last clinic appointment, at which she had a new doctor. Ann entered the room and immediately talked about Sunday's endless problems [parallel discussion]. Leader wanted to connect back to Sally, who was looking withdrawn and tense, without stifling Ann and undoing all the reinforcing she had been doing with her [good discussion-leading technique]. She grabbed for a connection with Sally through the feeling of strangeness Ann described having had on Sunday and Sally's upset with a strange new doctor—i.e., it is upsetting when we find ourselves in strange situations [finding a commonality]. Leader suggested that Sally share with Ann what she had been telling leader. It worked a bit. Sally shared and Ann made a small attempt to listen before she interrupted and started on a new track of how upsetting it was at emergency welfare center [continuation of parallel talk]. Leader emphasized how good it was that Ann could tell group about this incident [reinforcing] and noted that the man at the emergency welfare center did not seem to want to listen to her [approaching here-and-now focus].

Leader: "That was the same kind of thing that Sally was saying. Remember? Sally was talking about how she felt when the doctor seemed to ignore her?" [finding commonality]
Ann: "Yeah."
Leader: "I think it is important to listen to each other; it is natural to be angry when people ignore us or pretend we're not there."
Members: "Yeah." "Well."
Ann: "Yeah! I mean, I'm a good person. Right? I give to charity. I mean, I don't want to brag, but . . ." [utilizing grandiose narcissistic defense]
Leader: "It is terrific that you can brag, Ann." [reinforcing narcissistic task]
Ann: "I give to Children's Aid Society. I don't even put it on my taxes . . ."

Sally began speaking of a painful experience involving one of her grandchildren who has breathing fits when she does not get her way and how upset this makes Sally and how her daughter is reluctant to leave the grandchild with her.

Leader: "It sounds like a frightening thing." [empathy]
Sally: "I was so scared."
Leader: "Like when Ann discovered her dog was dead?" [finding commonality]
Sally: "Yeah."
Ann : "Sally, can you understand why your daughter might not want to leave the children with you if you get so upset yourself?" [First time a member has asked another a question out of concern for object!]
Leader (to herself): "This is more than I could wish!"
Leader: "Ann, I think you have said something to Sally that is really important. I'm glad you could say that—it means you have been listening to Sally. Sally, can you hear what Ann is saying to you?"
Sally: "Yeah." "What?"
Ann: Repeated statement.
Leader: Repeated her statement.

Sally: Nodded.
Leader: "Can you repeat what Ann said, Sally?"
Sally: Repeats statement.
Leader: "That is wonderful! You really heard what Ann had to say!" [Both members get approval from leader for listening.]

The two members left the group together and went for coffee in the hospital cafeteria.

SELF-ESTEEM REPARATION TECHNIQUE

EMPHASIZE INDIVIDUALITY OF MEMBERS

It is common in hospitals to hear patients referred to by their illnesses and also to hear patients refer to themselves in this way. Thus the patient appears to become the illness being treated. Crookshank (1923) wrote about the fallacy of "hypostatization," whereby one can mistake a word that is shorthand for an entire entity. A doctor threatened by the chaotic presentation of a patient's emotional and social problems and lacking guidelines to deal with these areas might automatically turn to aspects of the illness for which he or she is prepared: the well-structured scheme of purely medical management. For example, referring to a 19-year-old girl who is about to lose her hair from chemotherapy as "a leukemic" is depersonalizing. A surgeon about to operate on a 63-year-old grandmother referred to her, in her presence, as "this gallbladder case." An even more horrifying example was described by a group member who was a physician with cystic fibrosis. He remembered making rounds when he was a resident, and the attending pointing to someone and saying, "Oh, that one is just another cystic dying." Social workers and nurses typically complain that physicians do not see patients as persons and treat them like objects. Interestingly, when one nurse and social worker became co-leaders of a group, they were surprised at how *they* had been objectifying patients so that they would feel less insecure in the face of patients' catastrophic illnesses.

Despite the fact that groups are usually focused on hospitalizations or illnesses, when patients find themselves interacting with peers, their old selves can spontaneously emerge. Without realizing it, they seem to momentarily forget their illnesses and be themselves. When this happens, the patient becomes more than a sick person, but a person who has a long history, with unique characteristics, and someone capable of contributing to other people. The recollection of this reality in the group can be helpful in beginning to repair damaged self-esteem.

Leaders at St. Vincent's Hospital reported feeling differently toward patients after seeing them in the group. In group, patients were all participants in interaction with peers and staff—one human being to another. They had histories to share, some of the details were captivating, and the staff began to identify with and appreciate them in a new way. Qualities of patients emerged as they interacted that helped the staff see the patients more comprehensively. A male patient who was passive on the floor was seen as active in his group when he reached out to help another member verbally. In another instance, a man who was depressed, withdrawn, and self-involved, and with whom no one on staff was particularly connected, came alive in the group (with much support and reassurance from the leader). He was 68 years old, had had six heart attacks, and he looked at the younger men disbelievingly when they said they were careful about having sex after their heart attacks. He described his desire for his wife with sparkling eyes and said sex to him meant living. Staff was surprised and delighted by the revelation of this man's personality and appreciated him in a new way.

With few exceptions, all leaders who put someone in group whom they had known previously learned something new about their patient. One man who appeared as a vegetable revealed that he was a musician. The leader was surprised and began to think about the man's total life. Of course, these kinds of revelations cause problems for staff, who are so used to defending themselves from identifying with patients who have serious illnesses. Some group leaders have to deal with existential questions as to the meaning of life, death, and illness for the patients and themselves. Others become depressed and have to work through their own emotional reactions to patients' illnesses in their individual or group psychotherapy. Others are briefly stunned or paralyzed by facing, with full emotional impact, such thoughts as: "I could be this patient with this illness," or "It could be my family," or "What would I do if I were this patient?" Because patients often emerge as total people in the group, and because group leaders' emotional reactions are evoked, a fair amount of supervision time must be spent discussing these issues.

STRESS COMMONALITY WITH OTHERS

Yalom writes that one of the curative factors in group is universality: people discover that they are not alone—that others have the same thoughts and feelings. In working with a group of cancer patients, Yalom reveals: "I was repeatedly struck by the realization that, in the face of death, our dread is...that of the accompanying utter loneliness. The dying patient's concerns are often chiefly interpersonal ones. He is distressed at being abandoned, even shunned, by the world of the living" (1970, p. 123). Similarly, Hacket and Cassem (1974) report that patients in an emergency room said they were most frightened by being left alone.

Kübler-Ross (1969) elaborates on Yalom's observations on how painful it is to patients with a terminal illness if friends and family withdraw from them. Seriously ill patients in groups at St. Vincent's have made similar comments: "You have to act happy when healthy people call you or they will stop calling; they don't like to hear about sickness," or "The doctors should tell us the truth about our illnesses, not our families."

When I was beginning the group program at St. Vincent's, I encountered reluctance on the part of group leaders to form groups. Some people said, "I'm not a group person," or "How do I know this is valuable?" or "Why not leave the poor patients alone?" I asked leaders to pretend that they were in the patients' place and tell me how they felt. They all found this task somewhat frightening, but because of their courage and professional motivation, they proceeded. They began to think about what they were most afraid of: "What if this illness happened to me?" I asked what their needs might be, what they would want. Every person had the same thought: "I wouldn't want to be alone." With this realization, they proceeded to form their group.

Repeatedly, in the groups at St. Vincent's people said, "I thought I was the only one who felt this way," or "I have no one I can *really* talk to about my illness," or "Only sick people can really understand." The leader can capitalize on these expressions and introduce a group meeting by saying: "Patients have said that it is different talking to one another than to staff because you have actually experienced being sick and in a hospital and staff haven't," or "Patients have told us that they get something from one another that they don't get from us—a kind of understanding," or "We believe you have a lot to offer one another; there is a huge collection of individual experiences in this room."

It has been touching for me to see people who were formerly isolated and preoccupied, lying in their hospital beds beginning to find themselves part of a human interaction system in which they were not only accepted but also had status. Fisher and Laufer write the following about post–myocardial-infarction patients:

> It seems safe to say that, at the least, the high level of preconscious anxiety which stays with most heart attack victims for several years after their attacks can be reduced substantially by group psychotherapy. . . . The one thing almost all heart attack patients crave and respond to is the mutual airing of concerns—moving slowly from

practical matters to emotional ones as their tolerance for self-revelation allows. (1977, p. 229)

ENCOURAGE PEER HELPFULNESS

For the most part, patients assume a dependent position in the hospital; they are forced to assume a passive role and they often react by regressing. Independence, activity, and assertiveness usually reflect good self-esteem; dependency and passivity usually reflect low self-esteem. Blanck and Blanck (1974) define activity as the changeover from the passive, preoedipal state of receiver to the active, Oedipal position of giver of love. Some studies have revealed that patients who take a part in their hospital treatment show less regression and seem to feel better about themselves. Lubell describes an inpatient dialysis unit where patients were generally passive but became active participants after group attendance:

> They changed immediately into pajamas and, for most of their 48-hour run, remained on their beds and watched television or slept. Few of the patients made any effort to regulate their own equipment or to participate in their treatment procedures, but became overdependent on members of the staff for their care. After group treatments on the floor, patients began to wear street clothes while being dialyzed, several trained for home dialysis, most knew how to regulate their own equipment, and patients' depression seemed to have decreased. (1976, p. 161)

Group participation gives patients a chance to be active helpers, and for some patients this opportunity is the main attraction and value of the group. Yalom writes:

> In therapy groups, too, patients receive through giving, not only as part of the reciprocal giving–receiving sequence but also from the intrinsic act of giving. . . . It is a refreshing, self-esteem-boosting experience to find that they can be of importance to others. . . . Patients are enormously helpful to one another in the group therapeutic process. They offer support, reassurance, suggestions, insight, and share similar problems with one another. Not infrequently patients will listen and absorb observations from another member far more readily than from the group therapist. (1970, p. 23)

When Yalom (1980) worked with cancer patients, he referred to altruism as the most important way to find meaning in life and he observed that patients who experienced a deep sense of meaning in their lives faced death with less despair. Valliant found altruism to be a mature adult defense. He believed it "serves as a protective filter for the most searing emotions" (1977, p. 110). Group leaders and group process can facilitate the mobilization of this defense.

I have often expressed my respect and appreciation to patients for giving of themselves in the group. Once, patients were talking about how healthy people find them boring if they talk about their illness. Finally, one patient turned to me and said, "Do you find us boring?" It had been one of the most revealing and moving sessions we had had, and it was easy for me to say, "We have learned a lot from you today about what it feels like to be sick and in the hospital. The understanding you're helping us to obtain by sharing some of your deep feelings with us will help us do our job better."

Patients can begin to learn that there are many ways of giving, and that sharing one's own feelings with another is an important way. As Harper has indicated:

> Feelings . . . true grief, sympathy—are most supportive for the dying one, not only because he feels loved but because he sees that the living need his help. He feels called upon to soothe the physician's hurt, to comfort those who will mourn, to assure men of their dignity. Such a man will live his life to the end and as productively as he ever was able. (1977, p. 6)

Many of our patients formerly were able to perpetuate self-esteem by performing concrete and physical tasks that their incapacitation prevents them from continuing. Patients in group had the following to say about the role of the giver and how it relates to their feelings about themselves.

All said it was hard to be dependent; others do things differently than you. Everyone expressed their views about what it felt like to ask for help. Ms. L. said it was alright for her because she was able to reciprocate in some ways and consequently did not feel like a burden. Ms. D. "gives back" by caring. Ms. A. said that since she is always a burden, she can't ask for help. (She had recently been evicted from her apartment because she didn't go for proper SSI certification and didn't ask her social worker to help her.) Various members spoke of the frustration of being sick and the humiliation of not being able to do things for oneself. Ms. B. said that she was not anxious to go home: "I won't be working for the first time in my life; I will be a good-for-nothing." Ms. Q. said that she also worried about going home: "I will have to depend on my family for the first time in my life; I won't be able to travel alone to visit my daughter; someone will have to drive me." Ms. R. said,

"Well, I'll be alone soon and I'll just have to cope!" Leaders said that they probably would all make adjustments, but it sounded as though it might be difficult for them.

Mr. N. began the meeting by saying he had gotten some bad news in the morning. He had to have a brain scan and he was trying not to think of the worst. The leader asked him what the "worst" was. He said, "Being dependent on my family." Ms. K. said that she could take her illness, but she wanted no part of being old, feeble, and helpless. Ms. W. said that she liked helping the nurses and being useful in the hospital.

The importance of mutual helpfulness among the patients came up quite spontaneously in the group meetings. The leaders reinforced this kind of sharing, and the patients once again were reminded that their sensitivity to and concern for each other was a valuable contribution. Patients talked about how their roommate could make or break their hospital stay and gave examples of how they sometimes helped one another when no nurse was around. Occasionally, the discussion involved two people in the group, and it gave one a concrete chance to say "thank you."

Ms. D., a 50-year-old woman with chronic heart disease, was very anxious between group sessions as she awaited a cardiac catheterization. Prior to hospitalization her brother with whom she lived had died and her dog was killed. She met Mr. L. in the group—a 71-year-old man who had cancer, lived alone in a hotel, and did not seem to connect with the group process or any of the members. (The leaders wondered if they should have invited him to the group.) The following week Ms. D. told the group, with Mr. L. present, that he had listened to her ventilate during the week, and she needed a listener very much in order to take the edge off her intense anxiety. Mr. L. seemed pleased with Ms. D.'s comments; his face brightened for a moment. Mr. L. was discharged from the hospital the next day and died two weeks later.

The group leaders in this meeting were very moved by the fact that Mr. L. got some recognition that he probably would not have got from anyone if he had not attended the group. The leaders knew he was going home to his own apartment, had no existing family or friends, and would probably remain as socially isolated as he had been recently.

Two doctors said to patients in group meetings, "It would help us be better doctors if you could tell us what you respond to in a doctor, what feels right in terms of how a doctor relates to you?" Since doctors are often regarded with esteem, telling the patients that their opinions are valuable enhances patient self-esteem. Patients also have a chance to give something to the doctor. Doctors can usually tell patients sincerely that they learned something from them in the group meeting because usually they do. Doctors have said that they tend to see the patients more as total people in the group and their reactions make them more aware of alternatives in treating their patients. Some medical chiefs of service have considered group participation an important aspect of medical education.

Emphasize Individual Strengths

Group leaders have been consistently amazed at the strengths patients exhibit in coping with illness and hospitalizations. When the leaders see this exemplified in group discussion, they can reflect it back to the patients; the patients then look at their own strengths and self-esteem is enhanced, as in these two groups:

> Three women spoke of their difficulty with shortness of breath and their trouble before open-heart surgery: "It was no life!" They were glad they had had the surgery and survived. Members acknowledged how scared they had been before the operation. One leader said, "You all handled your situation differently, but you all did well." (universalization and differentiation) Ms. S. complained about her surgical pain at the site of incision. Another member showed her how she uses a pillow to sleep. One leader said, "It is nice how you help each other." Ms. N. asked Ms. S. why she didn't have her surgical stockings on. Ms. S. said they were dirty. Ms. N. said, "You can wash them; it would be good exercise." Members all said that they felt prepared for surgery and were grateful to hospital staff. Leaders pointed out that the patient's own part in the overall process was critical.

> Mr. N. said that being in the war was easier than being sick; at least in the army, he was the head of his platoon and could think of the men and their needs. Members talked about how people often face terrible tragedies— war, indebtedness, retirement. Mr. N. said being sick was harder than being in a war because you have no distractions and end up thinking about yourself all day. The group moved on to the strengths people have in coping with such things. They all try to keep their mind off their illness. The leader said, "Are you surprised at how much strength you have shown in facing your illness?" Ms. M., a 28-year-old nonverbal woman on dialysis for one and a half years, said that when she was told she would have to be dialyzed, she never thought she could cope with it. She was amazed at what she has been able to handle. The leader said, "A number of patients in groups have said the same thing."

Sometimes the leader needs to recognize and acknowledge members' strengths that are unrelated to patients' coping with illness but connected to the individuality and life experience of the members. For example, in a

long-term geriatric group for people with emotional-adjustment problems, members related to the leader as a grandchild. They would refer to
her as a "kid" and minimize some of her interventions; *they* were the
experienced ones. Instead of the leader trying to prove her worth to the
members, she acknowledged that they were indeed older and had more
life experience than she. She was learning a great deal from them. These
members were in desperate need of self-esteem boosting; afterward the
members responded more to her interventions. She was conveying that
she valued them as people; behind their devaluation of the group leader
was their need for recognition.

LEADERS' NARCISSISTIC STRUGGLE

Leaders often complain of boredom and inordinate demands on their
patience in working with the pregroup. Working with the severely disturbed is a long, tedious process. Sometimes it takes years to see any
results. Kernberg suggests that one should "not treat many of these
patients at the same time, because they put a great stress and many
demands on the analyst" (1975, p. 247). If leaders look to such groups for
their own narcissistic needs to be met, they will be disappointed and
angry. Patients' transference to the leader often triggers a countertransferential response of inadequacy. Oremland and Windholz state that the
therapist defends "against sensing the nothingness in the patient's relationship to the analyst. . . . Often the analyst himself becomes uninvolved
in the material and, in a sense, narcissistically withdraws into and becomes
fascinated by his own mind wandering. Often he feels bored and de-
tached in response to the aloneness" (1971, p. 272).

The following are aids in helping leader's morale: large groups, supervision that meets learning needs, peer exchange, short-term goals, and
supervisory or administrative approval. Large groups (10 to 12 members)
as opposed to small groups of 4 to 6 often add to intellectual and emotional stimulation for the leader. Supervision or peer consultation that presents intellectual and conceptual demands and helps define the leader's
learning needs also helps relieve boredom. It is very important that a staff
group be able to share their private successes with one another and that
supervisors support limited, short-term goal successes.

Supervision of pregroup therapists should include week-by-week
planning. A task should be outlined each week and a supervisor should
give approval when the task is accomplished. I tell these leaders that they
should not expect to see any results in fewer than six months. Rewards
from a supervisor or administrator have to substitute for rewards from

the patients during the first six months. Eventually, a positive cycle can develop, whereby the patient can be accepted and a staff group can begin to interpret to their community and administration how treatment works.

Despite the aids for the group leader outlined here, nothing will help a leader be satisfied with the pregroup unless he or she is a person who has achieved the developmental stage of generativity, as described by Erikson (1950); that is, he or she is comfortable in the nurturing role and feels rewarded by minimal progress or growth that is often not seen or applauded by others.

SUMMARY

Hospital patients who are severely disturbed or have a medical illness suffer from wounded self-esteem. The group is a treatment tool to treat self-esteem; if patients' self-esteem elevates, their prognosis for physical and emotional recovery improves.

Self-esteem-boosting technique includes: emphasizing the individuality of members, stressing commonality, encouraging peer helpfulness, and emphasizing individual strengths. In groups where damage to self-esteem of members is severe, members will form a pregroup. They will talk in parallel fashion and hardly take note of each other's presence, except to see others as extensions of themselves. In these groups additional pregroup technique needs to be employed. Leaders must understand, recognize, and respect narcissistic defenses such as idealization and grandiosity. They must help members be aware of and relate to their external environment.

The pregroup is often draining for the group leader; members tend to focus on the leader and not see the leader as a real person. For this reason, the leader has to be aware of his or her own fluctuations in self-esteem and narcissistic need to repair wounds to self-esteem.

Chapter 9

Mobilizing Group Members'
Coping Devices

People who are severely ill are coping with extraordinary stress on their psychological and biological systems.* In coping with such stress the psyche calls forth ego defenses to deal with irrationally based inner anxiety and adaptive mechanisms to deal with the reality-based threat of illness and hospitalization. Some people can adapt, that is, they can mobilize healthy, life-promoting drives, more easily and more effectively than others. Group members who are superb adapters can be used as models for others. Members who utilize maladaptive (life-threatening) mechanisms can be helped in the group by:

1. Exposure to alternatives represented by the variety of coping behavior displayed in the group.
2. The lessening of anxiety because of support attained in the group.
3. The influence of group norms, which stress positive adaptation.
4. The opportunity for modeling and reinforcement that the group provides.

Since the range and degree of coping behavior (defenses and adaptive mechanisms) for the severely ill often differs from that of people coping

*Some authors refer to ego devices designed to cope with life-threatening events as "emergency" or "recovery" defenses. (Hamburg, Hamburg, and DeGoza, 1953; Visotsky et al., 1961). Valliant (1977) includes defensive and adaptive mechanisms in one scheme and thinks defenses change with maturation. Although theorists such as Fenichel (1945) and Hartmann (1958) see defenses and adaptive mechanisms in constant interplay, I am separating the two for purposes of clearer discussion.

171

with normal amounts of stress, it is important for the group leader to study how group members cope and appreciate the value of the coping devices members employ.

This chapter will:

1. Define defenses and adaptation and discuss how severe illness and hospitalization is a threat from which the psyche has to protect itself.
2. Review the literature on coping devices of the medically ill and illustrate the use of such devices by medical and psychiatric patients who attended groups.
3. Show how groups can help to facilitate members' positive adaptation.
4. Outline some of the ingredients of positive adaptation and give examples of ego defenses which are frequently used by members to protect themselves from overwhelming anxiety.

DEFENSES AND ADAPTATION

One of the ego's main tasks is to protect the organism from internal and external danger. Internal danger comes from conflict within the intrapsychic system: id, ego, and superego. The ego employs defenses to limit the anxiety such conflict arouses. Greenson writes: "The concept of defense entails two constituents: a danger and a protecting agency" (1967, p. 78).

Psychoanalytic theorists have ranked defenses according to "high level" and "low level" (Kernberg, 1976). High-level defenses are those that are the most flexible and reality oriented (they allow maximum reality testing with a minimum of anxiety). For example, with sublimation, aggression can be channeled into socially acceptable activity. High-level defenses are resources available to the ego after it has been fully developed and differentiated from the id and superego. When the ego is still immature, weak, and undifferentiated, it has to pull upon more primitive defenses such as projection (projecting one's unacceptable impulses onto others) and denial. These defenses distort reality more than high-level ones, and thus the person who utilizes them appears more disturbed. Stolorow and Lachmann (1980) refer to the possibility that such low-level defenses can be prestage defenses. They clarify that these defenses are often utilized when the ego is in an embryonic stage of development and cannot possibly deal directly with overwhelming reality demands. For example, if a child is hospitalized for a severe illness at an early age, he may not be able to comprehend the changes in his life or manage the flood of anxiety aroused. He could resort to whatever defenses were available to him to assuage his fear; projection or denial would be possibilities, and if he employed these defenses he would be less afraid.

When mature adults become ill they often regress to styles of coping used in early childhood. Part of this regression is adaptive. Patients are forced into situations where they must be dependent on others in order to have their needs met. As patients retreat into dependency, they might use defenses employed in early childhood when the ego was weaker and less developed. Thus one might see patients utilize projection and denial who ordinarily would have excellent reality testing. Anna Freud (1942) thinks that children use denial more than adults. They can deny in certain areas and still function quite well. When adults become severely ill they can utilize "adaptive denial" in the service of preserving life-promoting drives.

Adaptation involves the ego's struggle to deal with external threat and demands. Hartmann defines adaptation as "the [ego] functions which are more or less closely related to the tasks of reality mastery . . . primarily a reciprocal releationship between the organism and its environment . . . brings about a relationship . . . which is favorable for survival" (1958, pp. 22, 24). Hartmann explains that one of the four regulatory functions of the ego is to find an equilibrium between the individual and the environment. As an individual matures and develops ego defenses, he or she can use those defenses in the service of adaptation. In other words, a defense such as denial, which was originally utilized to block out reality so that the anxiety aroused from one's impulses or fantasies would be contained, might later be employed to cope with a real situation that is dangerous or overwhelming. This might be the fact that one's life is threatened by an impending operation.

Is severe illness an internal or an external threat? It is internal in that it is within one's corporal boundaries, which includes a constant interaction between psyche and soma. Excluding psychosomatic illness, (although the line between somatic and psychosomatic is vague and constantly changing as we learn more), we can say that physical illness is a threat external to the psychic system. A germ invades from outside the body and threatens the physical body. It then threatens the body ego and thus all parts of the psychic system, since the ego originates from the body ego. Hence, the relationship between body state and ego state is a primary one. Any danger to one's physical self is also a danger to one's psychic self. Illness (whether medical or psychiatric) and injury threaten one's entire sense of well-being. Besides the external threat of illness, the ego has to deal with internal anxiety that arises in response to the external. Internal pressures with which the ego has to deal include: increased aggression (aggressive impulses which need to be discharged because of anger over illness); guilt (the individual feels he or she is being punished for a bad deed); and threats to the ego. The positive body ego is threatened by mutilation or threat of mutilation, and as self-esteem is threatened—as self-representation becomes negative—the ego's regulator of self-esteem (narcissism) has to work harder. In addition, there are of course new reality demands: hospitalization, surgery, possible rejection of family and friends, loss of job, financial problems, etc.

This list may seem overwhelming, but the severity of the tasks involved varies greatly with the individual. Emotionally weak people have a hard time, since their self-esteem is on shaky ground to begin with. Stronger people may regress, as they reexperience the feelings of helplessness they faced as infants, at times overwhelmed by frightening experiences beyond their control.

If one believes that schizophrenia has a biological basis, one would have to acknowledge that the schizophrenic's ego has tasks similar to those of the severely ill medical patient. He has the disadvantage of a long history of weak and damaged ego strength, but he too has to live with the effects of medication, hospitalization, social and financial consequences of illness, and intrapsychic pressure from flooding of the ego with instinctual material (which is a central part of the illness). Most important, the schizophrenic has the challenge of getting through a day against tremendous inner and outer pressure. Valliant writes: "Let us entertain the possibility that mental illness, like measles, is not a deficit state . . . the symptoms of mental illness reflect unconscious effort at mastery through an aggregate of defense mechanisms" (1977, p. 238). Menninger writes: "Disease [mental] may be seen, then, not simply as *lack* of 'ego strength,' an absence of normality, but as a positive expression of the survival efforts of the organism, inept and costly as they may be" (1954, p. 420).

When I first started studying the coping devices of the severely ill, I limited my inquiry to the medically ill. I later realized that the severely ill psychiatric patient used many of the same defenses out of a similar rationale; the ingredients of positive adaptation were often the same and were mobilized in the group meeting. Certainly both groups of patients (can we really separate them?) demand our admiration for their courage in finding methods of coping with the most difficult life situations. Their struggle is a reflection of the potential we all share. Bringing people together in a group simply reinforces and encourages a natural process— the potential for human beings to use interpersonal contact to enhance human growth.

The Literature

Although there is no literature specifically on coping devices of the medically ill revealed and mobilized in hospital groups, there are references related to hospital groups where coping devices are mentioned. There is also extensive literature on how people cope with illness from various professionals' individual work with medical patients and observation of them as they interact in an institutional setting.

Strain and Grossman (1975) write that successful adaptation to illness includes: ability to regress, maintenance of adequate defenses, access to feelings and fantasies and ability to communicate needs, and basic trust in the medical caretakers, as well as empathetic and flexible medical staff. Jacobson writes that developmental-phase specificity, capacity of the ego to integrate the experience, and capacity of the regulatory mechanisms of the superego to maintain self-esteem have to be taken into account. For example, regarding the significance of the developmental phase, a child hospitalized for a tonsillectomy might experience it as castration if he has reached the phallic phase (Blanck and Blanck, 1974). Younger children, whose sense of self is not yet consolidated, might experience it more as a loss of part of themselves. They might also be more concerned about the separation from the mother if they are still symbiotically tied to her.

Research on how the medically ill cope focuses on patients with specific disease entities: cancer, cardiac, polio, burn, stroke, and dialysis patients. Although each researcher is reporting on patients' coping devices when dealing with a specific serious illness, certain trends emerge when one looks at the combined data: there is a great variety of coping activity, and some coping devices are more adaptive than others; patients' trust in staff, staff responsiveness, group membership, and group interaction are important factors in successful coping. Two groups of researchers are studying cancer patients who are exceptional copers—those patients who live longer than expected and who maintain quality of life during their illness—Achterberg, Matthews-Simonton, and Simonton, 1978; Weisman and Worden, 1977.

The Achterberg study includes the "superstar" cancer patients: those individuals who "defy the odds, who either stabilize for long periods of time or who undergo complete remission of the disease" (p. 416). They reported on 12 such people and compared them to 10 patients who died within a year. On the M.M.P.I.* the superstars scored higher in ego strength than the group who died quickly. Analysis of item content

*Minnesota Multiphasic Personality Inventory

reflected psychological insight, absence of rigidity, and freedom from overconventionality. They exhibited a strong sense of reality, feelings of personal adequacy and vitality, a permissive morality, intelligence, and lack of ethnic prejudice. They felt more in control than their less fortunate counterparts.

Weisman and Worden studied 163 cancer patients' coping capacities and mechanisms. They found that patients fell into two categories: high emotional distress (HED) and low emotional distress (LED). The HED patients used more submissive and suppressive tactics. The LED patients confronted problems directly, shared concerns, and within realistic limits, did something about them. As with the Achterberg study, the LEDs scored high on ego strength on the MMPI. HED patients were sick with advancing stages of illness and complained of many symptoms. They had little support from others and used passive coping strategies, such as suppression, fatalism, withdrawal, and blame. A variance of 40 to 60 percent in emotional distress could be accounted for by medical variables. The rest was attributed to nonmedical factors.

In looking at survival rates and correlates, Weisman and Worden found the following:

> Short survivors had: more suicide themes on the T.A.T.*; poorer overall scores; higher repudiation of and by significant others; feelings that physicians were less helpful through the course of illness; higher peaks of vulnerability; more frustration at first follow-up after hospital discharge; greater dissatisfaction with medical progress; failed to comply with medical regimen and were considered "uncooperative" by staff.
>
> Long survivors had: fewer references to suicide on T.A.T.; better resolution scores; little or no signs of alienation by significant others; regard for physicians as more helpful even though outcome was fatal; fewer complaints about medical condition; satisfactory compliance with physicians and staff; and lower peaks of vulnerability. (1977, p. 35)

Weisman and Worden categorized strategies as to their overall effectiveness in bringing relief and resolution. The most effective coping strategies were: confront with action based on present understanding of problem; redefine problem, find something favorable in it, and rise above it; comply with authority, especially in dealing with medical problems. The least effective coping strategies were: try to forget the problem

*Thematic Apperception Test

(suppression); stoically accept the inevitable (nothing I can do about it); act out by doing something, *anything*; reduce tension by eating, drinking, drugs, etc.; withdraw; blame others for the problem; blame oneself.

Those authors who believe group membership, group interaction, and hospital environment are important variables in a medical patient's capacity to cope optimally have studied patients with severe injuries (Hamburg and Adams), severe rehabilitation problems (Visotsky et al.), polio (Kiely), and burns (Hamburg, Hamburg, and DeGoza). They observed patients interacting with peers and staff in an institutional setting and found that positive relationships seemed to facilitate recovery.

Hamburg and Adams (1967) studied people who were coping with severe injuries. The "importance of group membership" was one of four factors they felt were important in discerning a person's ability to cope. After the initial phase of accepting the injury, people increasingly identified with groups.

Kiely, after working with polio victims, states that "hospital environment" is one of four variables contributing to the coping capacity of patient. In discussing his research with polio patients, Keily concludes: "Perhaps of greatest importance is the interaction with other patients with similar disabilities and illnesses, which leads to overcoming the sense of isolation and loneliness and assists in the development of a sense of security" (1977, p. 289).

Visotsky et al. (1961) studied respiratory centers and were impressed at the importance of interaction for the patient and the importance of staff involvement.

Hamburg, Hamburg, and DeGoza (1953) studied severely burned patients. They felt that the mechanisms that facilitated recovery were: mobilization of hope, frequently derived by interaction with other patients with burns and members of staff; and restoration of interpersonal relationships through personal assistance (staff) and group activitivies (patients and staff).

Kimball stresses the importance of interaction in assessing coping success: in "interpersonal situations, the ward, outside groups, and family, there is the opportunity for pooling of information, support, ventilating, trying out new ideas, and testing out new models or role complementarity. This active effort supports the capacity for optimism and may overcome passivity and inactivity, which may lead to pessimism" (1977, p. 286). He continues to write that one of the four tasks of coping is "rewarding continuity of interpersonal relationships" (Ibid., p. 286).

Literature on small hospital groups where coping mechanisms are referred to fall into four categories: long-term therapy groups composed of medically ill with heterogeneous (Stein and Weiner, 1978) or homogeneous (Yalom, 1970) medical diagnoses; outpatient group programs (Coven, 1980; Schniewind and Needle, 1978); specific disease entity groups (Cooper and Cento, 1977); and hospital community groups (Hallowitz, 1972; Harm and Golden, 1961). These authors see group attendance as having improved the coping capacity of their patients.

ALTERNATIVE COPING DEVICES

People cope with illness differently, depending on their character structure, nature of illness, economic, cultural, social factors, etc. Some patients in a group meeting verbalized this observation themselves.

> The group was composed of four women and one man, all with serious illnesses. They talked about how hard it was to accept their illness. If you have a problem with depression, self-pity, lack of assertiveness, it affects you even more when you're sick. The group acknowledged that Ms. F. had an assertiveness problem and Ms. P. and Ms. L. had problems with depression.

> In a meeting composed of six women, all with serious illnesses, Ms. T. said, "even healthy people can be depressed and morbid—it really has to do with personality, not illness." Everyone agreed.

With any given situation presented in group, there are myriad coping reactions from group members. Yalom writes about therapy groups:

> Therapy groups invariably contain individuals who are at different points along the coping–collapse continuum. . . . They also often encounter patients who have had problems very similar to their own and have coped with them more effectively. . . . I have often heard patients remark at the end of their therapy how important it was for them to have observed improvement of others. (1970, p. 9)

People usually don't "think" before choosing a coping device, but in a group a member can select among various alternatives presented by various group members.

> Women in the Hispanic prenatal group spoke of their fear of getting to the hospital "on time." Most were from other countries and had been in New York City two months or less. Some of them had no phone and stayed alone in their apartments while their husbands worked. The group went from one member to the next, explored their situation, and devised a suitable plan for them. They all seemed relieved after the meeting.

In a general-medicine, male, inpatient group, a 76-year-old chronic complainer who lived in a nursing home, befriended a 78-year-old, wheelchair-bound man who was looking forward to going to a nursing home and consistently looked on the bright side of things.

> Mr. L. said that he was awaiting nursing-home placement; he was looking forward to it because he had been alone all his life. Mr. P. said that he lived in a single-occupancy dwelling and hated it. "Hope your experience is better than mine. The problem with being old is that people have to care for you." Mr. L. responded, "I'm 78 years young; I refuse to think of 'old age.'" Mr. P. began thinking of his parents: "They had a hard time and I never understood them. I would think, 'they're just old' but now, I feel I understand them." The leader felt that Mr. P.'s negativism was lifted somewhat because he was feeling good (young) that he was two years younger than his new friend and not in a wheelchair. She noticed that the two men moved their chairs closer together. At the end of the meeting they didn't want to leave.

Mr. L. was exhibiting the attitude of optimism that so many of the authors feel is connected with successful coping. Mr. P., who was depressed and negative, seemed to benefit by the exposure to Mr. L. He briefly moved away from his totally negative, depressed stance, confirming the leader's idea that Mr. L. was having some impact on him. One could speculate that he was able to give up some of his defensive anger because he was in a supportive environment and therefore less fearful.

STAGES OF ADAPTATION

Defenses and adaptive mechanisms can change as patients go through stages of adjusting to illness and as a result of interaction with peers and staff. Kübler-Ross (1969) says that patients go through the same stages in accepting traumatic illness that they go through in accepting death: denial and isolation, anger, bargaining, depression, and acceptance. Kimball states that the stages of adjusting to illness are the same as the stages of grieving: shock, ventilation, defensiveness, and rehabilitation. If this is true, patients change coping devices as they move to new phases of their illness.

The heart-attack group was most illustrative of the changes people go through in accepting illness. Members seemed to change their behavior in the group from one meeting (when they first came down from the intensive-care unit) to the next (when they had been on the intermediate floor for a week). Staff learned to have different expectations of patients at different points in their hospitalization. The following examples illustrate differential stages.

> *Meeting 1*: Members were complaining about the care they were getting in the hospital. Mr. T., who was reluctant to come to group, joined others in

interpreting orders for bed rest or decreased activity as simple neglect and ignoring of patients by staff. He blurted out his thoughts angrily.

Meeting 2: Mr. T. was waiting anxiously for the group to begin. As the meeting progressed, he said thoughtfully and calmly, "I feel I'm learning to cope with my problems—to accept that I have had a heart attack and I will have to make some changes in my life. The group has been very helpful. I'm not a verbal person, but I can see that talking helps. Maybe when I go home, I should start by talking to my wife more."

Meeting 1: Mr. M. was very anxious in group, fidgeting a lot and talking nervously. It seemed as though the more he talked, the more agitated he became. Members told him that he was "working himself up," and he finally calmed down.

Meeting 2: Mr. M.'s affect was depressed. He was quiet, looked sad, and alluded to not being happy about having a pacemaker or not improving in the hospital. He seemed to be oblivious to his external needs, as he walked away without his intravenous pole.

As these examples illustrate, it is often hard to know whether changes in behavior are due to patients' increasing comfort or discomfort with the group process, mood swings, or patients' further adjustment or lack of adjustment in accepting their illness. It is important that the group leader not jump to conclusions in diagnosing a behavior but use the group meeting to observe and ask new questions about the patient.

In the group, members often participate who are at different phases in accepting their illness: one may be angry, another depressed, another accepting. This variation in composition can be useful in helping patients to prepare for future phases or accept past ones. Patients have expressed some shame over crying for days, or "acting crazy," or "being evil"; the group leader should say: "Such behavior is common and often necessary in adjusting to a difficult situation." If one patient attacks another because the other patient represents a forbidden part of himself, such as an angry patient attacking a depressed patient, the leader might say: "Group is very interesting because we see how people facing a similar situation can feel differently. People's feelings can change, too, by the minute or by the day, and sometimes you can even feel two feelings at the same time." This statement combines both differentiation and universalization. The leader is trying to say, and may do so explicitly or implicitly, "All feelings are all right here; they are all natural; none of them are cause for alarm." A patient who is frightened by her anger and thus inhibited from moving to the next phase of accepting her illness, might take note of the leader's calm acceptance of the other patient's anger. A patient who is actively denying may find his anxiety lessening in the group because of the group support and acceptance of feelings. Some may move to the acceptance phase out of admiration for a member who has achieved this phase, through inspiration and identification. In these ways, group participation can result in behavior or attitude change.

THE EXCEPTIONAL COPER

I first became interested in groups for medical patients when the following case was presented to me:

> A 35-year-old man was stabilized on renal dialysis for two years. During this period he got divorced. In the following two and a half years he had a renal transplant that failed, a gastrointestinal stomach ulcer which hemorrhaged, a stomach removed, more infections, and finally two broken shoulder blades from a collision with a truck on his way to the hospital.

This man made an impression on his physicians because he continued to have a sense of humor and looked forward to the future. He did not deny the severity of events that occurred and was reality oriented. He always found something in reality to give him some hope; for example, with the car accident, he looked forward to the insurance settlement he would get. With the traumatic illnesses and concomitant misfortunes, he would express being glad that he survived. He was determined to continue his work as an editor and he succeeded. He would also say, "What is done is done."

My reaction to this man was that he should be used as a teacher for other patients on how to cope. If the doctors are inspired by him, why wouldn't patients be? Such people should be the real gurus of our society. They should not go unnoticed and their resources untapped by medical staff. Wouldn't it be nice if such a person could enjoy some status and recognition from the hospital in the last phase of his life? Yalom comments on patient models in therapy groups:

> Patients may model themselves upon aspects of the other group members as well as of the therapist. The importance of imitative behavior is difficult to gauge, but recent social psychological research suggests that we may have underestimated its importance ... Even if specific imitative behavior is short-lived, it may function to help the individual 'unfreeze' by experimenting with new behavior. (1970, p. 14)

In a later publication, Yalom (1980) describes the benefits of being a model in a group of cancer patients:

> "She [Eva] ... found meaning until the end of her life in the fact that her attitude toward her death could be of value to many other

patients who might be able to use Eva's zest for life and courageous
stance toward death as a model for their own living and dying . . . .
The idea of being a model for others . . . of helping them to diminish
or remove the terror of death can fill life with meaning until the
moment of death." (p. 433)

By helping others in the group Eva found meaning for her own existence.

Two exceptional copers, Ms. Bell and Ms. Kay, were in group meetings
on an inpatient service. Ms. Bell was a 53-year-old woman who had poly-
myolitis—a degenerative disease of all the muscles in the body. She had
been sick since she was 10 years old but had worked at an office job
consistently. She was on large doses of cortisone, which softens the bones.
Her last hospitalization resulted when she broke her spine in three places
and was totally incapacitated. Because of her strong motivation and her
participation in the rehabilitation process, she walked out of the hospital,
without help, four months later. Staff described her as consistently motivated and cooperative and never bitter, jaded, or self-involved. She
always seemed interested in other people—staff and patients. She seemed
to have accepted her illness with dignity and always faced the future. Ms.
Bell's participation in the group was as follows:

Meeting 1: Ms. Bell participated actively in the group meeting. Members
were talking about how they cope with pain. Ms. Bell said that she had
unbearable pain at times. Since she had had it for years she had learned to
cope with it when it was happening, and forget about it when it was over.
After a hospitalization she pretends she'll never have a recurrence of illness;
in this way she can enjoy part of her life. All the members went on to talk
about Thanksgiving—what they *do* have in their lives—and how they all had
nice families and wanted to be with them. Ms. Bell knew she might still be in
the hospital; despite her disappointment, her trust in her doctor was paramount. Later, members talked about things they gave up for their health,
that they never thought they would. Ms. Bell said that giving up her
chocolate cake was the hardest thing she ever did. She was surprised at her
strength in accomplishing this feat. She felt "life is very precious" and she
envies people like Ms. O., who could have an operation and then be better.
"It's the chronic illness that is the most horrible; it never goes away."
Meeting 2: Ms. Bell said that it is taking all of her will power not to use her
walker to go the bathroom. She and Ms. A. expressed how hard it was to be
bedridden and have to use the bedpan. Ms. Bell continued to say that she
was getting discouraged by her long hospitalization. When she fell and
broke her hip during the week, she felt like a fool.
Meeting 3: Group members talked about how they work to keep their spirits
up so they can continue to fight for their health. Ms. Bell said that she is
beginning to find it hard, since her hospitalization has already lasted six

weeks and she wants to be home for Christmas. She can't wait to take a shower and is frustrated by her incapacity, even though she knows she is doing her best and making progress. She said that work is very important to her, and as she lays in bed she wonders if she will be able to return. Later, Ms. Bell joined Ms. A. in talking about the confusion they feel sometimes: not knowing what day or time it is. Ms. Bell said that she could take her illness, but she wanted no part in being old, feeble, and helpless. The group picked up on Ms. Bell's hesitance to assert herself with staff and encouraged her to "speak up." She then talked in the group about her financial worries (of which staff had been totally unaware), and the social worker was able to assist her.

Ms. Bell's group participation revealed trust in doctor and family involvement as sources of support. She readily took advantage of the opportunity for interaction and free expression of feeling. She revealed an active orientation by her desire to get out of bed and work as soon as possible. She was not narcissistically involved, as demonstrated by her interest in others, illustrating advanced character development. Ms. Bell's free expression of feeling (anger) helped other patients to express their frustration. The other members, in turn, supported Ms. Bell to be more assertive with staff. Ms. Bell then stopped being a "good" patient and voiced a real need for help with her finances. The social worker immediately responded, rewarding Ms. Bell for asking for help.

Ms. Kay was a 49-year-old woman who had scleroderma for 24 years. This disease hardens and contracts tissue, and for at least 10 years Ms. Kay had been severely disfigured. She gave the appearance of being a stick figure: very malnourished, drawn, and emaciated, with skin pulled tightly over her bones. Her fingers were rigid in a clamped position. Despite these problems, she was able to take care of her personal needs, run a household, raise a daughter, and maintain a marriage. These tasks were not without their problems. Her daughter had trouble in school, and Ms. Kay was actively involved with the child and the school administration to work it out. Ms. Kay was referred to the social work department for help with her marital problems. Her husband became repelled by her as she moved from being a beautiful woman to a deformed person. He began seeing other women and rejected her sexually. She was able to talk about her feelings about her femininity and sexuality with her social worker, face her situation realistically, and be patient with and understanding of her husband's adjustment problems. Ultimately, the marriage was maintained, and both partners were satisfied with it.

Ms. Kay's attitude was usually, "It happened so I have to live with it." She had no tolerance for self-pity and was rarely depressed. Instead, she had a sense of humor, expressed direct anger over symptoms, and maintained an interest in the people around her. She said that she liked coming to group because it gave her the opportunity to give and to share. Following are excerpts from her group participation.

Meeting 1: Ms. Kay described her anger at her husband. "He says my coughing is all in my head." This comment of his infuriated her. She described how sometimes she gets so angry, she "cuts off her nose to spite her face." Other times she feels like throwing things. The group was supportive. She later expressed her ambivalence about leaving the nurses in the hospital to go home. Others felt that it was frightening to go home where they weren't assured of good care.

The leader wrote after the meeting: "We were struck by Ms. Kay's healthy expression of feelings and insight into herself. She seemed very insistent on being part of the group and identifying with the group rather than allowing others to isolate her because of her disfiguration or her isolating herself for this reason. She used the group to ventilate and the group was supportive of her. We all felt admiration for her, and I'm sure this feeling was conveyed nonverbally."

Meeting 2: Ms. Kay described her routine at home—how she cleans, washes dishes, makes beds, cooks, etc. She said she pushes herself too hard and "is stupid" about it; she insists on making perfect corners on her sheets as she makes her beds. She described herself as fussy and compulsive. (The leader couldn't imagine Ms. Kay being able to function in this way, given her deformity and her difficulty ambulating.) Ms. L., who was totally self-involved during the meeting, perked up and said, "You look too weak to do all that." Ms. L. said that she barely manages to get the absolute necessities done; it is hard for her. She said she felt better after coming to the group because she thought she was the worse off, but now she sees that Mr. M. has it worse—he has a "false heart" and hers is good (she had advanced cancer). Ms. Kay said that the exams she had to take during this hospitalization were especially hard. She was glad she could come to group and get her mind off of things; group relaxed her. She liked being active in the hospital. The nurses were always surprised to see her up doing things, like making her bed.

As with Ms. Bell, Ms. Kay was open about her feelings of anger and frustration, which encouraged others to express themselves. At the same time, she got support from the group and a chance to have a diversion from her usual preoccupations. As with Ms. Bell, she demonstrated an active approach to coping with illness. When Ms. Kay described her daily routine, she was such a strong example that the narcissistically withdrawn Ms. L. woke up. Ms. L. was able to use Ms. Kay to see her own passivity. Ms. L. became less withdrawn and was able to compare herself favorably to another group member, lifting her spirits.

DENIAL

Denial, the lack of full or partial conscious awareness of reality, can be adaptive (life promoting) or maladaptive (life threatening) for the medical patient. It can be life promoting by diminishing anxiety and the accompanying physiological changes and by regulating the integration of a trauma in doses that can be tolerated. Fenichel writes:

> Postponement of fear may have a lifesaving effect because it makes possible purposeful action which otherwise might have been paralyzed by fear . . . .Frightful experiences may be calmly accepted by the person in question . . . .During these moments, the ego has been able to prepare itself, to protect itself from being completely overwhelmed. (1945, p. 162)

Weisman writes that, "Denial helps us to do away with a threatening portion of reality, but only because we may then participate more fully in contending with problems" (1972, p. 60).

Most patients who cope successfully with illness use adaptive denial. In other words, they use denial when it will help them feel better, but they do not use it if it is going to interfere with their necessary capacity to assess reality and make good judgments, especially in regard to self-care. Denial can be maladaptive if the medical patient does not heed severe symptomatology or follow the prescribed medical regimen.

The Literature

The literature on the value of the defense of denial appears contradictory. Kernberg (1976) classifies the defense of denial as a low-level, primitive defense. Anna Freud (1942) thinks it is part of the "preliminary stage of defense" and commonly used by children. Stolorow and Lachmann (1980) think it might be a "prestage" defense. However, most patients who cope successfully with illness use adaptive denial. Most of the literature espousing the value of this defense has resulted from research with cardiac, intensive-care unit, dialysis, and burn patients.

Hackett and Cassem questioned patients on the intensive-care unit who had observed a cardiac arrest during their hospitalization. It was the rare patient who identified with the victim of the arrest. Most found some comfort from the event, such as the quick and efficient care the patient got, and denied the life-threatening aspects of the event. Hackett and Cassem continue to write that patient anxiety is difficult to identify in the coronary care unit because so many patients deny anxiety (Cassem and Hackett, 1978; Hackett and Cassem, 1974).

Stern, Pascale, and McLoone (1976) did a one-year follow-up study on 68 patients, who fell into two groups—depressives and deniers—when they were first hospitalized for myocardial infarctions.

> Seventy percent of those who were depressed postinfarct remained so throughout follow-up. These patients failed to remain at work and/or function sexually and had a higher hospital readmission rate. The denial group, although still functioning with minimal psychosocial distress, was not distinguished from the remainder of the study population who generally also functioned well. The good responders were those patients (25%) who denied being apprehensive or tense from the time of onset of their symptoms through their hospital stay. They did not experience any infarct-related anxiety or depression *and* with only one exception returned to work and sexual functioning.

Hamburg, Hamburg, and DeGoza (1953) viewed denial as a major "emergency defense" for burn patients. Stein and Wiener (1978) report on a therapy group of medical patients with mixed diagnoses who needed this defense.

A number of authors refer to the value of the defense of denial at the beginning stages of coping with severe illness. These authors represent studies of a variety of medical patients, including patients with severe injuries, burns, end-stage renal disease, and polio.

Hamburg and Adams, in studying patients who had severe injuries, noted that in the first phase of the injury patients exhibited avoidance defenses preventing overwhelming catastrophic reactions and allowing for a gradual acceptance of facts preparing for the transition to the tasks ahead. Gradually the patients accepted reality and periods of depression set in (1967). Hamburg, Hamburg, and DeGoza (1953) in working with severely burned patients, made the following observation of patients' initial reactions to the trauma: "a conscious effort is made to avoid thinking of unpleasant experience . . .there is an automatic exclusion from consciousness of affect associated with a known and remembered traumatic experience" (1953, pp. 7-8). Seligman (1972), in studying the emotional responses of children with burns, related positive factors in survival to early denial and withdrawal.

Some authors appreciate the use of denial in the initial phase of accepting illness, but see problems in the continuous maintenance of the defense. Short and Wilson note the "ubiquitous presence of denial" in the dialysis patient suggesting that at least initially "it may serve as an effective mental mechanism helping him [the dialysand] to cope with a continuing unsatisfactory situation" (1969, p. 437). Halper (1971), also working with dialysis patients, found that denial was often adaptive at the beginning, but adds that it can be restricting and even destructive in later stages. He associates denial with suicidal behavior. Kimball, in reviewing work with polio victims, states that "too rapid an acceptance of disability may lead to despair and despondency which may result in lack of maximum participation in the treatment program. On the other hand, expectations that are maximally discordant with reality may result in dashed hopes and total resignation at a future time, with failure to accept a limited recovery" (1977, p. 289).

Hackett, Cassem, and Raker (1973) cite a disadvantage of the use of the defense of denial: the delay in seeking help with cancer is less when the patient referred to the condition as "cancer," "tumor," or "growth." Hackett and Cassem (1970) expressed concern over cardiac patients who typically deny chest pain and do not come to the hospital for help. This behavior is an example of maladaptive denial. Visotsky et al. (1961) warns that denial can interfere with patients' cooperation with the medical regimen.

Kimball, after reviewing literature on severely ill children writes: "Positive factors in survival related to early denial and withdrawal. However, subsequent studies suggest that while these may be adaptive in some children they are not so in all and behavior such as protest may be more advantageous in others . . ." (1977, p. 293). It becomes obvious in reviewing the research or reflecting on one's own clinical work that one cannot assess defenses and their value out of context. One cannot simply state that projection of anger or denial are "bad" or "good" or "healthy" or "sick." One must assess its adaptive value at a certain moment in time and under specific circumstances.

Adaptive Denial

Valliant emphasizes that a defense cannot be evaluated apart from the context in which it takes place and its effect on relationships with other people. He gives an example of adaptive denial utilized by a cancer patient:

A man with cancer might dream that he is well and so *deny* the reality that he is fatally ill. Clearly, the comfort gained from denial in dreams has no harmful consequences. But let us suppose that this man persisted in his denial. If he went to a faith healer to escape the

pain of surgery, some might label him crazy, and he might compro-
mise his biological adaptation to his cancer. But if under special
circumstances, let us say *after* he was in the hospital receiving optimal
care, he were to deny that there was anything more wrong with him
than a bad cold, denial might once again become adaptive. He might
facilitate his own and his family's enjoyment of his last days. (1977,
p. 85)

Valliant gives another example where a man did not acknowledge that he
took medication. Valliant explored the issue further and asked whether
he was taking medicine for stomach spasms. "Oh," he said, "I had forgot-
ten all about that." But, in fact, each evening he took his medicine without
thinking, and his stomach problems abated (Ibid., p. 273).

An example of adaptive denial was Ms. Bell's description of how, when
she left the hospital free of severe pain and discomfort, she forgot she was
sick and lived as though she would never see the hospital again. When
severe debilitating symptoms reappeared she started facing her illness
and rehospitalization. When hospitalization occurred, all her energy went
toward coping on a day-to-day basis with hospital procedures.

The following process is from a cystic fibrosis outpatient group that met
for one year. Members are told two pieces of traumatic news: (1) their
nurse Sally, the co-leader of the group, will be leaving the program; (2)
Michael, a peer leader, is dying. If one studies the details of these few
meetings, one can see how some very sick people defend themselves,
using denial sporadically so that they can deal with painful material in
small doses.

Meeting 1: Six patients and one relative are present. Sally told the group she
was leaving the unit and would be at one more meeting. Members asked her
questions about her plans; she told them she was going back to school. A
discussion of school versus work proceeded. Mac said, reluctantly, that all of
them probably had things to say to Sally, and they would say them privately.
Tom said, "Yeah, I'll write a letter." Social worker asked, "Why?" Mac:
"Because we don't want our feelings to show." Social worker: "I don't
understand. We're really here for all of you to express your feelings and for
us to hear you." Mac: "I only came to group because of the leaders. I was
always negligent in self-care, and I didn't want to think about my illness."
Ivan: "You both deserve a lot of credit. We all owe you a lot of thanks."
Leaders: "But you had a large part in the group being a success; you all
participated." Ivan: "I used to be afraid to come to the clinic, but with Sally
there I felt cheered up." Sally: "Do you resent my cheerfulness sometimes?"
"No. Some people's cheerfulness we resent because it is phony, but we know
you are sincere and you really care about us." Group talked about naming
upcoming picnic for members and parents: "Farewell to Sally."

Leaders told group that Michael was very sick and may not "pull through." Silence. Tom changed the subject and began to talk of somatic preoccupations. The group followed and after comparing complaints went into a theoretical discussion. Social worker: "I guess the news of Michael is too painful for the group to talk about." Bruce (formerly considered the strongest denier in the group) said, "I guess it is. I don't want to face it. I feel for Michael, but it is so scary to think that it could be one of us. We don't want to face it." Neil: "If we don't talk about it here, where can we?" Lela (only relative in group) asked about Michael's wife. "Please tell Joyce we asked about her and if there is anything we can do, please tell us." Others nodded. The group ended and no one got up to leave.

Sally went with Mac to take a blood sample. Others approached Social worker and said they wanted to have a party the following meeting, in honor of Sally. They enthusiastically planned it. Everyone left, excited about the party.

One can see in this process how the group moves back and forth, from facing issues that are painful to blocking them out. Members respond to the leader's interventions because they are a cohesive group and strong enough to touch on their feelings. Despite their sorrow, fear, and anger (which is not recognized in this meeting) they end meeting on an "up" note. There is a strong pull in the group to reinforce a positive optimism.

Meeting 2: Composed of eight members, including one spouse, Lela. Everyone brought refreshments for the party, and there was an atmosphere of festivity. Lela baked a cake that said to the nurse: "Good Luck, We Love You." The departing leader was teary-eyed. Tom asked about Michael. The leaders said that he was not getting better. The Social Worker said, "Am I the only one who is angry at Sally for leaving?" No one responded, and the group continued to joke, laugh, and be festive. They all began talking excitedly about the picnic and making very thorough plans.

The next day, Michael died. Leaders called the members to tell them, so they would not be told the day of the picnic. Members expressed sadness, pain, and fear. Most had a desire to reach out to Michael's wife and comfort her. Tom commented: "It is pretty close to home; it could be me." Ivan: "Being in group is like love; you have to take the chance of being hurt (losing someone)." Bruce: "Being in group has helped me deal with death." No one seemed to question that they would have the picnic and make the best of it, even though the picnic was Michael's idea, and he had helped plan it. They decided to tell the truth if anyone asked about Michael.

The picnic included group members and their relatives, families who had cystic fibrosis children, and all the members of the interdisciplinary team. The atmosphere was one of festivity and play—a celebration of life and the present. Michael was remembered, but not in a morbid way. A few group members and the leader noted that the weather rapidly changing from sunshine to hail was symbolic of life: the show had to go on, and somehow they all found strength to live for the positive. Three members and the group leaders attended the funeral services.

MASSIVE DENIAL

When massive denial appeared in the groups at St. Vincent's, it was so strong that it was maintained despite confrontation. One woman with cancer said she had a lump in her throat. A man with a heart attack, said he had a "little" heart attack. One patient's interaction in a heart-attack group meeting was as follows:

> The patient demanded to know from the doctor present exactly how long he had to live. He had a friend who was in the insurance business and had acturial tables, and he felt everyone in the room should be told how long they had to live. The leader (social worker) got very tense and wished the patient would be quiet, thinking that these patients could die at any time and this subject was too frightening for the group to handle. Members responded: "You shouldn't listen to insurance men. There are other things you have to take into account." Members did not appear intimidated by the question. The members actually reached out and tried to help the worried patient feel more comfortable.

Mr. D. also attended the group. During his first group meeting, he did not acknowledge that he had had a heart attack; he said he had indigestion. The following discussion took place during his second group meeting.

> "I know now it was indigestion. It was the glass of orange juice I had." The group responded: "Did the doctor take an electrocardiogram?" "Yes." "Well, then what more do you want?" "If I want to think that I haven't had a heart attack, I'll think that way. This way I don't have to worry about it because I don't think I had a heart attack."

The group was stunned and intuitively did not pursue the subject any further. The group members respected the man's defense, probably with some awareness that the person could not and should not be budged.

MALADAPTIVE DENIAL

Maladaptive denial can also occur, as in this report from the heart-attack group:

Mr. N. and Mr. P. both said that it took them a long time of discomfort before they sought medical help. Mr. N. said that for years he got medicine from friends for chest pain and never went to see a doctor. Mr. P. said that once he got severe chest pain outside a hospital, and he never went inside for help. Ms. C. said when she became aware of her illness she went to a smoking clinic to stop smoking instead of going to see a doctor. Mr. O., who was hospitalized with a second heart attack, said that he knew smoking contributed to his attack; he just ignored his doctor's advice. "Why didn't I go for a check up?" He answered the question himself: "I wanted to be okay, not sick."

One question group leaders often ask is: "When do I probe and confront?" It should never be necessary for the leader to probe when the defense of denial is operative. For patients to use this defense, their underlying fear must be enormous. The group process has a natural confrontive component, and it also offers support. If patients feels supported and becomes less fearful, they will naturally be more open to the group's acknowledgment of reality. If the group members confront the denier and he or she begins to appear overly anxious, the leader must support the patient.

ANGER AND AGGRESSION

When faced with an illness people commonly become angry that this is happening to them. Illness and hospitalization are real threats and require a response. People handle anger in different ways: They can turn it against themselves, causing masochistic behavior, depression, or anxiety; they can express it directly when faced with a reality-based threat ("Why me?"); they can use the defense of projection, where expression of anger is a projection of their own aggression or assumed negative attributes onto the subject of attack; or they can displace anger from its target (illness, doctor, relative) to another object (bedpan, nurse). Fenichel (1945) explains that the person using the defense of projection would prefer to see danger as outside the self rather than within. This section will discuss the display of "irrational" anger, review the literature on expression of anger as a coping device, and describe the difficulty staff has with patient's expression of anger. The section "Sense of Mastery and Activeness" under "Positive Adaptation" will more fully discuss and illustrate positive expression of anger.

Cassem and Hackett (1978) and Halper (1971) report expression of anger as adaptive for medical patients. Halper and Hamburg, Hamburg, and Degoza (1953) describe the difficulty burn patients and dialysis patients have in expressing anger because of their dependency on staff and possible retaliation. Achterberg et al. (1978) and Weisman and Worden (1977) have differing reports on the usefulness of anger for cancer patients. Achterberg et al. write that exceptional copers have been known to be hostile. Weisman and Worden define "blaming others" as one of the least effective coping mechanisms.

PROJECTION AND DISPLACEMENT

Use of projection and displacement is most commonly viewed when hospital patients attack one another or staff. Expression of anger can be an alternative to complete withdrawal, which can lead to death. Fried writes of the value of projection as a defense, even if it reaches the extreme of paranoia:

> Patients with paranoid character traits fight, scheme, litigate in the courts, and invent distortions. They are, to be sure, in constant danger of being fired or confined or abandoned. Yet, I believe that the people who incline toward the paranoid . . . strategies take a good deal of pride in their conduct, self-destructive as it is. Compared with the masochists who give in to passivity and complaining, the paranoid patients are more active. Their arrogance does not stem solely from grandiosity but also from a conviction that they are maintaining some measure of action and initiative. Rarely do people with paranoid inclinations part with their pathological activity, unless they have been helped to form a core of true self-esteem and have started to apply their initiative in constructive areas. (1970, pp. 6–7)

Kiely (1972), working with a variety of medical patients, emphasizes the protective importance of the psychotic defenses, which may include projection in its most severe form.

Displacement of anger and paranoia is maladaptive to the extent that it prevents the person from getting necessary optimal medical care, including emotional support from others. The challenge of the group leader is to appreciate the protective nature of the anger and also to enable patients to get more of their needs met. Severely withdrawn patients' anger can be mobilized and their depression temporarily relieved. For example, Ms. O. was depressed and withdrawn on the floor. She rarely spoke, and when she did, it was a monosyllabic response. She seemed to come to the group out of passivity and "going along" with her social worker, which is typical of the disturbed patient. She had cancer.

The leader wheeled Ms. O. around so that she could see the other three women members in the group. Ms. O. muttered, "Thank you." As the meeting progressed, the members spoke about how they hate it when their blood is drawn. Ms. O. blurted out, "I hate it too! They're always coming in for something! Just when you get rid of one, another comes in! I have no peace!" Others agreed and chimed in.

After the meeting staff was amazed: Ms. O. joked with them for the first time. Ms. O. responded to the group process by spontaneously coming out of her withdrawn state—a response that was not elicited by community living on the floor or one-to-one contacts with staff. The group leader capitalized on Ms. O.'s passivity by bringing her to the group. In the group she placed Ms. O. in an advantageous position, making sure she was physically part of the group. The leader nonverbally expressed approval of the members joining together in a criticism of staff. As anger in the group was externalized, group cohesiveness developed. Ms. O. was a part of the camaraderie that developed. The leader did not interpret the displacement of anger but chose to allow the group cohesiveness to be the curative factor.

It is difficult for staff when they are attacked in the group. It is hard not to take patients' anger personally. The following meeting took place on a general-medicine inpatient floor. Five men were present: all of them had a history of alcoholism. The group was led by the social worker. Mr. N. attended group the week before and was a constructive and active group participant. However, during the week he was frustrated by the social worker, who could not help him appease his landlord:

Mr. N. attacked the group leader. His anger appeared intense and everyone in the group seemed nervous. "I'm sick of the hospital and am going to leave. You didn't help me with my landlord. You're not doing your job. You have been of no help to me at all!" The leader suggested he explain to the group what was bothering him; maybe other members could be useful. Some said that it was possible that the leader was at fault, but a few volunteered that she had been of help to them. The leader clarified what she could and could not do, given her role. She verbalized the frustration they must feel when "nobody helps" but emphasized the importance of staying in the hospital despite this frustration. She suggested that maybe other members could help, where she could not. Mr. A. told of his frustrations in the hospital and gave Mr. N. some suggestions. Mr. N. calmed down for a moment and then continued his tirade. Finally, in exasperation, the leader asked, "Has anyone had any positive experiences in the hospital?" Mr. H. immediately responded and told the group how wonderful the psychiatry program for alcoholics was for him. Mr. R. who was referred to this program and was extremely depressed, looked up. Mr. N. enthusiastically told

the members how important it was for them to all help themselves (not
seeing the contradiction). At the end of the meeting, Mr. N. said to the
leader, "I hope you're not angry at me. I was direct." The leader responded:
"This is the place to express your feelings."

It is difficult for a beginning group to handle direct interpersonal
attacks; members are usually threatened even if they are not the target of
such an attack. Usually the leader has to limit such expression of anger or
the group process becomes stymied. Each angry individual has to be
assessed as an individual; anger can be the expression of various kinds of
problems or strengths. In this case, the group leader was very aware that
the patient had an entrenched character disorder and had a low frustration tolerance. Her intellectual understanding of the patient helped her
deal with her emotional response to this attack. She stayed calm during
the meeting and maintained her professional role. (Many of the group
leaders that were hesitant to start groups told me that their worst fear was
that they would be attacked by a group member in the group and they
would not be able to handle it with good judgment. Once we had a nurse
who was so provoked by a patient in the group that she yelled at him. She
said later that her reaction was a subdued one compared to what she
wanted to do to the patient. Fortunately, a co-therapist, who was not so
emotionally involved, brought the patient back into the interaction and
reinforced the patient's more positive behavior.)

One of the fears nurses and doctors expressed when we were discussing
group formation was that the group would use their cohesion to band
together and attack staff. When groups first started to meet, staff members would corner the social work leaders and ask timidly: "Did they say
bad things about me?" The leaders then explained to staff that groups
often do express a lot of anger, and sometimes this anger is directed to
staff, but it usually is the group members' way of helping themselves feel
better; often it means not having to face their anger toward their own or
their relative's illness. In the relatives' group for neurology and neuro-
surgical patients, anger that belonged to the sick patient was externalized
onto staff. It was probably too frightening for the relatives to face their
anger toward the severely ill patient.

Every professional staff member in a hospital has to learn that expression of patient anger is usually not a personal attack but the patients'
attempt to feel better. But no matter how much we are trained, patients'
anger and demands (sometimes assertiveness) are sometimes hard to
take. In one group meeting, there was a "model" patient, Ms. Bell, whom
staff loved and admired. She prided herself on not asking the nurses for
anything unless she really needed it. She understood the nurses were very

busy (identified with them) and was proud of her own independence. She was also stoical in the face of pain and discomfort. Ms. R., on the other hand, was seen by staff as very demanding, and staff often became irritated with her. A nurse was present in the group meeting and Ms. R. had the following to say:

> "No one in this group responded to my idea of someone always being available for questioning that I expressed earlier. I am 80 years old, have some memory loss, and am not a sweet, charming person. People who are sicker than me get more sympathy from staff. Maybe I'm too direct for people's comfort. I feel like I'm being treated like a piece of trash in this hospital and wish someone would answer my questions (which are repetitive). I am a person with feelings and I can't help it if I have memory loss." As she left the group, at the conclusion of the meeting, she said lightheartedly, "Better I say something now than when I go home and am alone."

After the group meeting the nurse realized that staff had responded to Ms. R.'s assertiveness with annoyance, and staff decided to start rewarding the patient for her assertiveness. Some staff admitted that they would probably be demanding and provocative if they were in a similar position. If Ms. R. was indeed viewed by staff as a "piece of trash," it is not so dissimilar to staff seeing the patient as a "case" or "disease" or "thing." Through the mechanism of hypostatization staff protects itself from worrying about and identifying with the sick person. At the same time, however, staff members cripple their therapeutic efforts because they are dealing with a fictional entity rather than with the real problem; that is, they are not treating the total person.

IDEALIZATION AND GRANDIOSITY

When medical patients' self-esteem is weakened, there are two basic ways they can make themselves feel better: they can believe they are omnipotent, so the effects of illness cannot disturb them; or they can believe a staff member (usually a doctor) is a god and if they can stay closely connected to the staff member, they will be protected. Kohut (1971) calls the former "grandiosity" and the latter "idealization" and describes them as effective narcissistic defenses. Stolorow and Lachmann (1980) think these can be labeled as "prestage" defenses. Cooper (1976, 1978) illustrates how group therapy can help to mobilize these defenses. Lonergan (1980) shows how hospital groups can help medical patients' self-esteem.

Since protection of basic self-esteem is an essential to psychic survival, it is crucial that group leaders be able to identify and appreciate narcissistic defenses. They are often difficult to handle in the group because they are seen as obvious distortions of reality by other patients, and an attempt is made to confront them. In such instances, it is important that the leader protect and support the patient. This can often be accomplished by the leader stating, "Everyone is different; what works for one person, may not work for another." These defenses are often essential for psychic survival, but their effectiveness in coping with physical illness must be determined. Idealization is usually adaptive (life promoting) because the patient follows the prescribed medical regimen and anxiety is lessened. A number of authors see "trust in doctor" as a necessary coping device. Grandiosity is often maladaptive (life threatening) in that the patient attempts to determine his or her own treatment.

One example of a patient who used grandiosity as a defense was Ms. Y., a patient suffering with hypertension.

> Ms. Y. described herself in group as a supersensitive person, accounting for her hyperactivity. She seemed proud of the fact that she took life seriously, and the problems of the people around her, so that she was a nervous wreck. She said that people who were hyperactives were worthwhile people because they were supersensitive, and people who weren't hyperactives were not so good because they didn't have feelings for others.

One can imagine how difficult it would be to treat Ms. Y. for her hypertension and get her to take her medicine as an outpatient. It is common to hear doctors admonishing such patients for poor self-care. And yet, if a doctor understands that Ms. Y. is using the defense of grandiosity—a narcissistic defense designed to boost low self-esteem—the doctor might learn to affirm her self-esteem before making demands on her.

In this particular group meeting, the members go on to utilize idealization as a defense.

> All of the members expressed the importance of accepting illness and not dwelling on the morbid aspects. Ms. L. said, "If you become morbid, you end up alone—no one wants to be with you." All six memembers agreed. Ms. B. said when friends call, she always asks how *they* are and plans activities with them, and they keep calling. All agreed they should protect relatives from their despair. The group leader asked, "Do you also have to protect staff from your despair?" There was a loud, "No!" "Staff is different!" Members gave a lot of examples of nurses sitting with them for an hour offering comfort, acceptance, and help when they were unhappy. "Doctors and nurses have heart!" They began talking about how afraid they were to leave the hospital, because they were getting such wonderful care.

There was some reality to the fact that the nursing and medical care on this floor was superb. Many of the staff felt that if they were to be hospitalized, they would want to be on this particular floor. But we also know that all nurses and doctors don't convey "heart" to the patients. Staff, like relatives, have a hard time coping with their emotional reactions to patients' despair and fate. Yet it is probably too frightening to face the vulnerabilities of staff because the patients feel totally dependent on them for their medical care. They continue to talk of how they don't want to leave the hospital because they won't have the protection of their idealized figures: the nurses and doctors. When a patient idealizes, it is important that he or she continue to feel intimately connected to the idealized object. It is this connection that gives the patient a feeling of safety.

In the following group meeting, one can see the defense of idealization operating with Ms. Bell, resulting in her calm state. One can also see the anxiety of Ms. J., who does not idealize or even trust her doctor. (One can trust a doctor without employing idealization. In this way it is possible to see the doctor's limitations and capacity to make mistakes.)

> Ms. Bell knew she might still be in the hospital at Christmas; despite her disappointment her trust in her doctor's judgment was paramount. She had absolute trust in him and never questioned him. Ms. J. said that she trusted her sister's judgment much more than her doctor's. Her doctor wants her to have a shunt put in her arm *in case* she needs dialysis, and Ms. J.'s sister says that operations should be performed only when necessary. Other members seemed very concerned about Ms. J. because her anxiety was evident. They said that Ms. J. had to do what she felt was best, but they and their families always listened to their doctors. They seemed to be hinting that Ms. J. do the same, but she interrupted them. She said that when she was a little girl living in the woods in the South, she was jealous of children who got to go to doctors. Her dream was to be able to go to a doctor some day. Now she is 70 years old, and she has every doctor in the hospital coming to see her in order to get her to change her mind about surgery. She has never had an operation, and no one in her family has had one. Ms. Bell told her about her operations and how she felt much better afterward. Ms. J. said that she doesn't mind dying when the time comes; if she comes to the emergency room and needs dialysis and there is no time to put a shunt in, she'll die and that is okay. The group leader asked the other members how they would feel being in Ms. J.'s position: not trusting their doctor. The members responded with an emotional "Awful!"

Ms. Bell and other group members seemed to be nervous about Ms. J.'s questioning of her doctor because, at the same time, their defense of idealization was being threatened. Ms. Bell and others tried to make Ms. J.

more like them: "Operations are wonderful" and "We listen to our doctors." These comments were indirect advice giving that Ms. J. didn't heed. The group at the same time had compassion for Ms. J. and tried to reach out to her and "take her pain away." It was hard for them to deal with Ms. J.'s pain without having their own pain touched upon. The leader intervened to move the group toward a commonality that was not too threatening for the patients. They all seemed to appreciate Ms. J.'s dilemma.

If one can believe that one is omnipotent and impervious to disease, one can feel better than if one experiences the wounded self-esteem that often accompanies illness. Grandiosity was used by many patients in the heart-attack group, and all leaders were taught to accept and respect it, although it was difficult. Visotsky et al. (1961) write that their most problematic staff–patient experience involved a patient who used this defense.

The group leader should try to use the group process to support members' coping devices but also allow the natural confrontive aspects of the group process to take place. Members then have the opportunity to absorb new information in the group but are not pushed to do so. If a patient's anxiety elevates, the leader can always step in and offer support.

POSITIVE ADAPTATION

Some of the ingredients of positive adaptation to being hospitalized and having a severe illness include: sense of mastery and activeness; hope; fight for life; relatedness to staff; existential resolve; and faith.

SENSE OF MASTERY AND ACTIVITY

Mahler, Pine, and Bergman (1975) give a detailed account on how the infant utilizes aggressive energy in moving from dependency to independence. An enormous amount of work goes into becoming autonomous and individuated and experiencing a sense of mastery. When people become sick and are hospitalized, their sense of mastery is often threatened; they can enter a state of helplessness, dependency, and inactivity. Fried writes: "One of the most basic needs of the human race is activeness . . .)" (p. 3) and "Genuine activeness is a necessity of life" (1970, p. 6). When faced with serious illness, there is an understandable sense of frustration and rage that something so unwelcome could occur against one's will. The extent to which one understands and can accept, without guilt or anxiety, this anger and fights for those things he can do something about, markedly effects how successfully he adapts to the illness.

Emotionally healthy patients can channel anger into assertiveness; aggression is utilized to secure the best possible medical care. When assertiveness is combined with interpersonal skill, staff is not alienated. Patients become active participants in the recovery process and approach a sense of mastery over their situation. In this way, they counter the feeling of helpless dependency which can bring on the "giving-up complex" that ultimately leads to severe withdrawal (Colligan, 1975). Instead, they feel autonomous, independent, and active in the determination of their fate.

Most people working with the medically ill advocate encouragement of patient activity and autonomy. However, few authors recognize the potential of group participation in this process. It can be a powerful antidote to patients' feelings of helplessness. The simple act of attending the group is active rather than passive, and for this reason it is a treatment for depression. Assertiveness can be reinforced in the group through group support and exposure to peer models. Tanaka describes an inpatient psychiatric floor before and after the institution of group meetings:

> *Before:* Patients were "sleeping during the day and pacing the hallway aimlessly at other times. It was by no means unusual for these patients not to know anyone on the ward. They expressed boredom, yet refused to attend hospital activities prescribed for them. Those few who did attend occupational therapy seemed very indifferent, cared little about the program and were seemingly uninterested in staff. (p. 53)
>
> *After:* A sense of vitality emerged and social roles emerged that helped define people as part of a social interaction system. Patients took initiative to be helpful. They became volunteers in the community and helped peers control their self-destructive behavior. They began helping regressed patients feed and clothe themselves. Occasionally, they made home visits to discharged patients. (1962, p. 55)

It is important to appreciate patients' feelings of helplessness and allow them to articulate these feelings.

> Mr. B. said that having a heart attack was the same as having an atomic energy plant move on your property. You knew eventually it would kill you. Some people would fight it being there, but he wasn't the type. He just accepts it and will have to wait to see when death actually seizes him. Mr. S. said that if he had some broken bones, he would feel better than if he had a heart attack. At least, with broken bones, you can see them on an X ray and

picture it in your head. With a heart attack, there was nothing to picture; he wishes he knew what it looked like.*

Ms. Bell and Ms. Kay were always trying to do things for themselves, and the nurses and they commented that this activity made them feel better. Ms. Bell had one bout of depression in her long hospitalization. She had coped with severe pain and major setbacks in her recovery from a debilitating disease. Her depression came, however, when she was totally bedridden and could in no way participate in her rehabilitation. As soon as she was able to get up, her depression lifted, despite her poor prognosis: she felt she could do something to help herself.

At St. Vincent's, patients' desire for and pride in independence was always evident in spontaneous discussions about the bedpan. Private and nonprivate inpatients talked about having to use the bedpan as the most humiliating and degrading experience. In the following group meeting, four inpatients (three with cancer and one with a pending colostomy) support each other, with humor, in the expression of frustration about the bedpan. Again, a feeling of camaraderie develops in the group, and there is an externalization of anger. The leader appreciates this process as therapeutic and does not interpret the underlying dynamics. The atmosphere of acceptance makes it possible for the patients to express themselves.

> Members talked about the aides and how they don't meet their needs. What really bothers them is that they can sit on the bedpan all day and nobody cares. They have to ring when they want the bedpan and ring to get the bedpan picked up and wait! It is terrible being dependent. You can't even go to the toilet by yourself. Staff is so mixed up that one of the patients is inundated with bedpans, and others can't get one when they need it. They laughed with the woman who was flooded with bedpans.

In other meetings patients often talked with pride about how they snuck out of bed in the middle of the night to use the bathroom, against their doctor's orders. One man got stuck between the rails of his bed as a result, but that didn't stop him from trying again. (The group laughed

---

*Actually it would be possible for medical staff to give Mr. S. the equivalent of an X ray: the electrocardiogram. In group, medical staff can obtain some new ideas as to how to alleviate anxiety of patients. Patients are often explicit as to how staff can help them better; sometimes all we have to do is listen. In this case, however, Mr. S. may have been asking for something concrete; while he had the idea that something tangible would help his anxiety, perhaps his feelings about his heart attack might have been the crucial therapeutic issue.

and identified with him.) Others reported telling their doctors that they refused to follow such an order. One man, just recovering from a heart attack and on the coronary intensive-care unit, told his doctor that he would rather die than use a bedpan.

Part of being individuated is the feeling that one is in charge of one's own life. The adult does not feel like a child and does not see authority figures as parents. Adults can be dependent if necessary because they knows they *are* adults. Group process can reinforce these healthy inclinations. Active assertiveness can be implemented, as is evident in a letter that a member of a cystic fibrosis group wrote to his fellow patients. Formerly isolated, he assumed a leadership role in the group, encouraging others to join him for the fight for societal recognition and support.

> Hi! We're the survivors of the CF group. These meetings have been productive, but we have a problem. Except for a couple of gatherings when up to nine people have come, our attendance has been poor. In fact, over the last three meetings, our average has been three people. We cannot continue to have productive meetings if so few people attend. Especially now, since we wish to approach the CF foundation in a desire to have them work together for *our* benefit.
>
> Our plan is to get a representative from each borough together to form a complete city effort against CF. But we cannot do this without you. We're sure you've seen telethons for muscular dystrophy and others. Wouldn't it be great to get that kind of publicity and possibly even get on TV?! True, these goals are huge, but it can happen. We need your help to approach the foundation. If we don't have it, we all lose.

Patients often bring up complaints and questions in the group. Members can consistently encourage one another to be assertive with staff. Moos writes:

> Consider the questions patients may ask themselves: Can I express my anger at the doctor for not coming to see me? How can I ask for additional medication for pain when I need it? How can I deal with the disagreements among different physicians regarding how I should be treated? How can I handle the condescension and pity I sense in the nurses who care for me? How can I tell the physical therapist not to give up on me even though my progress is disappointingly slow? How can I engage my doctor in meaningful discussion of how I wish to be treated if I am incapacitated and near death? These are problems which plague patients and their families. The frequent turnover and change in personnel, particularly those staff who come into more direct contact with the patient, makes this an unusually complicated set of tasks. (1977, pp. 9–10)

Despite the fact that inpatients at St. Vincent's Hospital are informed in writing of their right to information regarding their medical status, many meetings touch on patients' difficulty asking doctors for information. "They're too busy" is a common reply when the leader asks why so many medical questions are coming up in the group when they have doctors available. In these meetings, time is spent analyzing patients' hesitance to confront doctors, utilizing role playing, and inviting a doctor to join the group. Members support one another in their basic right to have information. In these examples, staff participation and patients' free expression in the group meeting resulted in changes of hospital procedure.

> In one group a dialysis patient complained that when he was dialyzed next to Mr. L. (not in the group) he got very sick because Mr. L. moaned, groaned, vomited, and masturbated. Staff never seriously thought about how this patient affected other patients because they were absorbed in handling their own negative feelings toward this patient. After the group a special effort was made to isolate Mr. L., so that patients wouldn't have to contend with Mr. L. in addition to their own dialysis.

> During a relatives' group of patients hospitalized in the intensive-care unit, relatives complained that they could not call the floor at night. They often could not sleep for fear of their relative's death. As a result, nursing staff made a policy that one member of each patient's family could call the floor.

In both these illustrations, staff was receptive to patients' and relatives' real complaints. The group leader can become an advocate for the patients, either directly by relating patients' and relatives' discontent to other staff with recommendations or indirectly by encouraging group members to be more assertive through use of the supportive and confrontive elements of the group process.

There are numerous examples of group participation enabling members to be more active and independent (Lipton and Malter, 1971; Monaster, 1972; Sorensen, 1972), but hospitals have not begun to exploit the opportunities available to help patients be more autonomous. Brown (1961) suggests that hospital patients be given tasks such as assisting the nurses or directly helping other patients by reading to them, writing letters for them, talking to them, and leading games. Members of a posthospitalized group of mental patients talked with pride about the jobs they did in the hospital. The fact that they were given jobs and could handle the responsibility separated them from others. They were able to leave the hospital and get jobs in the community.

HOPE

Patients repeatedly use hospital group meetings to search for models in order to be inspired. They also compare themselves with others, concluding that they are more fortunate. In these ways they support each other in mobilizing "optimistic," positive stances. Hackett and Cassem (1974) and Visotsky et el. (1961) observed that cardiac and rehabilitation patients needed models for hope. Hamburg, Hamburg, and DeGoza (1953) viewed hope as a crucial recovery defense for burn patients. Tiger (1979), an ethnologist, feels hope is an essential survival mechanism.

Since hope is well accepted as important for the medically ill, the question of group composition is relevant: Will patients be demoralized by belonging to a seriously-ill group and seeing other "depressing" cases? In one private inpatient group of seriously ill patients, 12 meetings were held involving 31 patients, and to the leaders' surprise, in almost every meeting members looked at one another, asked about each other's illnesses, and said openly or thought (as they revealed to the leaders after the meeting), "Thank goodness I'm not you." Many patients attributed the helpfulness of the group to just this dynamic: "I was depressed and feeling sorry for myself before the group, but now I know how lucky I am!"

> Ms. L., 84 years old with a widespread metastasis from lymphoma, said that she was glad she was not Mr. M., a middle-aged man who had a pacemaker: "Imagine having a machine in you!" Mr. N., a 71-year-old man who had advanced cancer, could not understand how Mr. U., a 62-year-old man, could undergo dialysis twice a week; Mr. U. could not believe the courage of Ms. S., a 50-year-old woman who was going to have open heart surgery; Ms. S. told us that "having cancer was the worst!"

Ms. Kay evoked my fantasy of what the worst fate would be: she was grossly disfigured and in chronic pain and discomfort. I couldn't imagine Ms. Kay finding anyone in the group worse off or more courageous than herself. She was in group with Ms. L. who just had her leg amputated and whose husband was rejecting her. In the group she presented a cheerful facade, which I assumed would be transparent to Ms. Kay. Two weeks after the meeting, I visited Ms. Kay, who was in a great deal of pain and discomfort. She said, "I was just telling my roommate about Ms. L. I think about that woman all the time. She has so much courage. Imagine having a leg amputated and having your husband reject you! And she was so cheerful and has such a good attitude! She has been an inspiration for me." I was struck by Ms. Kay's need for a model—someone more courageous than herself to look up to, to demonstrate: "You can be even stronger than you are, so keep fighting to work at it!"

In forming a group for cystic fibrosis patients, leaders were afraid to mix patients who appeared very sick with those who appeared healthy; they wanted to protect the "healthies" from seeing what they might look like in the future, and they didn't want the "sickies" to be depressed by seeing where they used to be. Staff's assumptions were tested out when two patients were hospitalized in the same room. One patient was very sick and needed oxygen; the healthier patient told his mother he did not want to be in the same room. The reasoning for staff's discomfort was confirmed. Staff later found out that the healthier boy talked incessantly about his sicker roommate after his discharge. He visited him and seemed to enjoy helping him. It is possible that he also enjoyed feeling superior to his roommate. At the same time, when the sicker patients were in groups with patients older than themselves, they expressed relief: "Maybe I'll live that long." One 14-year-old girl was going to the children's clinic and finally said to her mother, "They told me I could live long. I don't see anyone older than me." She was switched to the adult clinic and greatly relieved.

Members often found someone outside the group to be inspired by. By doing this, the patients in the group became the more humble, fortunate patients and the patient chosen outside the group became the unfortunate, courageous one who is both admired and pitied. Since the members in an inpatient group for the severely ill were very unfortunate, by most standards, it was hard to find a suitable person outside the group to fill this role. In one instance, it was Ms. D., a 94-year-old woman, who insisted on reading her menu and ordering her own food even though it took her three or four hours. The group seemed to say, "If she can do it, maybe we can do it," or "Let's not give up—let's be fighters like her."

All patients need hope. In a group of posthospitalized mental patients, one member said, "Tell me the truth. Is this all that I can expect from my life? Will I ever be able to drive or support a family? Is this the best job I can expect to get?" Rogers (1951), Traux and Wargo (1966), and Yalom (1970) all agree that the therapist must have hope for the patients or he should not treat them. Members should be encouraged to have fantasies and be helped to slowly move toward their dreams. In the same group members talked furtively about how they had sex in the bushes at the hospital and never told staff. They giggled like children over their sexual fantasies. The leader took their thoughts about sex seriously and conveyed the expectation that they have satisfying sexual outlets. The discussion then moved to how members could approach potential sexual partners. One member approached a member of the opposite sex after months of coaching by the group. In a geriatrics group, a 70-year-old man was obsessed about having an affair most of his waking hours. When he came to the group he felt it was unrealistic for him to have an affair because he was impotent with his wife. He asked the group, "Am I finished? This is my last chance. Should I give up?" The group encouraged him to take his sexuality seriously. In a group for patients recommended for nursing homes, some members were quite depressed. In the group one member had a positive nursing-home experience. Another member was uplifted and said, "Gee, I would want to live to be a 100 years old if life at the nursing home was good." She had gotten some hope for her future.

FIGHT FOR LIFE

Many of the patients walk a tightrope between life and death, and it appears that a will to live keeps them alive. Achterberg, Matthews-Simonton, and Simonton (1978) referred to their superstar cancer patients as "fighters." Visotsky et al. (1961) noted that certain polio patients fought for health despite tremendous odds. Kiely (1972) refers to the "courage to be" that some people possess.

Patients talk about fighting depression on a daily basis. They acknowledge that depression and withdrawal are appropriate at the beginning phase of a diagnosed illness, but they insist that one cannot wallow in it. Group members had little tolerance for self-pity. Instead, patients reveal ways they talk themselves out of depression, pep talks they give themselves, and how they force themselves to be active participants in their rehabilitation. Those who seem to fight the hardest talk about how precious life is. Their sincerity is evident.

It is possible that the medical patients who appear to have the will to live are those whom existential therapists would describe as having a free will (Yalom, 1980). For the existentialist, the concept of will as a psychological construct includes utilization of drive energy in the service of propelling one's wishes. These wishes are highly individualized: they provide meaning for one's existence and they incorporate a demand for responsible choices. Wishes lead to action and represent potential for the future. The medical patients that stand out as having the "courage to be" or "fight for life" are people who utilize drive (instinctual) energy in their fight for physical survival. They appear to be privy to a personal meaning of life which motivates them to fight for a future—even if that be one more day. They make the choice of wanting to live and take responsibility for this choice by cooperating with medical staff and embarking on their own effort to fight passivity and depression (e.g., talking to themselves each day).

RELATEDNESS TO STAFF

Medical patients need empathy and compassion from hospital staff, as well as attention paid to their physical needs. Certain patients elicit better responses from staff than others and consequently have more of their emotional and physical needs met. These patients demonstrate interpersonal skill and are very sensitive to staff's needs. They find ways of giving to staff, by acknowledging them or inspiring them by their "fight" and "courage." They accomplish this despite the personal threat of their severe illness to staff.

Most of the staff was able to respond to such patients as Ms. Bell and Ms. Kay very well. Both patients remained identified with, tolerant of, and openly appreciative of staff, though not obsequious. Staff couldn't do enough for them. After Ms. Bell's discharge, nurses continually asked the social worker how she was doing. When Ms. Kay was hospitalized, shortly before her death and soon after her doctor's death, the nurses and doctors separately (without knowing the others were doing it) planned an anniversary party for her.

One social worker described her feelings toward Ms. C. who demonstrated interpersonal skills and participated in a relatives' group.

> She took from me but didn't drain me. She always gave back something, and I felt *I* had gotten something from talking to *her*. She had a real sense of humor, and I would leave her feeling uplifted. Once I met her on the street, and she told me a joke. I went home laughing. Then I thought, "Gee, she made me laugh, and she's the one who has a sick husband!" Since she worked, I would stay at the hospital until 5:30 so I could see her because I knew she would appreciate seeing me and I would get a lot out of being with her. She was such an enjoyable person.

Ms. C. got the best service that this social worker had to offer.

EXISTENTIAL RESOLVE

The new medical patient with a severe illness has to adjust to a new and different life. One doctor says to his patients, "You are now a different person and have to live differently." Yet as Weisman writes, "Health means far more than simply not being sick. Similarly, recovery from an illness means more than merely being able to survive. There is a dimension of health that assures us of gratification in being able to do for ourselves . . . we die of many things before we die of disease" (1972, pp. 56–57).

Group discussion sometimes covers some basic questions about life, death, and illness: Is it alright to die? What price is worth paying to live?

What do we make out of illness hitting us? Weisman and Worden (1977) write that most of their cancer patients were concerned with existential questions. Group members cover basic questions, as in this heart-attack group. "How much can we give up and still feel that we are living? How much should we follow the doctors' orders, altering our lives, when we know doctors are not gods and they make mistakes?" They grapple with the fact that nothing in science is permanently established. (Magee 1975) The group was composed of Mr. B., with a second heart attack; Mr. S., with his sixth heart attack; and Mr. D., with a second heart attack.

> Mr. D. began the meeting by saying he had followed all the doctor's orders (lost 20 pounds, stopped smoking and drinking), and now he was back in the hospital with a second heart attack. He asked the doctor, "Tell me why this happened?" His doctor said humbly, "I can't explain it." The group said doctors are not God and they don't know everything. Eveyone agreed but seemed conflicted. Then someone asked, "Why should we follow the doctor's orders when it doesn't do any good?" Mr. S. said that he had the same experience as Mr. D.; he followed *all* the doctor's orders, and he's had six heart attacks! The leader said that there are many factors involved in getting a heart attack, and staff does try to share the information they have (including risk factors), but the group is right in that the doctors are not gods. "How does it feel when no one can give you absolute assurances?" Members said it was awful and frustrating. They graphically described the many things they gave up that were precious to them and made life worth living: favorite foods, sex, etc. Mr. S. said that the two years he was "the best" he gave up so much that life lost its zest, and he still got a heart attack. Leader reflected members' anger. Members talked about how much they could give up and still feel that life was worth living. Mr. B. said that he would modify his work but not give it up completely; Mr. S. said he would not give up sex with his wife: "What would be the point? That *is* life!" Mr. S. continued: if he has a bad prognosis when the results of his tests come in, he is going to leave the hospital and have a blast—"really live"—and die of a heart attack. They all spoke of wanting to die of a heart attack and not being "too good" and slowly and painfully deteriorating from another illness; i.e., if we are going to live, how we will live is important, and if we are going to die, how we die is important. Mr. S. was discharged from the hospital with poor test results and died of a heart attack a few weeks later.

In this meeting, the leader does not try to help the patients solve the problems they are presenting, namely, how rigid they should be in following the doctor's orders. She assumed that exposure to other patients' thoughts and feelings and the associative aspects of the group process (the stimulation of one's own associations—thoughts and feelings—by listening to others' new material) are enough to present any individual with new information that they can use in the service of their own adaptive mechanisms. The leader does try to reflect the feelings underlying the patients' concrete concerns, assuming that the feelings of helplessness and anger are difficult for them to accept and hence adding to their anxiety level.

FAITH

Faith in religion or another powerful external force that will rescue the medically ill patient can be seen as an extension of idealization or denial. It can also mobilize hopefulness because there is such comfort in knowing one will be cared for when one feels so helpless. Authors studying coping devices often do not include it as a separate entity, and yet most people have observed it as a powerful contributor to an optimistic state of mind. Katz et al. (1977), Friedman et al. (1977), and Visotsky et al. (1961) mention faith as an aid in coping. Kahn writes: "Medical social work must guard against ignoring religion. If religion brings peace to people, it cannot be destroyed, belittled, or even ignored. We must instead utilize what may be a real source of contentment and strength" (1958, p. 89). Kahn thinks that illness heightens religious feelings and helps adjustment to illness. It answers the question, "What caused this illness?" and this helps people feel more secure.

Religious references were made most in the open-heart-surgery inpatient group. Many patients described coming out of surgery as a "rebirth" experience. They spoke of their lives being in God's hands. One member had been resuscitated three times and said, "What will be, will be." Others felt God had given them a new chance to live and were euphoric (denying that they still had a serious disease with which to live).

As with other devices such as anger and denial, faith can be seen as negative if looked at out of the context. Faith can be seen as resulting from or causing passivity, which researchers feel hampers positive coping. Yet in the example just presented, one has to recognize that patients undergoing open-heart surgery often do feel dramatically better afterward and are euphoric. They can attribute such a good feeling to a kind of miracle. Is this maladaptive or pathological?

The following took place in a relatives' group for patients hospitalized on the head-and-neck surgical floor. Ms. B., 50 years old, is a middle-class Italian woman; Ms. R., also 50 years old, is a working-class Hispanic woman. Their husbands were having radical neck surgery for cancer and were roommates.

> Ms. B. said that she was happy about to coming to group. Ms. R. said that she knew her husband would be alright while she is in group. Ms. B. asked,

"How do you know?" Ms. R. said, "Because I believe in God." Ms. B. said, "I thought so." Then they discovered, to the leader's amazement, that they were both born-again Christians—a charismatic pentecostal and fundamentalist movement within the Catholic church. They excitedly compared thoughts and experiences. They then looked at the leader and said, "You must think we're crazy." The leader said, "No, I think it is wonderful that you have a common base with which to help your relatives deal with a difficult situation." They both disagreed with the leader and explained, "No; it's not difficult; it's Jesus Christ's will. God sends us experiences to test us and strengthens our faith." They smiled contentedly. They both said that they had had good lives and went to church regularly, but they didn't like the ritual of the Catholic church and wanted a more personal Christ. They now feel that they have a personal relationship with God. Ms. B. changed churches after her husband got ill. They continued to talk of their experiences with the illness, as other group members tend to do, but their expressions were encircled by mention of Jesus and "praise the Lord." Their experiences were not seen as bad or horrible, but all was positive. They were comforted by their relationship with Jesus. At one point, they tried to proselitize the leader. She said, "That's not why I'm here; I'm here to help you meet each other, and you've accomplished that. I'm just amazed that your husbands ended up as roommates and the two of you were the ones who could come to group today." They answered together, "That was the way Jesus wanted it."

Interpreting this meeting in light of coping devices is puzzling, and discussion of it may add to our confusion or clarity of the subject. One could say that these two members were denying in the same way, and consequently their meeting reinforced their defenses. But the mechanisms observed by the leader cannot be viewed as denial in the pure sense. These people sought good medical care and followed through assiduously with the prescribed medical regimen. They described feeling pain and suffering (did not deny this experience) but felt something good would come of it. In this sense, one could almost see their defense as similar to the superstars described in Achterberg's study: aggressively making illness a growth experience. However, even though these members talked of their pain and suffering, the affect was missing; instead, they appeared contented with minimum anxiety.

Bendio reports what a member of a cystic fibrosis group wrote after being informed of a fellow member's death:

It's very hard to talk about personal thoughts of death without mentioning religion because it is a very important part of the lives of many of us with C.F. I believe that trials come to us all for the sake of building character and helping us to understand the trials of others.

Through hardship and pain, we have been taught to endure. It is a human quality that must be practiced. We battle to the finish and are blessed in our weakness. (1978, p. 14)

SUMMARY

People with severe illness often use different defenses and adaptive mechanisms than they employ when coping with normal amounts of stress. An effective defense is not necessarily the one that ranks the highest on the reality-oriented or ego-strength scale. A coping device has to be evaluated according to its life-promoting effectiveness. Hartman (1958) writes that ego activity has to be viewed in terms of adaptiveness to reality tasks; thus a regressive coping device may be used in the service of reality mastery. Monat and Lazarus (1977) write that an evaluation of coping and adaptation must take into account diverse levels of analysis (psychological, physiological, and sociological), the short-term and long-term consequences, and the specific nature of the situation in question. They state that there is growing conviction that all coping processes (including defense mechanisms) have both positive and negative consequences. Thus for some people, primitive defenses such as denial and projection can be very effective in lowering anxiety or preventing withdrawal. An individual high in ego strength may use such defenses temporarily and effectively. The group leader must be able to evaluate the adaptiveness of coping devices, appreciate the variety of mechanisms patients use effectively, and take the opportunity to learn from patients as they spontaneously interact. Appropriate technique in leading medical groups includes the establishment of a supportive environment, where members are free to display their varying coping mechanisms, and the use of positive reinforcement to encourage each group member's potential for optimum adaptation. Positive adaptation—the successful adjustment to external threat—can include the patients' maintenance of the following: a sense of mastery and control over one's life, hope, a will to live, relatedness to staff and significant others, existential resolve, and faith.

Defenses and adaptive mechanisms are crucial for self-protection. Participation in the small group can facilitate patients' choice of optimum coping mechanisms. Members are exposed to alternative methods of coping and observe others at various stages of illness. The exceptional coper can be used by members as a model and as a source of inspiration. As the leader establishes a supportive atmosphere in the group, patients' anxiety may decrease, and they therefore may avail themselves of alternative methods of coping that they ordinarily could not afford.

Chapter 10

Humanizing the Hospital Experience

It is possible for hospital care to be a positive, humanizing experience. Contrasting dramatically with my own thesis, Goffman, in referring to mental institutions, had the following to say: "those who eat and sleep and work, with a group of fellow workers, can hardly sustain a meaningful domestic existence.... Upon entrance...he begins a series of abasements, degradations, humiliations, and profanation of self" (1962, p. 11). In terms of relationship between patients and staff he writes: "Each group tends to conceive of the other in terms of narrow, hostile stereotypes, staff often seeing inmates as bitter, secretive, and untrustworthy, while inmates often see staff as condescending, highhanded, and mean. Staff tends to feel superior and righteous; inmates tend...to feel inferior, weak, blameworthy, and guilty" (Ibid., p. 14). As for different kinds of people being thrown together for communal living: "The practice of mixing age, ethnic, and racial groups in prisons and mental hospitals can lead an inmate to feel he is being contaminated by contact with undesireable fellow inmates" (Ibid., p. 29). In brief, Goffman puts community institutions in the category of concentration camps, military camps, and prisoner-of-war camps.

By contrast, this chapter will illustrate how small-group intervention can help institutions meet the human needs of their clientele, even to the point of making hospitalization a positive growth experience. I am not condoning or denying the existence of the long-term psychiatric institution where human conditions are deplorable. But we have come a long way since 1962 in knowing how to improve such conditions. The cause of the problem is not institutionalization per se, or irreconcilable rifts between patients and staff, or different kinds of people being forced to live together. All of these factors can be turned into positives. Hospitalization does not have to be like a prisoner-of-war camp. This image is in direct contrast to one of isolated nursing-home candidates who attended a group and spontaneously at the end of the meeting smiled and held hands. However, in order to change dehumanizing conditions in institutions, increased support must be sought in the form of financial aid and improved professional commitment.

Although private and voluntary medical institutions are not as notorious for brutal conditions as public, long-term psychiatric facilities, a more subtle process of dehumanization has been of concern to professionals. In 1979, *Hospitals*, the journal of the American Hospital Association, published an entire issue on "Guarding the Human Ingredient." Howard and Derzon define dehumanization in hospitals as: "the perception of people as objects; the instrumental use and exploitation of people; coldness and indifference in social interactions; the repression and limitation of human freedom; and social ostracism and alienation" (1979, p. 76). Howard reviewed the literature that referred to dehumanization in hospital care and found that writers used the word to describe people as: things, machines, guinea pigs, lesser people, isolates, and recipients of substandard care. They were also viewed as people without options; "interacting" with icebergs; living in static, sterile environments; and denied preservation of life (1975, p. 60). Howard continues to outline what most people mean when they refer to "humanized health care." Hospitalized patients should experience: inherent worth, irreplaceability, holistic self, freedom of action, status equality, shared decision making and responsibility, empathy for and from others, and positive affect. (1975, p. 72). Howard (1978) feels that the larger the institution, the greater the danger of dehumanization.

As one can see by perusing the lists of ingredients of humanization and dehumanization, group treatment could be very effective in ameliorating dehumanizing elements. Yet authors rarely mention groups as an essential, helpful antidote. For example, Howard writes that "coldness and indifference in social interaction" and "social ostracism and alienation" are problems but does not mention group treatment as a partial solution. These omissions are all the more surprising since hospital care is a group-centered reality. Professionals often seem to deny that they are treating their patients in a group situation and cling to the illusion that their treatment of the patient is a solely private matter. Klein (1977) states that professionals act as though patients are not influenced by the world around them. He makes a plea to staff in psychiatric settings to consider the context of the therapy: the social system of the ward with its norms, expectations, and values and the role and status system among staff.

The small group can remind both patients and staff that they are all human. It is understandable why staff has to distance itself from patients while learning about the ramifications of physical disease. But at some point the depersonalization of patients by staff has to stop: the total patient has to be treated and considered in making diagnostic assessments. Group intervention is one vehicle through which patients and staff can further their communication and patients can draw upon their own strengths to support themselves and one another. The small group can offset the destructive consequences of dehumanization.

At St. Vincent's Hospital, clinic staff noted that patients spent hours in the waiting room, never reading or talking to one another. The potential for utilizing waiting time to introduce patients to their own resources and those of their peers was everpresent. Patients shared many common problems and concerns and yet represented all walks of life. On the hospital floors, staff reported that patients often stayed in their rooms, did not interact with one another, and seemed depressed and withdrawn. Many of the patients seemed to be responding to what might be perceived as an alienating environment that fostered patients feeling a sense of isolation. This realization was especially disturbing given the breakdown of family, social, and cultural supports in many of these patients' lives.

In reviewing the patient group meetings, I was struck by the difference they made in offsetting hospital staff's tendency to depersonalize patients. In addition to establishing mutual-aid networks among patients, the atmosphere of certain clinics and floors appeared more congenial and warmer after group was instituted. Patients interacted more freely with staff and one another. Many used the small group to learn about their own disease, hospital procedures, and community resources. Some extended their curiosity to learn about other patients, which, at times, stimulated their intellectual and social awareness. These results ultimately led to greater patient cooperation in following the prescribed medical regimen.

In one instance a doctor and social worker used the group to change the atmosphere of a pediatric outpatient clinic.

In the pediatric allergy clinic, preadolescent children sat for hours and never played or talked to one another. This behavior disturbed the social worker and physician assigned to the clinic. They formed a group for these children, with one goal being to change the atmosphere of the clinic. After months of trying to form this group, one could observe boys furtively looking the girls over and girls overtly giggling. Clinic became an additional place for these preadolescents to expand their social exposure. Many were shy and felt that in school their asthma made them "different"; in the clinic group they saw and were able to use the fact that asthmatics could be seen as desirable.

Patients often expressed through words and actions how group participation was filling a need for them. On a general-medicine floor composed primarily of geriatric patients, two patients were observed fixing their hair and polishing their nails before group meetings. Attending the group stimulated renewed interest in their appearance. Staff had not seen this behavior before. Patients came to meetings and complained of boredom, requesting from staff that more activity be instituted in their day, demonstrating increased patient assertiveness and more trust in staff. Patients seemed more alive as they were able to directly express their frustration. A group of diabetics complained about the new insulin needles used and administration was responsive. (Staff did not realize that these needles were hurting the patients and thus contributing to their poor compliance.) One gentleman openly spoke of his loneliness on the inpatient floor, saying he had nothing in common with his roommates. At the conclusion of the group meeting he said he liked the group and felt that he was together with people for the first time. Two groups which I led ended at lunchtime, and no one would get up to leave the meeting. Several people came in and said the food was getting cold, but no one budged. In forming a group of aphasics on an inpatient service, the leader asked them if they wanted arts-and-crafts activities in their group (so they could express themselves nonverbally). They all said, in faltering speech, "No, we want to talk to each other." One week, during the height of a heat wave, our air-conditioning system broke down. We assumed that our outpatient group would elect not to meet; members insisted on having their meeting despite the lack of ventilation.

FLOOR EVENTS AND DYNAMICS

In the following examples small-group intervention helped staff understand what was going on on a floor or clinic; these examples illustrate how the leader can use the small group to help patients deal with hospitalization.

PEDIATRIC INPATIENT UNIT

The children were exposed to a few critically ill patients on the floor. Ordinarily, staff would not deal directly with the children's anxiety and questions in observing this. Instead, they often "pretended" that patients were not aware of what went on behind closed doors. In this instance, the leader elicited questions and expression of feeling from children in a verbal and nonverbal manner. She helped to reassure the children that they would be taken care of despite emergencies on the floor.

Four children were present at this meeting, ranging from 7 to 15 years old. Two were boys and two were girls. Two were private patients and the ethnic composition was one Black, one Hispanic, and two white.

T.: "I want to ride a cyclone in Coney Island because it's so scary." M.: "I want to go to the beach." The group was interrupted because of the confusion on the floor, when two critically ill children had to change rooms. T.: "What is happening? What is wrong with those two children?" Leader: "They are very sick and need a lot of help right now." E. told about spilling some lighter fluid on himself and getting burned. "It was very scary; I couldn't put the flames out. Maybe I would have died if no one helped me." (E. could be identifying with sick patients relieved that they are getting immediate care. Patients on intensive-care units have similar reactions when viewing staff coming to the aid of a dying patient.) Leader: "When you get sick here, we know how to help you. Everyone here is sick in different ways and we help you in different ways. We know what you need." (Leader deals with underlying anxiety.) E.: "When do we have meetings? I missed having a meeting yesterday." Leader: "We will not have a meeting until next week, but now that you have met each other you can continue to talk together."

General-Medicine Inpatient Unit Example

One male general-medicine floor, which had a large alcoholic population, had an atmosphere that vacillated from depression to diffuse anger. In one group meeting, the group was composed half of alcoholics and half of men who functioned quite well and exhibited more ego strengths. In the group meeting, the alcoholics dominated. Essentially, they used the group to ventilate their anger: hospital staff wasn't giving them enough. The others, with whom the leader had had a number of lively and meaningful individual conversations, withdrew in the group, much to the leader's surprise and chagrin. In discussing this meeting, we realized that this interaction typified the floor; the alcoholics, rather than those with healthier personality configurations, dominated the floor. We decided that a strong effort would be made to bring out the healthier individuals in the group meetings; they should run the show. In successive meetings the alcoholics participated but discussed more what their problems had been and how they were struggling to cope better. The nonalcoholics could identify with this struggle, since they too were straining their coping capacities because of the stress illness had placed on them. Both groups found a constructive commonality and a more congenial atmosphere on the floor evolved.

Cardiac Intermediate-Care Unit

On a floor for private heart-attack patients, a patient died of a heart attack in the lounge. Two nurses had a spontaneous meeting with patients to discuss this event. Later in the year another patient died on the floor. During the meeting that week, the nurse noted that the atmosphere in the group was especially depressed and talk was more ruminative than usual. As we were discussing the meeting afterward, the nurse realized for the first time that during the meeting she had not mentioned the patient who had died. She was able to look at her own feelings toward the patient's death ("Death is something we're not used to on this floor") and her need to dismiss it. She was then able to recognize its potential effect on the patients and reach out to help them with it.

GENERAL-MEDICINE INPATIENT UNIT EXAMPLE

In one inpatient general-medicine group, it became clear that one 36-year-old member was psychopathic and dominating the other members by charming them. He told the group how he had just been released from prison after serving ten years because he shot some drugs into his leg and it got infected. One young man, 25 years old, had experimented with drugs and was particularly awed by his older friend. During rounds that week, staff could not figure out why the 25-year-old was not responding to his medication. The group leader suddenly remembered the meeting. It turned out that the older man was giving his young friend some drugs, thus complicating the medical picture. He had been dominating the floor as he had the group. The older man was discharged shortly thereafter.

CHARACTERISTICS OF FLOOR OR CLINIC POPULATION

When a group is formed, it caters to a specific population. As the group members interact spontaneously, themes emerge. Often new information is learned about the specific patient population that is directly related to increasing understanding of patients' treatment needs.

OUTPATIENT GENERAL-MEDICINE CLINIC

The dialysis group and the outpatient general-medicine group for patients with chronic illnesses, such as hypertension, diabetes, heart disease, and lung disease, were composed primarily of patients who were emotionally and socially isolated and had limited coping capacities. Many of these patients were chronically emotionally disabled and in need of outpatient supportive psychiatric care, yet they never received psychiatric care. It is possible that since they had a physical illness that brought them to a medical facility and they could focus on somatic concerns, they were not motivated to seek out psychiatric help. These groups required therapeutic intervention which made use of techniques suitable for disturbed people. The focus needed to be on breaking through the patients' narcissistic withdrawal by helping them make contact with other human beings. In this way patients might be stimulated to change their noncompliant behavior. The group helped clarify to medical staff why so many of these patients demonstrated poor self-care. Treating them medically was very frustrating because they would skip clinic appointments, not follow diet, not take medication as prescribed, and periodically need to be rehospitalized. Most were blatantly self-destructive, and medical staff were used by patients as additional partners in feeding their self-abasement. Coven described her outpatient population of diabetics well:

> The diabetic population . . . did not adhere to prescribed diabetic diets, changed their own medication levels, refused to test urine, and canceled clinic appointments when they felt they had "cheated" too dramatically. Yet coming to clinic was, for many, a most significant experience in their lives. The waiting time, the anger and annoyance with clinic procedure, the appointment itself filled a certain concrete and emotional space for them. Many viewed their physicians as parental figures; they could then respond childlike, to either what they experienced as "scolding" or "reward" that was the climax of the clinic visit. Generally, the patients would be "scolded" for not adhering to diets, or would diet strenuously—abstaining from even necessary levels of sugar and starch consumption—several days before the appointment, in order to receive praise. They seemed frightened by social-work intervention on an emotional level, breaking appointments or insisting on "no problems" in their lives. (1977, p. 3)

In order to understand these patients' plight better, one could use the analogy of workers who hold jobs that they dislike. Many people work at jobs that they dislike (as patients do not like having diabetes). They must fulfill demanding routines (as diabetics do) and failure to perform at some minimal level of competence carries penalties (as with diabetics who must follow medical prescriptions or they will get sicker). But most wage earners (unlike diabetics) are regarded as responsible for their task fulfillment, and are active and knowledgeable participants through constant feedback, unions, and peer pressure (unlike diabetics). In their jobs they are part of a well-defined population, which they see themselves belonging to (unlike the individual diabetic).

Once the problems of this population were obvious, a treatment plan could be made. Two outpatient medical groups were formed by this experienced group worker. Over a 32-month period, membership was consistent, with one member coming to as many as 75 group meetings. The leader felt that patients' ego strength improved with treatment. As patients began to demonstrate better self-care, medical staff was convinced of the value of the group sessions. After one patient attended 15 meetings, she said, "I feel terrific! This medicine really works when you take it!" However, one member, Laura, who was obese and diabetic, was a constant source of frustration to medical staff. She had not responded to any former overtures to help her, but with small group intervention, her behavior began to change.

> Laura said she had gone out to eat a piece of chocolate cake and then decided to leave it half finished. Leader asked how she felt about the experience, had it been new for her? "Well, you know, I did it because I wanted to. I was angry and went out to get the cake, and then I just left it." Leader reinforced her positive action and felt it might be important for her group to refer back to the fear she had expressed last week about her inability to maintain the diabetic diet. "You've been angry before, Laura, but you've said you have always eaten large amounts of sweets." "Right!" she replied. "Always when I'm angry I do!" "But you didn't this time," leader said. "That seems important for you—new for you." "Well, I guess so. . . . I, uh, I just decided not to. . . . Well, I said, 'Laura, you're a big fat slob and ya gotta lose weight!'" (Ibid., pp. 11-12)

The disturbed patient does not follow the prescribed medical regimen and demonstrates a kind of suicidal behavior. The patients were surprised that the leader's reactions to their behavior were different from their own. Coven (1979) continues:

> *Mr. E. to leader:* "You mean if I told you I was dying of thirst and the doctor said I shouldn't have water, you wouldn't give me water?"
> *Leader:* "That's right. I'd help you tolerate the thirst. That is part of what being in group is about."
> *Mrs. M. to leader:* "Well, when you go, you go, and that is all there is to it. You agree with that, don't you?"
> *Leader:* "If I believed that, I wouldn't be here. Everytime you put salt on your food you make a decision."
> *Another to leader:* "But what if we just got hit by a car. We couldn't help that."

Leader: "I would wonder if you looked for cars when you were crossing the street."

This group seemed baffled as the leader was introducing them to a new concept. However, they all started to change their behavior and follow the medical regimen more closely. One worked on alcohol intake, another smoking, and another salt and sugar intake. It was this kind of demonstration that led to groups becoming a basic part of the outpatient primary-care program.

PEDIATRIC OUTPATIENT CLINIC

In the outpatient pediatric allergy group, the youngsters, ages 9 to 16, appeared extremely shy and nonverbal. Staff had not realized the degree of social awkwardness and discomfort with budding sexuality that was among the children; many of the children were quite verbal in a one-to-one relationship with the staff members. In the group, staff began to remember their own feelings at a similar age, and they attained a more realistic view of where the children were at developmentally. The physician in the group attended an allergy conference at which another physician reported a hospital group for pediatric allergy patients where she separated the sexes, making a viable, verbal group possible. The leader followed this example and was also successful.

CARDIAC INTERMEDIATE-CARE UNIT

Group members frequently demonstrated a limited capacity for insight. Members tended to focus on concrete information given to them by doctors and their own concrete, simplistic explanations for their illness. Magee writes, "To know in advance that whatever happens you will be able to understand it gives you not only a sense of intellectual mastery but, even more important, an emotional sense of secure orientation in the world" (1975, p. 45). It was often hard to move the discussion from repetitive questions to the doctor to members' feelings about not getting the facts and answers that they were looking for; that is, the feeling of no one being able to give them "the truth." This observation was also reported in the literature by Ibrahim, Feldman, and Sultz (1974) who worked with post–myocardial-infarction patients in groups. The leaders and supervisor made the assumption that this characteristic resulted from fear and loss of self-esteem. Fisher and Laufer (1977) write of the underlying insecurity and self-doubt of such patients. Staff became more sensitive to the importance of reinforcing narcissistic defenses and were satisfied with the results.

STAFF FEELINGS TOWARD PATIENTS

In some instances group exposure helped leaders get in touch with their own feelings toward a patient population.

CARDIAC INTERMEDIATE-CARE UNIT

The leaders of a heart-attack group had been saying for weeks that they wished they had a group composition where patients did not deny and were open about their feelings of fear over having a heart attack. One meeting it happened. After the meeting, the leaders, an experienced nurse, social worker, and doctor, felt drained and exhausted. They were all surprised at how difficult it was to empathize with patients who were in the midst of a trauma. They said, "Their pain was so vivid. You could almost feel it." This meeting was composed of five men, three with their first heart attack and two with their second.

> Leader: "How do you feel?" Member: "Scared to death. How do we know we're not going to have another heart attack?" Each member told his story of how he experienced his heart attack. One member had his in a subway station. He needed oxygen. He remembered lying on the cold ground and young people tearing his shirt to help him. One member asked leader, "What do we do? Put it out of our mind?" Another: "I'm going to do that." Another: "I couldn't do that." Leader: "You're telling us what happened to you. How does it make you feel?" All started to ventilate at once. Members faced the fact that some had their second heart attack even though they followed doctor's orders. Someone blurted out, "We could drop dead at any minute!" At the end of the meeting, members did not want to leave. They were upset that they would have to wait a week for another group meeting. The leaders felt bad also.

PEDIATRIC OUTPATIENT CLINIC

In the pediatric allergy group an experienced social worker, doctor, and physical therapist had been trying to help latency-aged children relate to each other. In the clinic they had appeared shy and withdrawn, and for months in group they talked in a parallel fashion. Finally the leaders were rewarded: the children had a real group discussion. In the midst of it the doctor changed the topic. The supervisor was surprised by this, since he had wanted the children to talk openly for such a long time and had put a year's effort into accomplishing it. Finally the leader responded to the supervisor's questioning: "It was just too painful to picture these nice children in such horrible surroundings." The social worker talked of her own protective schooling and how frightening their stories were to her. In this excerpt from the meeting, six members were present. Their ages ranged from 9 to 15 years; there were five boys and one girl.

> Doctor to Larry: "Miss P. (social worker) tells me you have problems in school. What are they?" Larry shyly told his story and how his family had reported the teacher who was mean to him. Another member said a teacher tried to choke him in school, and another said his teacher was unfair to him. The discussion moved from "getting mad" to fighting to violence in the schools and how they handle it. Big kids picking on little kids and gangs were discussed. Soon members were freely sharing their encounters with violence. The leaders felt the children were being honest and sincere. One member told of witnessing a murder in the housing projects. They all agreed you had to stick with others in the housing project (the few people you trusted) for safety. (The leaders suddenly realized that this basic mistrust probably contributed to the members' initial reticence to interact with one another.) Members continued to say how important it was to carry a weapon. They then voiced their confusion about whether to fight in the face of danger or run. One thin, asthmatic child had sent away for a magazine to build up his muscles and look tough.

The leaders had an intellectual understanding of the ghetto life their patients were a part of, but it wasn't until these meetings that an emotional understanding was achieved. It became so common for patients to describe their feelings more vividly in group than in the one-to-one relationship that leaders and supervisor began to believe that patients were less protective of staff in a group experience.

AN ACCEPTING ATMOSPHERE

The institution of small groups on a floor or clinic can help to change the dehumanizing and stultifying atmosphere that commonly exists. This can be done by means of:

1. The mobilization of humor and pleasure in the small-group meetings.
2. The development of mutual-aid networks among patients.
3. The influence of a specific member who invests in the group.
4. The leader's conscious and unconscious reinforcement of positive norms.
5. The communication to patients that they are part of a community.

Whatever happens in the small group affects the floor or clinic because the group constitutes a change in the system and members become a core of leadership. Also staff is involved in the group, and they begin to change their attitude.

MOBILIZE HUMOR AND PLEASURE

Despite the fact that groups in hospitals often take place under tragic circumstances, the tone in the small-group meeting is usually a pleasant, optimistic one. It is almost as though there is a joy in people being able to come together and communicate. The leader should appreciate and encourage this natural occurrence, rather than feeling it is inappropriate and discouraging it. For example, in a group of relatives of patients hospitalized in the intensive-care unit, members jumped from talking of their feelings of despair to humor and light conversation. When this meeting was being discussed in group supervision, another group leader said that patients don't seem to stay on their feelings very long. Another group leaders was reminded of Kübler-Ross's statement that the terminally ill could not talk of death all the time: "You cannot look at the sun too long."

Sorensen (1972), reporting on a therapy group in a community hospital dialysis unit, wrote that the atmosphere of the patient group was one of confidence, hope, and often joviality. Most leaders at St. Vincent's found the groups more inspiring than morbid. The atmosphere was rarely depressed. In most of the meetings, most of the patients smiled at least once. Humor was an outgrowth of people coming together. One member said to another, "Thank you for making me laugh." Interestingly, Valliant found that humor was an effective "mature defense mechanism" for successful men that he studied.

> Humor is one of the truly elegant defenses in the human repertoire. Few would deny that the capacity for humor, like hope, is one of mankind's most potent antidotes for the woes of Pandora's box . . . it is difficult to study humor . . . humor is short-lived. Like a rainbow, even when reliably perceived, it forever evades our grasp. (1977, pp. 116-117)

DEVELOP MUTUAL-AID NETWORKS

Members have a great deal to offer one another. Staff could never provide the volume of support that a mutual-aid network among patients can. Self-help groups have become prolific because they fill a basic need for peer support. Yalom states that, "After hearing other members disclose concerns similar to their own, patients report feeling more in touch with the world and describe the process as a 'welcome to the human race' experience (1970, p. 10). Patients at St. Vincent's have said, "I never appreciated sick people before" and "You learn the value of people helping each other in a hospital."

A group for relatives of hospitalized patients provided one another with emotional support. For example, one woman was humiliated by the patient "throwing her out of the room," and others assured her that they had also had this experience on patients' "off days." They also had a chance to directly discuss floor issues with the nurse. Relatives reported feeling more comfortable in the hospital and less isolated. In one instance this comfort became a problem, as the relative was spending too much time at the hospital. Relatives were seen chatting and leaving the hospital together. Staff noted a new friendliness and camaraderie on the floor.

When the Hispanic prenatal group was formed, it was discovered that most of these patients were in the country two years or less and came from many different countries. Many were socially and emotionally isolated, with their usual source of support (families) far away. The group was a place where these patients could meet each other and make friends. A mutual-aid network developed within a year. Patients shared what knowledge they had acquired about New York City, went shopping together after group, readily socialized during clinic waiting time, introduced the group to potential new members, and visited each other when they were hospitalized under what they called a *madrina* (godmother) system. These patients were introduced to staff and procedures were explained. They felt quite comfortable when hospitalized, although before the group, hospital staff had found them "hard to manage," "uncooperative," and excessively "hysterical" during labor and delivery.

Use the Involved Member

Sometimes a member will become especially involved and invested in the group. The leader should not feel that it is exploitative to fully engage his or her participation. In hospital groups such an involvement is usually predicated by a need that the group can fulfill. The patient can acquire status, recognition, and acceptance by occupying a central position in the group.

Michael was diagnosed as having cystic fibrosis when he was 10 years old. Until he was 22 years old, he avoided a treatment facility and was able to maintain a job and a marriage. At 27 years he became a patient at the cystic fibrosis program at St. Vincent's. He had a recent hospital admission for pneumothorax and took a leave of absence from his job. Despite the fact that he was competent and well liked, he was gradually eased out of his job and was unable to find work. He attributed these rejections to his health. Staff saw him as extremely intelligent and empathic. He had a good marital relationship and sense of humor and became a dynamic peer group leader. His attitude was, "I'm not working, so I might as well give you the benefit of my talents." He and other patients called new patients to invite them to the group; some of them spent long periods of time on the phone with prospective members. He composed a letter to recently diagnosed children's parents, inviting them to a party where they could meet adult cystic fibrosis patients and ask them questions. The entire group became very enthusiastic about his idea. The party had an attendance of 68 patients and parents. The entire interdisciplinary team also participated.

Ms. T. was a 53-year-old woman with chronic heart disease and a hyperthyroid problem. She lived in a single-occupancy hotel in the Time Square area and had a long history of social and emotional isolation. She never knew her parents, was raised in a series of foster homes, never had any close relationships, and never came to a psychiatric facility for help. When she was 17 years old, she moved to New York from Philadelphia and worked as a waitress and a nurse's aid. She was invited to join the primary-care outpatient group; she attended 96 weekly group meetings and was only absent from group two times. The group leader described her as the "mother" of the group; she had finally found a role for herself. Her impact on the clinic was felt when staff noted that she would always smile at them and say hello even if she didn't know the staff member well. She also set a special tone for the group: when one other socially isolated member was hospitalized for a terminal illness, she visited the woman every day. She elicited the leader's help in coping with the feelings these visits generated, and her increasing openness helped the whole group cope with a group member's impending death.

REINFORCE POSITIVE NORMS

Change of atmosphere does not always occur spontaneously. Group leaders can influence the atmosphere in a group (and at the same time the floor or clinic) by reinforcing positive norms. Sometimes leaders are not even aware of the behavior they are encouraging; reinforcement can be subtle and nonverbal. Leaders can consciously and purposefully introduce and encourage growth-producing norms and can even stimulate motivation to change. Behavioral theory is very useful in understanding how leaders can do this.

Behavior therapy stresses the importance of modeling in a group: members often imitate the leader. Change of behavior occurs when the leader gives feedback and positive reinforcement. Rewards for behavior have to be appropriate, immediate, and specific. The power of the leader's interventions is made possible by the importance that members place on the role of the leader (their cathexis of the leader).

Liberman reports on an experiment that was conducted with nonpsychotic outpatients who were on a waiting list for group therapy. The experimental group leader used behavioral technique and consciously rewarded behavior that would lead to group cohesiveness. "The therapist's attention, acceptance, approval and interest—expressed verbally or through facial and postural cues—served to reinforce or strengthen selectively that behavior of the patient on which it focuses" (1970, p. 142). The control group leader used a conventional, intuitive, group-centered approach. The experimental group was more cohesive, and the cohesiveness was accompanied by relief of complaints from patients.

In the following process recording, a new member in an outpatient psychiatric group is introduced to certain norms: differences among members are alright, and people do not have to express deep feelings. Although the leader was not very active, he was expressing approval of these norms through facial expression and eye contact.

> Leader welcomed new member, P., and invited any questions she might have about the group. (Norm: new members will be welcome here, and there is space for them in the group.) P. asked how long people had been in the group. Members responded. Two others were new to the group, and one member, E., had been in the group one year. P. said she was glad there were other new group members; she would not feel pressured to hurry and catch up with group. (Norm: it is alright for people to be at different places.)
>
> E. said he came to the group to let off steam. P. said she was glad group was focused on work, because the last group she was in focused on feelings and it was painful. Leader asked about her work problems. (Norm: one member can discuss feelings, and one member can focus on concrete problems.) The group discussed work problems and whether or not to reveal one's mental illness to employer. P. said she would not tell. Leader asked W., "Would you want to do this?" W. replied, "No, I would not feel comfortable lying." Leader elicited differences of opinion. (Norm: differences of opinion are alright here.)
>
> E. said that people did not believe he was mentally ill. P.: "I can understand that; you look so strong." (Norm: we will support each other here.) E.: "People don't realize what it is like to have anxious feelings." (Norm: group members are good; others are bad.) E. said that he did not tell people he had been in a hospital: "It would only spread." Leader asked if E. was concerned about confidentiality in the group. E.: "No one would break confidentiality here." Leader: "Does everyone agree?" Heads nodded. (Norm: confidentiality will be respected in the group.) (Meehan, 1980)

This group developed and resolved the trust questions positively. Norms were being established that were nonthreatening and accepting so that the group was experienced as a safe place.

Norms are not only important in establishing or changing a group atmosphere but also in helping individuals behave differently so that their coping capacity increases. In the pregroup, the leader needs to motivate members to be more interested in their surroundings (often this is accomplished by the stimulation of being in a structured group and idealizing the leader). The leader must immediately reinforce any expression of interest of one patient toward another. For example, if one patient compliments another on the blouse she is wearing, the leader might say, "It is good that you noticed what Sylvia is wearing today and that you could let her know you like her blouse." As each patient is positively reinforced with attention from the leader, the other group members are also educated and eventually they provide reinforcement for one another. The group begins "catching on" if the leader is consistent and repetitive in his or her comments. As the group members learn, the leader needs to repeat less and the members repeat more.

Gruen gives an excellent description of how he uses behavioral technique in group therapy. He stresses that the leader must "carefully listen for *tiny* clues of first attempts at something new by the patient" and immediately reinforce new behavior. He points out that even listening to a patient's self-destructive episodes is a way of reinforcing their continuance: this is very crucial for leadership in medical and psychiatric groups. Noncompliance (slow suicide) is one of the biggest problems in the health field. Masochism is a great enemy of health in both medicine and psychiatry. Following are excerpts from Gruen's excellent article on the use of behavioral technique in group therapy.

> It is a common occurrence during the initial phases of a group that the patients dwell on their problems and their symptoms. They see themselves as "sick" and unable to cope, which is probably a reflection of the end state that drove them to help, partly the expectation that such ruminations are an entrance ticket to the group and to the leader's acceptance and caring. The alert therapist can wait for an aside where a patient quickly mentions a positive act or a compliment he has received. The leader can then interject quickly with, "That doesn't quite fit the gloomy picture you have given of yourself!" Another patient may relate woes of abandonment and neglect but visibly perk up and enjoy the attention others pay him during his narrative. The therapist can quickly ask the patient if he noticed how he enjoys having all the people take him seriously and that he

certainly is not abandoned now. In such cases the therapist can get the patient to introspect on this unusual behavior. He can ask him if it felt differently or better and whether it satisfied his needs and also gave him a better understanding of himself in the attempt at enlarging his perception.

If patients persist in their negative self-image or if they continue in an unbroken narrative of failure and negative traits, one can often interject one's faith in eventual change by sowing little seeds of doubt. These "doubts" put the therapist on record that he cannot completely share the patient's self-image. . . . An example of how the therapist can inject a seed of doubt might be the phrase: "Is it really necessary that you feel this way?" If others in the group are invited to comment here, the patient is at least reminded that his recital of self-condemnation may have raised some doubts in others.

Another way of sowing doubt is to remind the patient of his descriptions of testimony by others who have seen him differently. "I wonder why you feel this way when you have told us that others (friend, spouse, or colleague) have seen you differently?" If group members have expressed different reactions to the patient, one can substitute for the last phrase: "when group members have expressed different views of you?" The sowing of doubt is, of course, only a gentle nudge to the patient to consider the *possibility* of change. It should not be aimed at forcing the patient to launch into a thorough review of his present negative views. Such a course would only invite resistance and sometimes a more persistent clinging to masochistic defenses. The patient must decide for himself when he can venture out of the "safe, even if polluted," harbor of his old defenses and negative self-perceptions. However, the seed of doubt can act like a new light in the channel out of the harbor which might eventually make the passage outside safer.

Holding up new attempts at coping is another way that the therapist can get the patient in touch with different positive parts of himself. If a patient has had trouble voicing or even getting in touch with his needs but suddenly asks a second time for a clarification to his question during a maneuver by some patients to get the conversation onto another topic, the therapist can remind the patient with "You know, that is the first time you have asked for something that was important to you!" The patient who feels that he has nothing to offer to anyone can be asked to reflect on the disconfirmation after another group member thanks him for being so helpful and supportive in a previous session. Another example is that of a patient who cannot stand his own hostility and who has sabotaged all differences of opinion by jumping in at once as the "peacemaker." If for once he is suddenly silent while other members argue out their different perceptions of a problem, the therapist can turn to the patient and point out that he let this argument happen for the first time and then ask him what he felt.

The main force in fostering motivation in the patients to look for new ways of coping is the therapist's feeling of joy when this occurs. This is one time when he can inject his genuine feeling into his comments and his emphases. If, for instance, he accompanies the above-mentioned remarks with an obvious feeling of pleasure, or surprise, or friendly interest, he shows that these attempts are the proper thing to do. In this way, the patient learns that the therapist considers this behavior helpful and important. The therapist's feelings and reactions can eventually echo a similar motivation in the patient, especially if he follows up his show of feelings with opportunities to explain this theory of personality change.

The use of reinforcement utilizes an expansion of the example cited above. The therapist who is aware of his reinforcing qualities can marshall his posture, his facial expression, his attention, and the expression of his feelings as positive or negative reinforcing mechanisms. Therapists have done this anyway since the beginning of therapy, often without being aware of it, as has been shown in a number of observations and special studies. Here we are asking the therapist to become aware of his own behavior and to use it more consciously as a teaching and behavior-shaping device. For instance, when a patient with severe feelings of inferiority launches into another big account of how he failed at a social relationship, the therapist can let his eyes wander or appear less interested and even bored until the patient mentions in passing that he got mad for the first time and made a sarcastic remark at a colleague who reminded the patient of his lack of success. At this point, the therapist can "move to the edge of his seat" and appear more interested. His gaze can become focused on the patient. He might even nod his head and smile if another patient interjects with a "good for you!" Some therapists will at times express genuine emotions of joy or compassion, like showing tears or going over to the patient to touch him, in order to express their happiness and approval for some new behavior of a patient which left him and the group with good feelings or a new sense of accomplishment. . . . Eventually, the operation of modeling principles allows the transfer of this reinforcement activity from the therapist onto the group so that they begin to reinforce for each other. In this way, proper reinforcement of new and positive behavior becomes a group norm and a therapeutic goal for everyone. (1977, pp. 242–249)

STRESS COMMUNITY MEMBERSHIP

Patients in a hospital are, in fact, part of a community. It is a community where people of very different circumstances come together. Patients are often forced to live with people whom they would ordinarily never approach or with whom they would never associate. Some people are loners, and they are thrust into community living by hospitalization. This can cause some difficulties, but such a variety in composition can help to make hospitalization a growth experience. The fact that members of the community are in the same boat helps them to appreciate one another and overcome barriers that would ordinarily exist between them. If this does not happen, patients can be particularly pained by exposure to others. Patients often say that roommates can make or break their hospital stay. The small group is a place where the pluses and minuses of community living can be sorted out and dealt with.

The leader of a pediatric inpatient group used the group to create a family atmosphere on the floor. She included almost all the children in the group, so that ages often ranged from 3 to 17 years old. She was surprised at how well the children responded to his inclusion. Some older and younger children attached themselves to one another. Some from large families seemed to enjoy the similarity; some from small families seemed to enjoy the exposure.

Group compositions reflect the varied populations of the medical or psychiatric services. On inpatient adult services, it is not unlikely to have an age range of 19 to 85 years and a mixture of socioeconomic classes and ethnic groups. One observer of a pediatric group was surprised to see an upper-middle-class girl, an albino girl, and a lower-class girl talking as though they were best friends. Another group found no difficulty in including a shopping-bag lady (someone who lived on the streets or in public shelters, carried all her possessions in bags, and was disheveled upon admission)—someone staff felt was a typical societal reject. Almost anyone, despite his or her pathology, could have been considered for one of the groups.

In a group of private inpatients who were seriously ill with poor prognoses, the patients elucidated some problems of community living: having to see people that one finds frightening and repulsive; noise and other kinds of perceptual stimulation to which one is not accustomed, etc. Patients differed in what they found most difficult. Sometimes the discovery of these individual differences affects treatment planning. One woman who was admired by staff for her stoicism said that one thing she could not handle was an old roommate who was in pain. She felt totally upset and helpless in the face of such a person—much more so, she said, than by the severe pain of her chronic, long-term, debilitating illness. Staff was glad to have this information and readily changed her room, and she became calmer.

As in most communities, the problem of overt prejudice can occur. The following group is composed of Ms. M., an 82-year-old woman from Ireland, and two Puerto Rican women: Ms. R., 38 years old, and Ms. A., 64 years old.

Ms. M. began the group by saying hostilely: "These two speak Spanish. Maybe they need an interpreter." A few minutes later, she said negatively, "Puerto Ricans have a lot of visitors in the hospital, and they bring in a lot of food that I don't like, and I don't understand any of their language." The leaders became nervous, feeling Ms. M. was obviously prejudiced. Ms. R. immediately responded to Ms. M., saying calmly and patiently that all Puerto Ricans weren't the same. She shared some of the history of Puerto Rico, explaining why many clung to the Spanish language. They all talked about their immigration experience.

In all the cases we have had of overt prejudice expressed in groups, the leaders were surprised at how well members handled this issue themselves. Perhaps it is the unspoken and indirect prejudice that throws people the most.

Differences that often divide people are sometimes bridged in the groups because of the beginning group's mechanism of wanting to include all present in the group and define them as good and label all other people bad and outside the group. In this way, members of a beginning group externalize their mistrust and reassure themselves that they are safe with one another. If this happens, patients who normally might be excluded socially can experience being part of an in-group.

In a meeting of patients who were seriously ill, members talked of how horrified they were by the people they saw in the rehabilitation clinic; they really felt sorry for those people. (A number of people in the group went to the clinic regularly, but they didn't include themselves as part of this group.) One member of the group was an obviously paralyzed stroke victim and another was severely disfigured from advanced scleroderma. They went on to talk of Ms. K., a 22-year-old woman who was not in group. (Her illness was not considered "severe" enough—she presumably had hysterical seizures.) The group lamented about Ms. K., how sorry they felt for her, because she was young and sick. There was a feeling of camaraderie and closeness in the group, with all included.

In this meeting, members who were disfigured or handicapped and often shunned by those more fortunate were accepted as part of the more fortunate in-group. The group found someone whom they all could agree was less fortunate than themselves—Ms. K.—because she was young and they were not. Members seemed to be glad that they found such a person to feel sorry for, and their mood seemed to elevate.

SUMMARY

Unlike Goffman's view of institutions portrayed in *Asylums*, hospitals can be humanized and hospitalization can be a growth experience. Groups can be utilized to help humanize the hospital experience. Groups can facilitate communication and understanding between patients and staff. Often conflict is played out in the group that represents conflict on a hospital unit. Characteristics of certain populations can become clearer. As a leader leads a group, he or she often will become aware of personal, previously unconscious feelings toward patients.

Positive group experiences do not always occur spontaneously. The leader's interventions are crucial in establishing positive norms in the group so that an accepting atmosphere will evolve. The leader should appreciate and reinforce the natural humor and sense of pleasure that spontaneously emerges as members interact. The leader also needs to encourage the development of mutual-aid networks and stress the community membership which all the members and the leader share.

Chapter 11

Educating the Patients

THE VALUE OF PATIENT EDUCATION

Educating patients about their disease, the realities of their situation, and the therapeutic process is valuable because: it encourages and provides the tools for patients to take responsibility for self-care; it conveys respect for the patient and thus boosts self-esteem; it helps patients participate in decision making and thus contributes to humanizing the hospital experience; and it assists the ego so that the patient may more easily and effectively adapt to his or her illness.

Do Not Infantalize Patients

One of the problems in delivering health care is eliciting cooperation from the patient. Often the patient slips into an infantile role with the medical team and does not take responsibility for his or her own care. The staff may reinforce this process by infantalizing the patient and not sharing crucial information. Yet, when groups of patients are questioned as to the amount of information they they would like to have about their disease, they invariably say they want to know as much as possible. Hackett and Cassem (1974) interviewed patients on the coronary care unit, and none of them complained of being told too much. Patients often said they *they* should be told their true diagnosis, *not their relatives* (usually the reverse occurs). Patients wanted to protect their relatives, just as their relatives want to protect them!

RESPECT THE PATIENT

Educating the patient is a way for staff to acknowledge that the patient is a responsible adult. Since it conveys respect for the patient, it also boosts self-esteem. It gives the patients the information they need to make choices and participate in decision making, thus helping to humanize the hospital experience. The attempt to protect the patient by limiting how much information is provided can be infantalizing. Experience shows that most patients want to know as much as possible about their situation and they can make use of this knowledge. When a patient does not want to know, then we must respect that wish.

An example of how respect for the patient can be conveyed in psychiatry is education of the schizophrenic patient. Psychiatric patients are as interested in learning about their disease as medical patients. Many schizophrenic patients will never be cured of their illness and will have to live with symptoms and side affects from medication. Schizophrenics are often very interested in the theories of schizophrenia and the various ways that medication works, and patients can educate each other on how best to cope with symptomatology and the effects of medication.

ASSIST EGO STRENGTH AND ADAPTATION

As patients assume an adult, as opposed to a regressed, childlike role, the ego is strengthened and the ability to adapt increases. In one study, patients were educated before surgery as to the procedure and the kind of pain they would have (Egbert et al. 1964). The experimental group used less than half the narcotics required by the control group, and were discharged from the hospital sooner than control group members.

Children are usually curious about their surroundings. On a medical floor they are observant of the events taking place around them, such as nurses attending to critically ill children. When staff is reluctant to have direct discussions with children about such activity, children become fearful and anxious, feeling that the adults are responding to something that is too horrible to talk about. In the small group, patients' questions can be elicited and dealt with directly. In the following two inpatient meetings, children were free to ask any questions they wanted. They seemed to feel comfortable with the most morbid realities, as long as these realities were not so dangerous that they couldn't be spoken about. There is much truth in Shakespeare's statement, "Present fears are less than horrible imaginings." These children seemed to be helped by the leader's labeling of "dangers" or the "unknown." Verbalizing, having words put to vague or unknown things, is ego supportive. In discussing Popper's work, Magee underlines "the enormous importance of objectifying our ideas in language . . . while they are only in our heads they are barely criticizable. Their public formulation itself usually leads to progress" (1975, p. 71).

The age range in the group meeting was 3 to 13 years. The group was composed of one Black, two Hispanic, and five White children. Four were private patients and four were not; three were boys and five were girls.

> "Being in the hospital is like being in a stranger's house and not knowing the rules." "It's frightening, scary, and they do things that hurt," said Peter, who had been in a lot of pain. He turned to the leader, "Why are little girls in the hospital?" The leader said he could ask the girls. One said that she got hit by a car as she ran to the ice-cream truck, and she woke up in the hospital. The group seemed intrigued. As the girl spoke she was giving her Mickey Mouse doll shots. Peter then asked Clara why she was in the hospital. She said she spilled coffee on herself. Larry said he wished his dog could be with him in the hospital. Charlotte said, "Sh! You better not talk about dogs in front of Pat; he got bit by a dog." Leader said, "You can ask Pat how he feels about it." Charlotte and Larry did, and Pat said, "I like dogs; it's just this one dog. He's a wolf dog—a bad dog. Larry's dog sounds like a nice dog. I'd like him."

This meeting included 5 to 17 year-olds: four boys and three girls; one Black, one White, and five Hispanic patients; and four private patients.

> During the meeting, Glenda left the room. Jim said, "Where did she go?" Carol said, "Radiation therapy." Jim: "What's that for?" Paul: "So her cancer will stop growing," matter-of-factly. Jim seemed satisfied with this answer, and the group went on to another topic. Jim showed his bandages. Paul showed his. Jim asked Paul about eye surgery: "What happened to you?" Paul said he got hit by a baseball bat because he was in the way. Ann said that she is going to have eye surgery because her eyes are crossed. "Don't glasses correct that?" asked another member. "How scary to have something wrong with your eyes," said another. Paul: "I only have one bad eye—she has two." Anne: "I'm scared but I know what to expect." Paul: "After surgery I had trouble breathing, but they take care of you here. They know when you can't take care of yourself." Leader: "That's right. We will take care of you. You are all different and need different things, and we know how you're different and what you'll need."

PATIENT EDUCATION THROUGH GROUP
INTERACTION

Learning new information in an anxiety-laden area requires that emotional as well as intellectual needs be given attention. As members interact, the emotions that can block learning are revealed. Imparting of information is only one step in the teaching process. Interpretation of information is the other necessary step. A teacher may say something, and students may hear something entirely different; it is only through dialogue that the teacher can learn what is being perceived. The small group is the ideal format for patient education to take place. Shulman (1979) writes that the challenge of education in groups is to present information and elicit interaction to make the information meaningful. The small-group approach, where interaction (as opposed to straight didactics) takes place overcomes some of the limitations of "classroom" teaching, where people often have trouble remembering information.

Medical staff frequently complain that they repeat something over and over again to certain patients, and they never remember. Often only when the patient comes to the group does he or she actually register the information. For example, at St. Vincent's Hospital, there were several patients that never used the word "cancer" to refer to their disease until they were in a group. Sorensen (1972) reports that patients learned how to do home dialysis better from their peers than from staff.

USE SUPPORTIVE ATMOSPHERE TO ENHANCE LEARNING

One of the main values of the use of supportive technique is that it is designed to lower patients' anxiety. As anxiety lowers, the patient can risk being more open to external forces (people and information) because less psychic energy is needed to defend against anxiety. The supportive elements in the group include the patient discovering that others share the same fears and situation; he or she is not isolated and alone. Some people who are sick have the belief that they are being punished for some evil they have committed. In a group they find there are others in their predicament who seem like good people and not worthy of punishment.

USE GROUP NORMS TO ENHANCE LEARNING

Cohesive groups are interactive and establish norms; if the norms are positive ones, they can be a powerful influence in facilitating positive behavior change. Hare (1976) describes research that demonstrates how group norms changed people's behavior: community problems were solved, productivity raised, group skills improved, student attitudes changed, and personalities changed. Hare emphasizes that groups in which opportunities for discussion are maximized are found to be the most effective and adds:

> There is evidence that the important element in change is not so much having a chance to discuss the problem as it is providing an

effective method for breaking down the old value system before adopting a new one, . . . an emotional as well as an intellectual process. As the process of change takes place, group members tend to show the greatest resistance to change just before they yield to the new set of values. (1976, p. 47)

In order for this process to take place members have to have the opportunity to interact so that norms—the instruments of influence—can develop, and enough support from the group to lessen anxiety so that they can risk external influence. Taking in new information involves change: people need support if they are going to change during a stressful period.

Encourage Group Members to Be Teachers

It is often glibly stated that "the best way to learn is to teach," but the profundity of this statement may not be fully realized or appreciated. Tavris (1976) reports on the research by Zajonc who studied family size and birth order in relation to intelligence. He postulates that one reason first children have high IQ scores is that they have the opportunity to teach younger siblings. Youngest siblings do not have this opportunity and, therefore, score lower.

It is interesting to speculate why teaching may be crucial for learning. Perhaps the ego sorts out information better as it is forced to formulate it in order to communicate it verbally to another person. Also the status involved in teaching boosts self-esteem so that level of functioning heightens. At any rate, members teach each other in the small group. Group members become didactic with one another after the group has been exposed to information, with old members correcting misinformation of new members. As members spontaneously interact, gaps in members' knowledge are revealed and corrected, as can be seen in this group meeting, composed of three women: Lucy, age 24, treated for a ruptured ectopic pregnancy; Pam, age 22, treated for ectopic pregnancy; and Carol, age 15, admitted for recurrent intrauterine infection.

Members were involved sharing intimate feelings about pregnancy and boyfriends, despite the fact that this was a first group meeting for them. Carol suddenly asked if it was true that if you didn't have an orgasm, you could not get pregnant. Lucy and Pam started telling her "the facts." Carol asked why she had never experienced an orgasm; was there something wrong with her? Her boyfriend said she would have one when she got older. Pam agreed: it comes with experience. Lucy said, "It's important to know your own body." The leader said to Carol, "It sounds as though you have a lot of questions about your body and about sex." She nodded. Lucy told her

about a class being held in the community where she could get some good
education; the agency also had counselors who talk to you individually. She
also said that she would have a friend bring in a book for her. Carol looked
surprised and said, "That's nice; people don't usually do nice things like
that." The leader said it was time to end the meeting and she wondered how
people felt about it. Pam said it was helpful to know others felt as she did; she
didn't feel so alone. Lucy said she was glad she came because she now had
two new friends. Carol said she felt good talking—it made her feel better.

The following meeting is composed of six relatives of patients hospitalized in the intensive-care unit. It is a first meeting for all of them.

Members interacted easily and spontaneously. Ms. L. wondered if she
should get a private doctor to ensure the best care for her relative. Ms. M.
said that at the beginning of hospitalization, the house staff take care of the
patients and are very good. It is good to get a private doctor before transfer
to another floor. Ms. L. asked about clothes for the patient. Ms. M. responded. Members exchanged opinions on books they had read about heart
attacks, since most patient relatives were hospitalized on the coronary care
unit. Ms. M. said that the heart association was also very helpful and told of
her contact with them. The group continued to talk about what it must be
like for the patients to be in the hospital and reasons for heart attacks. At the
conclusion of the meeting, Ms. L. said that she "learned things and didn't
feel so alone."

The following meeting was composed of three Spanish-speaking
couples who had children with cerebral palsy. The group leader had tried
for two years to get one couple to place their child in a specially designed
school that she felt would greatly benefit the child. The couple would not
even visit the school, much to staff's chagrin.

During the meeting, two couples shared how wonderful this school had
been for their child; they were hesitant to consider school for their child at
first, but now they see the benefits. The resistant couple listened intently to
other's experiences.

After the group meeting, the couple visited the school and placed their
child shortly thereafter. The group leader was sure that the group experience was what made the difference.

PROVIDE INTELLECTUAL STIMULATION

Members of hospital groups are often bored by hospital routine and are
in need of intellectual stimulation. In an inpatient group of patients who
were seriously ill with progressive physical deterioration, members enjoyed the intellectual stimulation of learning about each other's disease:

Mr. D. (withdrawn prior to group participation) asked Ms. H. what having a cardiac catheterization was. She explained in detail, and everyone (five members present) appeared interested. She then asked Mr. D. what dialysis was like. She was horrified that one had to be on a machine five hours a day, three days a week, and the group not only showed interest but admired his courage. The tone of the group seemed to become more excited. They proceeded to go to the remaining three patients and asked for details of their disease. They all had questions for each other and afterward said, "Gee, it's so interesting; there is so much to learn about." They all said they enjoyed the group and left smiling.

On the pediatric floor, a group was used to orient the children to the floor: making introductions and explaining routine. Old patients told new patients what to expect (including the fact that they had to go to school—but it was alright—and that breakfast was the best meal). The children had tremendous curiosity about one another and the environment. The came from all sorts of backgrounds. One boy from the country asked someone in the city if it was possible to swim in the city. Children compared illnesses and life-styles. After one meeting, the children composed a play for staff that was reminiscent of a camp experience.

MAKE EDUCATION PART OF GROUP STRUCTURE

Beginning groups need structure, and sometimes the leader may choose leader-centered instruction as part of that structure. When this format takes place, the group may look more like a class; in fact, members may often incorrectly refer to it as such. But in a classroom the format stays constant. In the small group, the leader may introduce formality as a way of giving members a chance to distance themselves as they get used to each other's presence, but eventually discussion and peer interaction will take precedence. Examples of teaching being incorporated into structure are: the prenatal group, where the nurse explains fetal development with pictures; and the pediatric allergy group, where the physical therapist and doctor bring pictures of lungs to the group and explain to asthmatic children what their problems are.

The amount of information that group members can absorb is often impressive. The burn-unit group for relatives at St. Vincent's Hospial was a discussion group, but education was of top priority to the group leaders. This nurse and social worker geared education to the expressed needs of the relatives. Chetrick and Woods spell out their accomplishments:

Our groups included education regarding the medical, nursing, and psychosocial needs and treatment of burn patients. Some of the issues covered were: differences between first-, second-, and third-degree burns; important role of nutrition in healing; the burn as an injury to the total body (not just the visible skin); the role of the family during various stages of the illness (i.e., assisting in feeding, exercising, etc.); the impact of burns on the patient's body image; skin grafting; the necessity of the painful debridement; the role of exercise in the rehabilitation phase; coping with pain; the role of medication; and the adjustments involved in the posthospital period with respect to scarring and disability, family and social role, and possible unemployment for temporary or long-term periods. We noted that those relatives who attended more than one group were able to introduce some of the above issues and information to new members in a manner demonstrating they had understood and assimilated it well.

We found that in almost every meeting, particularly when patients were recently admitted or continued to be acutely ill, there were many questions about pain. The painful nature of the burn injury, coupled with the painful treatments (debridement), made families quite upset. They felt badly about "surviving" (not getting burned) and at times projected their feelings of guilt on to us for "not doing enough" for their loved ones and for "hurting them." The exploration of these feelings, the education about the pain and treatments, and the obvious concern we demonstrated, appeared to help relatives to feel less guilty, less anxious, and to strengthen their coping mechanisms. We always attended to every question, and explored the feelings behind it.

The topic of discharge planning was covered in all meetings and given increasing attention during the rehabilitation phase of hospitalization, as patients moved closer to discharge. In groups where there were newcomers and old-timers present, the newcomers got exposure to what patients needed to do to get better (i.e., wearing body stockings, exercising, etc.). The medical aspects of posthospital care of the burn patient were thoroughly covered ... in all of the meetings. (1979, pp.1-2)

EDUCATE PATIENTS ABOUT THE THERAPEUTIC PROCESS

Education not only takes place about the ramifications of disease but also about the therapeutic process. In any kind of therapy, psychiatric or medical, the patient is a student who learns from the therapist teacher.

Fidler states, "It is as though the patients (psychiatric) are trying to play the game of life, but they have not managed to learn the rules" (1965, p. 692). Fensterheim describes the assertive training group: "Perhaps the paradigm of the assertive training group is a noncompetitive advanced seminar with each student involved in his own project, yet learning from the experiences of his classmates, under the guidance of an experienced professor" (1972, p.165).

Even in the pregroup where patients tend to idealize the leader, education is a crucial piece of treatment. Members need to be educated as to how the therapeutic group process works. The leader cannot assume that the patient knows what is healthy and not healthy and what is helpful or not helpful.

Another example demonstrating the need for education in a therapy group is taken from a long-term geriatric group where members tended to give each other concrete solutions to problems. This was the way they were formerly taught to resolve difficulties: one defines a problem, figures out the solution, and acts on it. This approach was continued in the therapy group. While concrete suggestions had been helpful in other situations, the members had come to group to learn more adaptive ways of problem solving. Thus, concrete suggestions became resistances to group treatment. The leader had to educate members as to unconscious processes and the relationship between childhood experiences and present problems. These members in their 60s and 70s were amazed when they discovered that they were still plagued by parental prohibitions. They began making rebellious overtures for the first time in their life. One member confronted another who was rigid like his father. Another tried to have an extramarital affair. Another tried to "put herself first" and be selfish. Another tried thinking of herself as strong and not a baby. There was a sense of elation in the group that in the final stages of their life they could begin to free themselves from their parents' admonitions. They felt enlightened to learn that their parents were still acting as a central force in their lives and they had the power to fight these internalized persecutors.

SUMMARY

Patients cannot become equal partners in the treatment process if they are not educated. They need to know what is helpful and not helpful in the therapeutic process of group interaction, as well as the rationale for the medical regimen. Both psychiatric and medical patients struggle with compliance and self-care. Their treatment often entails the taking of medication, following a special diet (restricting intake of alcohol, sugar, salt, and nicotine), and keeping clinic appointments. Staff often feel frustrated in not having time or energy to educate patients.

Patient education can take place in groups and be a crucial part of the group structure. Often patients are better able to absorb information in a group, where they are supported by their peers, than they are in individual encounters. In the group patients may be less anxious because there is some distance between them and the threatening authority figure; consequently, they can absorb more information.

Part IV

THE POTENTIAL OF A HOSPITAL GROUP PROGRAM

Chapter 12

Benefits and Cost Containment

The dramatic effect of the psyche on physical recovery and well-being (and vice versa) has been documented in the literature (Usdin 1977). Self-esteem is intimately connected to the psychological state of the patient, and for this reason most hospitalized psychiatric and medical patients are in need of treatment specifically designed to treat their wounded self-esteem. Small-group intervention is such a treatment.

Given the potential of a hospital group program to help staff with the most basic problems in delivering health care (compliance, bridging the traditional psyche–soma split), it is remarkable how the field of medicine, in particular, has underutilized this treatment tool. There are a number of reasons for this, but most importantly hospitals are not going to add or change any services unless they are cost-effective. Various studies have demonstrated that groups can improve quality of inpatient and outpatient care: obese patients can lose weight, patients can accept illness better, patients can be easier to manage, patients can improve medically. But do groups save the hospital money?

DO GROUPS COST LESS?

This book has illustrated how the provision of small groups for medical and psychiatric patients increased quality of care: information obtained from the group enhanced diagnostic and treatment planning; and treating wounded self-esteem countered the tendency toward depression, thus facilitating the recovery process. But do groups cost less? To answer this question, we must ask, "Less than what?" If staff people can accom-

245

plish in a group what they can by seeing people individually, and if this service is part of their job description, then they would be saving time and money. For example, a social worker might be responsible for doing intake on ten people a week. He might be able to do good intakes by having patients participate in an intake group meeting. Besides the leader getting valuable information on the patients, he could facilitate peer support among members, which would be an added benefit. The group approach would be more efficient than seeing members individually and many hospitals do this in psychiatry. In a medical setting social workers can use group for screening cases, and nurses and doctors can use groups for patient education. Staff often get tired of repeating the same thing to one patient after another. If education is done in a group, patients can have the additional advantages of peer exchange (see Chapter 11).

Departments of psychiatry are gaining experience in utilizing the group modality to contain cost, but since use of groups in a planned manner is relatively new in medicine, groups often do not save staff time but open up new areas of need and service and upgrade quality of care. For example, a physician who co-led an inpatient group for heart-attack patients said, "This is so enlightening. I finally can sit down and *hear* patients in a relaxed way. I now wish I had more time to talk to my patients. I'm always so rushed." In this case, the group increased the doctor's sensitivity to patients' needs. If he does listen more to his patients, he will be adding something to his provision of services. The quality of care he provides will be better, but the cost of his time will go up. Another example is the head nurse who leads a group and learns more about the patients hospitalized on her floor. Patients emerge more as people and less as objects. She is more attracted to them and follows the meeting up with personal, friendly visits. Her increased interest and warmth contributes to the patients' comfort on the floor, and they respond by having a smoother recovery. Again, the nurse is spending more time relating to the patients and, in this sense, raising costs for the hospital. *It is cheaper in the short run if the staff sees the patients more as objects and less as people.* Another example is the social worker who has a floor group. Because he is seeing a broader range of the population than he would ordinarily (he might just see patients referred to him or do chart screening), he will no doubt pick up more cases that are in need of his services. Patients will learn who he is and what his role is and even self-refer. Again, amount and quality of work will increase, but the additional time required to meet these patients' needs will cost the hospital money.

Even if groups are used to help staff be more efficient, this cannot be accomplished without supervision and recording. Thus evaluation of group cost has to include: supervision time; recording time; recruitment time; follow-up time (if the patient expresses an individualized need, the leader has to see him afterward); and group meeting time. Schniewind and Needle write about the cost of a group in a primary-care setting:

> An ideal group in our setting generates about $2,600 a year. The cost of a social worker's time for this is about $1,000 per year in salary, fringes, and overhead. Having groups led by two leaders is still cost-effective and is often necessary for on-the-job training or for coverage in a busy medical setting where one worker may be called away. (1978, p. 11)

The statement that a group "generates about $2,600 a year" brings us to the important topic of funding hospital groups. The harsh reality of hospital groups is that *even* if groups are cost-effective in terms of time saved and secondary benefits, the hospital will not benefit unless its funding source financially rewards it for being more efficient.

HOW ARE HOSPITAL GROUPS FUNDED?

INPATIENT GROUPS

Cost of inpatient groups is usually calculated as part of the total cost of provision of services. Hospitals used to be able to request funds according to their needs; thus, if hospital staff added a service, they could simply request more money. The result of this policy was an escalation of hospital costs, to the point that they appeared unmanageable. Insurance companies began setting limits on what hospitals could spend in the next year. In the late 1970's, hospitals in eight states were bound by mandatory prospective reimbursement. A sum of reimbursement for the coming year was derived by the formula method, the budget review method, or the case mix method; if a hospital's cost exceeded that sum it would not be reimbursed for the loss. Thus a ceiling was placed on possible reimbursement. The ceiling was often below the cost of providing comprehensive medical care. In New York City 25 hospitals were forced to close (Schwartz 1981). Imposed ceilings affect hospital groups in the following ways:

1. If a hospital is funded according to present expenditures and if groups are added with less cost for provision of services, the hospital will be reimbursed less the following year. Thus there is no advantage to the hospital for cutting cost.
2. If groups increase quality of care but increase cost, even minimally above the ceiling, the hospital will not be reimbursed for the in-

creased cost. If the hospital can find an additional funding source, and the hospital has not reached its ceiling, it might be reimbursed one, or even two, years later.

3. If a hospital has reached its ceiling and is spending more than is allotted (i.e., the hospital is operating with a deficit), any cut in cost in providing services will be very helpful. (In New York State nine out of ten voluntary hospitals operated in the red for at least two of the five years from 1974–1978 [Schwartz 1981].) In this case, "cost-containment groups" should definitely be exploited by the hospital.

4. A hospital such as Kaiser Permanente which is composed of private organizations and minimally affected by ceilings will be directly rewarded by any cost effective measure, including the advantages of hospital groups. Kaiser is funded primarily by patients coverage fees and the hospital is rewarded by any successful attempt to keep their population healthy. In contrast, Schwartz concludes the following about the data on ceilings: "The unit of payment employed in prospective reimbursement may create perverse incentives that have an important and unwelcome influence on hospital behavior." (1981, p. 1252)

OUTPATIENT GROUPS

At one time (over a three-year period, Medicare and Medicaid rates for inpatient care changed more than seven times per year [Schwartz 1981]), funding for outpatient groups differed in psychiatry and medicine. There was some effort made to equalize it. In both divisions, self-pay participants drained the hospital's funds. The method of funding by third-party payments greatly affected how and when the group is held.

In psychiatry, outpatient group attendance was funded by Medicaid if the patient came to clinic for the sole purpose of attending a group, and if the group was at least 50 minutes long. Medicaid reimbursed a hospital according to the number of clinic visits and a group visit counted as a clinic visit. Various members of the interdisciplinary team led the group, but they had to be properly supervised and their work had to be evaluated. Group treatment or education had to be prescribed as part of the physician's plan of treatment. If two people from different disciplines led the group, increasing quality of care, the hospital would not get a larger reimbursement. If the leader saw an individual after the group because he or she had a pressing need, the hospital would lose money since only one visit per day was reimbursable. If the patient was given an appointment for the following day, providing he or she had no other hospital appointments, the hospital would be reimbursed for two visits: the individual visit and the group visit.

Unlike psychiatry, medical outpatient groups were not funded separately from individualized clinic visits. Groups were considered as part of the cost of providing professional service. For example, if a nurse led a group, it was calculated as part of the cost of the nurse's salary. Part of the nurse's provision of professional service, which she was being paid for, was leading the group. Other professionals' participation was viewed similarly. Thus the hospital did not gain financially by providing groups. Instead, professionals who already felt overworked crowded group leadership into their schedules.

Medicaid experimented with reimbursement for group attendance, approaching a policy similar to that of outpatient psychiatry. Members had to make an additional trip to the clinic for group attendance. A member of the interdisciplinary team could lead the group (nonmedical) if group attendance was prescribed by the physician or part of a treatment plan. Evaluations of treatment had to take place. Patient education and counseling was considered a reasonable rationale for group attendance. Unlike policy in psychiatry, in one pilot program the *physician* had to be present in the group for at least half of the group session and the physician had to document rationale for attendance and evaluation of treatment in the medical chart each time the group met. (This requirement was consistent with Medicaid's policy of paying for patient education if it is done by a physician.)

It may occur to the reader that a staff member could bring together a large number of patients, show them a movie, and send Medicaid a sizable bill. This misuse is called "ganging" and is not permitted. The physician had to have a face-to-face encounter with each patient and discussed his or her disease in a personal way. Each patient had to get some individualized attention; this could be done in the small group.

If Medicaid continues to fund outpatient medical clinics for patients' group visits, hospitals will be encouraged to add such a service, particularly since it is known that good patient education can cut down the rate of rehospitalization. Mildred Morehead, (1976) in her study for the legislature of Hawaii, clearly demonstrated that implementation of access to outpatient facilities reduces the need for, and therefore the cost of, inpatient care.

Even with Medicaid's effort to reimburse outpatient groups, there are problems with their methods of financing in terms of group practice. Quality care may entail two staff members leading a group (a medical and a psychosocial resource person); reimbursement is the same whether one or two people lead the group. Quality care also may entail the group being integrated into the clinic schedule. This may be the best way to integrate the results of the group into the immediate diagnosis and treatment planning. Medicaid's plan of reimbursement discourages this kind of integration. In one pilot program, physician attendance in the group was mandatory, thus escalating the cost of providing a group for patients. Cost of group would be less in psychiatry where a physician merely has to sanction the group and participate in periodic evaluations. On the other hand, if doctors participated in asking patients to come back to the clinic for an additional group visit, it certainly would be an effective way of impressing upon patients that group participation is, in fact, part of their medical treatment. It would also be a way of encouraging doctors' participation in the groups, which has proved to be extremely valuable for both doctors' education and patients' well-being.

BENEFITS

If we simply look at the cost effectiveness of hospital groups in light of requirements of funding sources we would be seriously remiss in our method of inquiry. The group leader is, after all, a member of the hospital and society as well. The group leader will be affected by the eventual fate of both.

Funding policy is made by our representatives and we pay the price of the long-range results of inadequate or adequate provision of medical care. Cost does not just involve hours of labor power required to run a group or provide other services. It involves staff turnover, number of hospitalizations per patient, amount of medication required, law suits against hospital, etc. Schwartz (1981) concludes: "Money has been saved, to be sure, but only at considerable political and social cost" (p. 1254).

Hofmann (1979), in an article on the financial benefits of humanizing hospital care, cites the following:

1. If there is more job satisfaction among staff the economic benefits would be:
    • increased staff productivity and morale
    • lower staff turnover, resulting in less time spent recruiting and training people
    • less absenteeism
    • less burnout
    • fewer grievances, so that less hours would have to be spent in supervision
    • less likelihood that staff would unionize, lowering time spent negotiating
    • less staff time and energy spent on counterproductive inter-departmental rivalry, competition, and jealousy.

2. If patients are happier, they will be:
   - more likely to cooperate with the medical regimen and be less likely to sign out
   - more likely to pay the uninsured portion of their bill
   - less likely to sue the hospital (a number of people feel increasing suits are the results of poor relationships between patients and staff).
3. If both patients and staff are pleased with hospital care, more physicians will want to admit their patients to the hospital. Public support of the hospital would increase, and this support would aid fund-raising.

RESEARCH ON COST-EFFECTIVENESS

The public is concerned about escalating hospital costs and the necessity of controlling inflation. Legislators are not as interested in general statements about the long-range economic benefits of quality medical care; they want to know the results of disciplined research. For this reason, it is very important that group leaders document the cost of the care they provide and try to measure the benefits in a controlled manner.

Efficacy studies of psychiatric group patients' use of psychiatric facilities are discussed in Chapter 20. In an unpublished study conducted at the Tremont Crisis Center of Albert Einstein Medical Center, Youcha and his colleagues followed 87 schizophrenic patients, some in a group and some not. Those people attending group were hospitalized less frequently for shorter durations, and used less medication. Group patients were able to take more "drug holidays" and were also on lower maintenance dosages.

Jones and Vischi (1979) reviewed the literature on the impact of alcohol, drug abuse, and mental-health treatment on medical-facility utilization. They reviewed 25 studies, and the results are enlightening. With one exception, use of medical facilities decreased.

A pilot study conducted by the Group Health Association of Washington, D.C. (GHA) revealed that patients who received short-term outpatient psychotherapy reduced their usage of general medical services and of X ray and laboratory services by approximately 30 percent.

A pilot program conducted by a clinical social worker at a Kennecott Copper plant in Salt Lake City, Utah, showed the cost-effectiveness of an on-site outpatient mental-health program. Over

a one-year period, the employees involved in the program showed
significant reduction in absenteeism (from 5.8 working days per
month to 2.93 days, a 49.5 percent drop), and in hospital, medical,
and surgical costs (from \$109.04 per person per month to \$56.51
per person per month, a 48.7 percent reduction). Over the same
one-year period the control group showed a 2.9 percent *increase* in
absenteeism and a 7.7 percent *increase* in hospital, medical, and
surgical costs.

A study of Kaiser-Permanente's 16-year experience with mental-
health benefits found that patients who underwent short-term
psychotherapy showed a reduction of almost 75 percent in medical
utilization over a 5-year period. (Adams and Miller, 1980, p. 3)

Table 12-1 shows Jones and Vischi's summary of all the studies.

Additional research documenting the interrelationship between psychiatric and medical care in terms of utilization of facilities is found in
Shepard (1980).

Twenty years ago, Querido conducted a six-month follow-up study
of 1,630 former general-hospital inpatients to assess forecasts made
by clinicians. . . . They found that regardless of the physical diagnosis, the outcome of illness was significantly worse among "distressed" patients, and that the predictions of the observing team,
which included psychosocial factors, were correspondingly more
accurate than those based on purely clinical considerations. . . .

It is relevant to refer to the Florida Health Study. . . . They found,
to their surprise, that whereas only about one-quarter of their psychiatric cases made use of the mental-health services, almost 90
percent utilized the physical-health services. They drew the conclusion that the primary-care physician performed a much greater role
in the provision of mental-health care than had been appreciated.
(1980, p. 12)

Certain medical patients who attend groups make less use of a medical
facility (see Chapter 2). Groups for cardiac and asthmatic patients probably fostered greater compliance and therefore affected rehospitalization
rate. Schoenberg and Senescu (1966) treated medical patients who had
multiple somatic complaints in weekly group sessions for 18 months.
Group meetings were held in the medical clinic. They measured rate of
utilization of clinic facilities before, during, and after group attendance.
These patients were considered "high utilizers" of medical clinics; they
made at least 10 clinic visits per year, prior to the group. Average clinic

TABLE 12-1
Summary Table for 25 Studies

Study	Setting	Time — Before ADM Care	Time — After ADM Care	Study Group Size	Comparison Group — Size	Comparison Group — Psych. Match	Comparison Group — Utiliz. Match	Comparison Group — Demogr. Match	Impact on Medical Utilization (Study Group vs. Comparison Groups)
Mental Health									
1. West German (Duehrssen) (1962)	Clinic	unstated	5 years	845	none	—	—	—	85% reduction in days of hospitalization.
2. Kaiser Permanente (Follette) (1967)	HMO	1 year	5 years	152	152	yes	yes	yes	62% decline for all medical visits vs. +13%; and 68% decline for all inpatient days vs. −6%.
3. HIP (Fink) (1969)	HMO	1 year	2 years	112	106 / 116 / 97	yes / no / yes	no / no / no	no / no / no	8% decline for physician services vs. +5%, +3%, −6%; and 15% decline for lab and X ray services vs. −25%, −3% and +1%.
4. GHA (Goldberg) (1970)	HMO	1 year	1 year	256	none	—	—	—	31% decline for physician services and 30% decline for lab and X ray visits.
5. Kaiser Oregon (Uris) (1974)	HMO	1 year	1 year	45	45 / 45	yes / no	yes / yes	yes / yes	11% decline for medical visits vs. −16% and −28%.

TABLE 12-1 (continued)
Summary Table for 25 Studies

| | | Time | | Study Group Size | Comparison Group | | | | Impact on Medical Utilization (Study Group vs. Comparison Groups) |
Study	Setting	Before ADM Care	After ADM Care		Size	Psych. Match	Utiliz. Match	Demogr. Match	
6. Puget Sound (Kogan) (1975)	HMO	5 years	2¼ years	148 / 171	148 / 165	no / no	no / no	yes / yes	17% and 20% declines in total outpatient visits (including psychotherapy) from year before psychotherapy to 2nd year after vs. +5% and −3%.
7. Blue Cross W. Pennsylvania (Jameson) (1976)	CMHC	about 2 years	about 2 years	136 / 26	1,500 / 521	no / no	no / yes	no / no	57% decline in inpatient and outpatient medical expenditures; 87% decline for high utilizers vs. −61% for comparison high utilizers.
8. HIP Medicaid (Fink) (1977)	HMO	1 year	1 year	169	141	yes	no	no	12% decline for all physician services vs. +7%; and 25% decline for lab and X ray services vs. +28%.
9. Mexican-American (McHugh) (1977)	health center	about 6 months	about 6 months	119	none	—	—	—	72% increase in medical encounters.

TABLE 12-1 (continued)
Summary Table for 25 Studies

| | | Time | | Study | Comparison Group | | | | Impact on Medical Utilization (Study Group vs. Comparison Groups) |
| | | Before ADM Care | After ADM Care | Group Size | Size | Psych. Match | Utiliz. Match | Demogr. Match | |
Study	Setting								
10. 4 Settings (Regier) (1977)	HMOs; health center	Mental Health care received at some time during the one year period studied		987 541 258 957	172 379 555 491	yes yes yes yes	no no no no	no no no no	6%, 30%, 28% and 21% fewer medical visits respectively by the four study groups.
11. GHA (Patterson) (1978)	HMO	3 months 12 months	3 months 12 months	952 426	none none	— —	— —	— —	declines of 19% (medical services), 14% (lab), and 30% (X ray) for 3 months after; declines of 5%, 16%, and 33% for 12 months after.
12. Minority Children (Graves) (1978)	health center	1 year	1 year	21	21 21	yes no	yes no	yes yes	36% decline in medical visits vs. +30% and −9%.
13. Columbia Medical Plan (Kessler) (1978)	HMO	1 year	1 year	1,155	none	—	—	—	8% decline in medical visits.
Alcohol									
14. Illinois Bell (Hilker) (1974)	employee-based	5 years	5 years	402	none	—	—	—	cases of sickness disability down 46%.

TABLE 12-1 (continued)
Summary Table for 25 Studies

| Study | Setting | Time | | Study Group Size | Comparison Group | | | | Impact on Medical Utilization (Study Group vs. Comparison Groups) |
		Before Adm Care	After Adm Care		Size	Psych. Match	Utiliz. Match	Demogr. Match	
15. Philadelphia Police Dept. (1975)	employee-based	unclear	1-2 years	170	none	—	—	—	sick days down 38%; injured days down 62%.
16. Philadelphia Fire Dept. (1975)	employee-based	unclear	6-12 months	77(51)	none	—	—	—	sick days down 47%; injured days down 2%.
17. Oldsmobile (Alander) (1975)	employee-based	1 year	up to 1 year	117	24	yes	no	no	33% decline in S & A benefits vs. +66%; and 52% decline in lost manhours vs. +10%.
18. Kennecott (1976)	employee-based	1 year	apparently 1 year	12	18	yes	no	no	48% decline in hospital, medical and surgical costs vs. +8%.
19. ATC (JWK Int.) (1976)	ATCs	1 month	6th month	4,777	none	—	—	—	reduction in hospitalization pointed to total health care savings of more than $1,000 per client.
20. G.M. Canada (Lunn) (1976)	employee-based	about 1 year	about 1 year	104	48	yes	no	no	48% decline in S & A benefits vs. +127%; and 64% decline in WC benefits vs. +79%.

256

TABLE 12-1 (continued)
Summary Table for 25 Studies

| | | Time | | Study Group Size | Comparison Group | | | | Impact on Medical Utilization (Study Group vs. Comparison Groups) |
Study	Setting	Before ADM Care	After ADM Care		Size	Psych. Match	Utiliz. Match	Demogr. Match	
21. California Pilot (Holder) (1976)	employee-based	1 year	3-20 months	240+	none	—	—	—	26% reduction in medical utilization; $.41 savings in medical expenditures for every $1.00 spent on alcoholism treatment.
22. U.S. Navy (Edwards) (1977)	rehabilitation program	2 years	2 years	148	none	—	—	—	hospital days down 69%, all illness diagnoses down 79%.
23. AHP (Hunter) (1978)	HMO	6 months	1 year	90	90	no	no	yes	38% reduction in inpatient and outpatient medical expenditures vs. -9%.
24. GHAA (Brock)	HMO	0-24 months	6-31 months	704	none	—	—	—	40% reduction in outpatient medical care utilization.
25. Kaiser S. California (Sherman) (1979)	HMO	2 years	2 years	64	85	yes	no	no	27% reduction in inpatient and outpatient medical care expenditures vs. +53%.

Source: Jones and Vischi

257

visits per year dropped from 13 to 3 during the treatment period. This was a significant decrease and it was maintained at a 5-year follow up.

The studies on psychiatric patients' utilization of medical care and the financial benefit of group and individual therapy is certainly better researched than the effect of group treatment for medical patients on future utilization of medical services. There is need of research which samples a large variety of medical patients attending hospital groups and eventual outcome. However, the literature that does exist and the observation of those involved in the clinical practice of groups in a medical setting point in the same positive direction. It is important to remember that the medical population *includes* the psychiatric population, and the size of this population is contingent on the utilization of the psychiatric facility.

It is of special interest to note that the psychotherapy provided to patients in most of the studies is brief. Thus, it has been demonstrated that even one psychotherapeutic intervention can affect outcome. In discussing the Kaiser-Permanente study, Jones and Vischi write: "The finding that a single psychotherapy visit or even just a few such visits could lead to such large and continuous declines in medical care utilization was totally unexpected (1979, p. 31). The group intervention I have been advocating in this book can also be very brief. My thoughts on the value of the single-session group are substantiated by this research. It is possible to help people in crisis in a short period of time. For the same reasons that brief individual therapy may affect medical utilization, brief group intervention may affect it as well.

The economic benefits of individual psychotherapy for patients with emotional problems has been justified; the economic benefits of group psychotherapy may be even greater because the cost of providing such a service is less. At the same time patients get the added benefit of peer support. I must clarify, however, that group intervention should not exclude the possibility of individual attention. Often members will reveal problems in the group that require individualized help.

SUMMARY

The group leader must recognize that although the time and skill involved in beginning and maintaining a hospital group may appear great, it is a relatively small input when compared to the magnitude of output. The group can be the fulcrum of a machine and the group's results can reflect a mechanical advantage. The input or force is the leader's knowledge and guidance. The multiplied accrued effect of hospital groups can include: better patient–staff relationships, patients accepting more responsibility for self-care, and less utilization of medical facilities *because people can become healthier*. The problem of providing total patient care, where the traditional psyche–soma split is bridged and there is greater patient compliance with the medical regimen, may begin to look solvable. For optimum prevention and treatment, group intervention should be an integral part of inpatient and outpatient care. Given hospitals' increasingly limited resources, the provision of groups may make the best use of staff. In this way, the highest number of patients have the advantage of receiving comprehensive medical and psychiatric care.

References

Achterberg, J., Matthews-Simonton, S., & Sumonton, O. C., 1978. Psychology of the exceptional cancer patient: A description of patients who outlive predicted life expectancies. *Psychotherapy: Theory, Research, and Pjactice, 14*(:6–422.

Adams, K. & Muller, A., 1980. State society presidents urge senators to vote for Medicaid bill. *Newsletter of National Federation of Societies for Clinical Social Work, 1*(7):3.

Adams, M., 1976. A hospital play program: Helping children with serious illness. *American Journal of Orthopsychiatry, 46*(3):416–424.

Allen, K. S., 1976. A group experience for elderly patients with organic brain syndrome. *Health and Social Work, 1*(4):61-69.

Anthony, E. J., 1971. The history of group psychotherapy. In Kaplan & Sadock (Eds.), *Comprehensive Group Psychotherapy*. Baltimore: Williams & Wilkins.

Anthony, E. J., 1973. The group of two. In Wolberg & Aronson (Eds.), *Group Therapy: 1973*. New York: Stratton Intercontinental.

Apaka, T. K. & Sanges, K. B., 1962. Group approach in a general hospital. *Social Work, 7*(4):59–65.

Astrachan, B. M., Flynn, H. R., Geller, J. D., & Harvey, H. H., 1970. Systems approach to day hospitalization. *Archives of General Psychiatry, 22*:550–559.

Attanasia, F., 1976. Process recording, Department of Social Work. New York: St. Vincent's Hospital and Medical Center.

Auerswald, E. H., 1968. Interdisciplinary versus ecological approach. *Family Process, 7*(2):202–215.

Bailis, S. S., Lambert, S. R., & Bernstein, S. B., 1978. The legacy of the group: A study of group therapy with a transient membership. *Social Work in Health Care, 3*(4):405–418.

Bednar, R. L. & Melnick, J., 1972. Risk, responsibility and structure. *Journal of Counseling Psychology, 21*(1):31–37.

Bendio, J., 1978. Reflections of a consumer. *C.F. Social Work Highlights, 1*(4):14.

Bennett, L., 1979. Group service for COPD outpatients: Surmounting the obstacles. *Social Work with Groups, 2*(2):145–160.

Berengarten, S., 1957. Identifying learning patterns of individual students: An exploratory study. *Social Service Review, 31*(4):407–417.

Berger, M. M., 1958. Problems of anxiety in group psychotherapy trainees. *American Journal of Psychotherapy, 12*:505–507.

Berger, R., 1975. Process presentation, Department of Social Work. New York: St. Vincent's Hospital and Medical Center.

Berne, E., 1966. *Principles of Group Treatment.* New York: Oxford Univ. Press.

Bion, W. R., 1959. *Experiences in Groups.* New York: Basic.

Blanck, G. & Blanck, R., 1974. *Ego Psychology—Theory and Practice.* New York & London: Columbia Univ. Press.

Bloom, N. D. & Lynch, J. G., 1979. Group work in a hospital waiting room. *Health and Social Work, 4*(3):48–63.

Bloomingfeld, I., 1970. Psychotic and borderline patients in outpatient groups. *Group Analysis, 3*(3):144–147.

Borriello, J. F., 1976. Group psychotherapy in hospital systems. In Wolberg & Aronson (Eds.), *Group Therapy: 1976.* New York: Stratton Intercontinental.

Brautigam, W. & Ruppell, A., 1977. Group psychotherapy. In Wittkower, Warens, & Hagerstown (Eds.), *Psychosomatic Medicine, Its Clinical Applications.* New York: Harper & Row.

Brickner, P., 1978. Primary care program. *One-Year Report. Department of Community Medicine.* New York: St. Vincent's Hospital and Medical Center.

Brickner, P., 1977. Workshop on primary care, Department of Community Medicine. New York: St. Vincent's Hospital and Medical Center.

Brickner, P., Burnstein, M., Coven, C., Crimmins, C., Harnett, E., Lechich, A., Mellendick, G., & Scharer, L., 1978. Development of the primary care program at St. Vincent's Hospital. *Statistics and Health Review, 3*(1):2–11.

Brown, E. L., 1961. *Newer Dimensions in patient Care (Pt.1).* New York: Russell Sage Foundation.

Burstein, E., 1975. Group psychotherapy: A treatment of choice for narcissistic disturbances. Paper presented at the American Group Psychotherapy Association Annual Conference.

Cassem, N. H., & Hackett, T. P., 1978. The setting of intensive care. In T. P. Hackett & N. H. Cassem (Eds.), *Handbook of General Hospital Psychiatry.* St. Louis: C. V. Mosby.

Chetrick, C. & Woods, B., 1979. Evaluation memo on burn unit group, Department of Social Work. New York: St. Vincent's Hospital and Medical Center.

Colligan, D., 1975. The Dangers of Stress, *New York Magazine*, July 14, pp. 28–32.

Cook, W., 1975. Unpublished reports, Department of Social Work. New York: St. Vincent's Hospital and Medical Center.

Cooper, E. J., 1976. Beginning a group program in a general hospital. *Eastern Group Psychotherapy Society Newsjournal,* July: 6–9.

Cooper, E. J., 1978. The Pre-group: The narcissistic phase of group development with the severely disturbed patient. In Wolberg & Aronson (Eds.), *Group Therapy: 1978*. New York: Stratton Intercontinental.

Cooper, E. J. & Cento, M., 1977. Group and Hispanic prenatal patient. *American Journal of Orthopsychiatry, 47*(4):689–700.

Coven, C. R., 1976. Process recording, Department of Social Work. New York: St. Vincent's Hospital and Medical Center.

Coven, C. R., 1977. Fantasy to reality—beginning group treatment in a medical setting, Department of Community Medicine. New York: St. Vincent's Hospital and Medical Center. Unpublished mimeo

Coven, C. R., 1977. Group treatment in primary care: A social work contribution to comprehensive medical care. New York: St. Vincent's Hospital and Medical Center. (Unpublished abstract.)

Coven, C. R., 1978. Fantasy to reality: Beginning group treatment in the medical clinic, Department of Community Medicine. New York: St. Vincent's Hospital and Medical Center. Unpublished.

Coven, C. R., 1981. Ongoing group treatment with severely disturbed medical outpatients: The formation process. *International Journal of Group Psychotherapy, 31*(1):99–116.

Crookshank, F. G., 1923. The importance of a theory of signs and a critique of language in the study of medicine. In Ogden & Richards (Eds.), *The Meaning of Meaning*. New York: Harcourt, Brace & World.

Davis, J. M., McCourt, W. F., Courtney, J., & Solomon, P., 1961. Sensory deprivation: Role of social isolation. *Archives of General Psychiatry, 5*(1):84–90.

Delbanco, T. L., 1975. The hospital and primary care. *Journal of Medical Education, 50*:29–38.

Detre, T. P., Kessler, D. R., & Jarecki, H., 1963. The role of the general hospital in modern community psychiatry. *American Journal of Orthopsychiatry, 33*(4):690–700.

Devereaux, G., 1949. The social structure of the hospital as a factor in total therapy. *American Journal of Orthopsychiatry, 70*(3):492–500.

Durkin, H., 1975. The development of systems theory and its implication for the theory and practice of group therapy. In Wolberg & Aronson (Eds.), *Group Therapy: 1975*. New York: Stratton Intercontinental.

Egbert, L. D., Battit, G. E., Welch, C. E., & Bartlett, M. D., 1964. Reduction of postoperative pain by encouragement and instruction of patients: A study of doctor–patient rapport. *New England Journal of Medicine, 270*(16):825–826.

Eisenberg, L., 1980. What makes persons "patients" and patients "well?" *The American Journal of Medicine, 69*:277–286.

Engel, G. L., 1976. The predictive value of psychological variables for disease and death. *Annals of Internal Medicine, 85*(5): 673–674.

Enquist, C. L., Davis, J. E., & Bryce, R. H., 1979. Can quality of life be evaluated? *Hospitals, 53*(22):97–102.

Erikson, E. H., 1980. Ego development and historical change: Clinical notes. In Scheidlinger (Ed.), *Psychoanalytic Group Dynamics*. New York: International Univ. Press.

Erikson, E., 1950. *Childhood and Society*. New York: W. W. Norton.

Fenichel, O., 1945. *The Psychoanalytic Theory of Neurosis*. New York: W.W. Norton.

Feinstein, A. R., 1963. Boolean algebra and clinical taxonomy. *New England Journal of Medicine, 269*:929–938.

Fensterheim, H., 1972. Behavior therapy: Assertive training in groups. In P. Sager & H. Kaplan (Eds.), *Progress in Group and Family Therapy* . New York: Brunner/Mazel.

Fidler, J. W., 1965. Group psychotherapy of psychotics. *American Journal of Orthopsychiatry, 35*(4):688–692.

Fisher, B. & Laufer, G., 1977. A survey of the literature on psychological factors in heart attacks, the response of the heart attack patients to group psychotherapy, and recommendations for further investigation. In Wolberg & Aronson (Eds.), *Group Therapy: 1977*. New York: Stratton Intercontinental.

Frank, J. D., 1952. The effects of interpatient and group influences in a general hospital. *International Journal of Group Psychotherapy, 2*(2): 127–138.

Freud, A., 1942. *The Ego and the Mechanisms of Defense*. (2nd ed.) London: Hogarth.

Freud, S., 1914. On narcissism: An introduction. *Collected Papers*, 1925 edition, 4:30–59. London: Hogarth, 1949.

Freud, S., 1921. *Group Psychology & the Analysis of the Ego*. New York: Bantam Books, 1971.

Freud, S., 1904. *The Standard Edition of the Complete Psychological Works of Sigmund Freud*, (1953). London: Hogarth.

Freud, S., 1960. *A General Introduction to Psychoanalysis* (1917). New York: Washington Square.

Fried, E., 1970. *Active–Passive: The Crucial Psychological Dimension*. New York: Grune & Stratton.

Friedman, S. B., Chadoff, P., Mason, J. W., & Hamburg, D. A., 1977. Behavioral observations on parents anticipating the death of a child. In Monat & Lazarus (Eds.), *Stress and Coping*. New York: Columbia Univ. Press.

Frey, L., 1966. *Use of Groups in the Health Field*. New York: National Association of Social Workers.

Galinsky, M. J. & Galinsky, M. D., 1967. Organization of patients and staff in three types of mental hospitals. In Thomas (Ed.), *Behavioral Sciences for Social Workers*. New York: Free Press.

Galton, M. A., 1959. The beginning casework practitioner; A categorial delineation. *Social Service Review, 33*(3):245–252.

Garland, J. A., Jones, H. E., & Kolodny, R. L., 1965. A model for stages of development in social work groups. In Bernstein (Ed.), *Explorations in Social Group Work*. Boston: Boston Univ. School of Social Work.

Garma, A., 1973. Gruppenpsychoanalyse bei Patienten mit Ulsus Pepticum. *Dynamic Psychiatry, 18*:2–10.

Gifford, C. G., Landis, E. E., & Ackerly, S. S., 1953. The rise of social group work as a therapeutic factor in the hopital setting. *American Journal of Orthopsychiatry, 23*(1):142–155.

Grinnel, R. Jr. et al., 1976. The status of graduate level social workers teaching in medical schools. *Social Work in Health Care, 1*:317–324.

Gitterman, A., 1979. Development of group services. *Social Work with Groups in Maternal and Child Health*. New York: Columbia Univ. & Roosevelt Hospital.

Goffman, E., 1962. *Asylums*. Chicago: Aldine.

Gombrich, E. H., 1956. *Art and Illusion*. New Jersey: Princeton Univ. Press.

Grand, H., 1973. Treatment of the chronic schizophrenic. Paper presented at group therapy staff conference, New Medical College, Metropolitan Hospital, Department of Psychiatry.

Greenson, R. R., 1967. *The Technique and Practice of Psychoanalysis*. New York: International Univ. Press.

Grobman, J., 1978. Achieving cohesiveness in therapy groups of chronically disturbed patients. *Journal of the Eastern Group Psychotherapy Society, 2*(3):141–148.

Groen, J. J. & Pelser, H. E., 1960. Experiences with, and results of, group psychotherapy in patients with bronchial asthma. *Journal Psychosomatic Research,* 4:191–205.

Gruen, W., 1977. The encouragement and reinforcement of coping strengths as a therapeutic goal and strategy in group therapy. In Wolberg & Aronson (Eds.), *Group Therapy: 1977.* New York: Stratton Intercontinental.

Hackett, T. P. & Cassem, N. H., 1974. Psychology of the C.C.U., Monograph. Department of Psychiatry, Massachusetts General Hospital. Supported by contract PHS 43-67-1443 and HE 13781 of the National Institute of Health, Public Health Service, US Department of Health, Education and Welfare.

Hackett, T. P. & Cassem, N. H., 1970. Psychological reactions to life-threatening illness: Acute myocardial infarction. In Abram (Ed.), *Psychological Aspects of Stress.* Springfield, Ill.: Thomas.

Hackett, T. P., Cassem, N. H., & Raker, J. W., 1973. Patient delay in cancer. *New England Journal of Medicine, 289:*14–20.

Hackett, T. P., & Weisman, A. D., 1977. Reactions to the imminence of death. In Monat & Lazarus (Eds.), *Stress and Coping.* New York: Columbia Univ. Press.

Hallowitz, E., 1972. Innovations in hospital social work. *Social Work, 17*(4):89–97.

Halper, I., 1971. Psychiatric observations in a chronic hemodialysis program. *Medical Clinics of North America, 55*(1):177–191.

Hamburg, D. A. & Adams, J. E., 1967. A perspective on coping behavior: Seeking and utilizing information in major transitions. *Archives of General Psychiatry, 17:*277–284.

Hamburg, D., Hamburg, B., & DeGoza, S., 1953. Adaptive problems and mechanisms in severely burned patients. *Psychiatry, 16:1*–20.

Hare, P. A., *Handbook of Small Group Research* (2nd ed.). 1976. New York: Free Press.

Harm, C. & Golden, J., 1961. Group worker's role in guiding social process in a medical institution. *Social Work, 6*(2):50–57.

Harper, B., 1977. *Death—The Coping Mechanism of the Health Professional.* Greenville, S.C.: Southeastern Univ. Press.

Hartmann, H., 1958. *Ego Psychology and the Problem of Adaptation.* New York: International Univ. Press.

Heath, E. S. & Bacal, H. A., 1972. A method of group psychotherapy at the Tavistock Clinic. In P. Sager & M. Kaplan (Eds.), *Progress in Group and Family Therapy.* New York: Brunner/Mazel.

Hirsch, S. & Lurie, A., 1969. Social work dimensions in shaping medical care philosophy and practice. *Social Work, 14*(2):75–79.

Hofmann, P. B., 1979. Can hospitals afford to care less. *Hospitals,* *53*(22):80–83.

Horn, B. 1976. Process presentation, Department of Social Work. New York: St. Vincent's Hospital and Medical Center.

Horn, B. & Haselman, L., 1976. Memo, Department of Social Work. New York: St. Vincent's Hospital and Medical Center.

Houlihan, J. P., 1977. Contribution of an intake group to psychiatric inpatient milieu therapy. *International Journal of Group Psychotherapy,* *27*(2):215–224.

Howard, J., 1978. Humanization and dehumanization of health care. In Reich (Ed.), *Encyclopedia of Bioethics II*. New York: Free Press.

Howard, J. Humanization and dehumanization of health care. In Howard & Strauss (Eds.), *Humanizing Health Care*. New York: Wiley.

Howard, J. & Derzon, R. A., 1979. Prospects for humane care are hopeful. *Hospitals, 53*(22):76–79.

Howell, G., 1953. The art of collaboration. *Proceedings of an Institute on Teamwork in the Medical Setting*. Eastern Canada District of American Association of Medical Social Workers, 52–61. P. 56-57.

Ibrahim, M. A., Feldman, J. G., Sultz, H. A., et al., 1974. Management after myocardial infarction: A controlled trial of the effect of group psychotherapy. *International Journal of Psychiatry in Medicine, 5*:253–268.

Jones, K. R. & Vischi, T. R. Impact of alcohol, drug abuse and mental health treatment on medical care utilization. *Medical Care, 27*(12): -21–82. (Supplement)

Kahn, M., 1958. Some observations on the role of religion in illness. *Social Work, 3*(3):83–89.

Kane, R., 1975. The interdisciplinary team as a small group. *Social Work in Health Care, 1*:19–32.

Katz, J. L., Weiner, H., Gallagher, T. F., & Hellman, L., 1977. Stress, distress and ego defenses: Psychoendocrine response to impending breast tumor biopsy. In Monat & Lazarus (Eds.), *Stress and Coping*. New York: Columbia Univ. Press.

Kellerman, H., 1979. *Group Psychotherapy and Personality*. New York: Grune & Stratton.

Kennedy, J. A. & Bakst, H., 1966. The influence of emotions on the outcome of cardiac surgery: A predictive study. *Bulletin of the New York Academy of Medicine, 42*:811–845.

Kernberg, O. F., 1970. Factors in the psychoanalytic treatment of narcissistic personalities. *Journal of the American Psychoanalytic Association, 18*:51–85.

Kernberg, O., 1975. *Borderline Conditions and Pathological Narcissism*. New York: Jason Aronson.

Kernberg, O., 1976. *Object Relations Theory and Clinical Psychoanalysis*. New York: Jason Aronson.

Kernberg, O., 1978. Leadership and organizational functioning: Organizational regression. *International Journal of Group Psychotherapy*, 28(1):3–26.

Khantzian, E. J. & Kates, W. W., 1978. Group treatment of unwilling addicted patients: Programatic and clinical aspects. *International Journal of Group Psychotherapy*, 28(1):81–94.

Kibel, H. D., 1978. The rationale for the use of group psychotherapy for borderline patients on a short-term unit. *International Journal of Group Psychotherapy*, 28(3):339–357.

Kiely, W. F., 1972. Coping with severe illness. *Advances in Psychosomatic Medicine*, 8:105–118.

Kimball, C. P., 1977. Psychosomatic theories and their contribution to chronic illness. In G. Usdin (Ed.), *Psychiatric Medicine*. New York: Brunner/Mazel.

Kindig, D. A., 1975. Interdisciplinary education for primary health care team delivery. *Journal of Medical Education*, 50:97–110.

Klein, R. H., 1977. Inpatient group psychotherapy: Practical considerations and special problems. *International Journal of Group Psychotherapy*, 27(2):201–214.

Kohut, H., 1971. *The Analysis of the Self*. New York: International Univ. Press.

Kolb, D. A., Rubin, I. M., & McIntyre, J. M., 1974. *Organizational Psychology*, 2nd edition. New Jersey, Englewood Cliffs: Prentice-Hall, Inc., pp. 23–30.

Kübler-Ross, E., 1969. *On Death and Dying*. New York: Macmillan.

Lamberts, H., 1975. Working together in a team for primary health care. *Journal R. Coll. Gen. Pract.*, 25:745–752.

Laudon, J., 1977. Face sheet, Department of Social Work. New York: St. Vincent's Hospital and Medical Center.

Liberman, R., 1970. A behavioral approach to group dynamics. *Behavior Therapy*, 1:141–175.

Lipton, H. & Malter, S., 1971. The social worker as mediator on a hospital ward. In Schwartz & Zalba (Eds.), *The Practice of Group Work*. New York: Columbia Univ. Press.

Lonergan, E. Cooper, 1980. Group intervention for medical patients—A treatment for damaged self-esteem. *Group* 4(2):36–45.

Lonergan, E. Cooper, 1980. Humanizing the hospital experience: Report of a group program for medical patients. *Health and Social Work,* 5(4):53–63.

Lubell, D., 1976. Group work with patients on peritoneal dialysis. *Health and Social Work, 1*(3):159–176.

Magee, B., 1973. *Karl Popper.* Glasgow: Great Britain—Fontana/Collins.

Mahler, M., Pine, F., & Bergman, A., 1975. *The Psychological Birth of the Human Infant.* New York: Basic.

Manley, M., 1976. Follow-up memo, Department of Social Work. New York: St. Vincent's Hospital and Medical Center.

Manley, M., 1976. Leader's group evaluation, Department of Social Work. New York: St. Vincent's Hospital and Medical Center.

Manley, M., 1976. Original memo, Department of Social Work. New York. St. Vincent's Hospital and Medical Center.

Marks, R. M. & Sachar, E. J., 1973. Undertreatment of medical inpatients with narcotic analgesics. *Annals of Internal Medicine, 78*:173–181.

Meehan, N., 1980. Process recording, Department of Social Work. New York: St. Vincent's Hospital and Medical Center. (Adaptation)

Menninger, K., 1954. Regulatory devices of the ego under major stress. *International Journal of Psychoanalysis, 35*(4):412–420.

Moffet, A. D., Bruce, J., & Horvitz, D., 1974. New ways of treating addicts. *Social Work, 19*:389–395.

Monat, A. & Lazarus, R. S., 1977. Some current issues and controversies. In Monat & Lazarus (Eds.), *Stress and Coping.* New York: Columbia Univ. Press.

Monaster, A., 1972. Therapy with the senile patient. *International Journal of Group Psychotherapy, 22*(2):250–257.

Moos, R. (Ed.), 1977. *Coping with Physical Illness.* New York: Plenum.

Morehead, M. A., 1976. Ambulatory care review: A neglected priority. *Bulletin of the New York Academy of Medicine, 52*:60–68.

Morrissey, P., 1978. Memo, Department of Social Work. New York: St. Vincent's Hospital and Medical Center.

Muir, J., 1911. *My First Summer in the Sierra.* Boston: Houghton Mifflin.

Nason, F. & Delbanco, T., 1976. Soft services. *Social Work and Health Care, 1*:297–308.

Nugent, K., 1977. Memo, Department of Social Work. New York: St. Vincent's Hospital and Medical Center.

O'Brien, C. P., 1975. Group therapy for schizophrenia: A practical approach. *Schizophrenia Bulletin, 13*:119–130.

Oradei, D. M. & Waite, N. S., 1974. Group psychotherapy with stroke patients during the immediate recovery phase. *American Journal of Orthopsychiatry*, *44*(3):386–395.

Oremland, J. & Windholz, E., 1971. Some specific transference, counter-transference and supervisory problems in the analysis of a narcissistic personality. *International Journal of Psychoanalysis*, *52*:267–275.

Panepinto, W. & Kohut, S., 1971. Alcoholism: Treatment through under-standing. *Hospitals*, *45*:56–58.

Parloff, M. B. & Dies, R. R., 1977. Group psychotherapy outcome re-search. *International Journal of Group Psychotherapy*, *27*(3):281–320.

Patrick, P. K. S., 1979. Burnout: Job hazard for health workers. *Hospitals*, *53*(22):87–90.

Payn, S. B. Reaching chronic schizophrenics with group pharmacother-apy. *International Journal of Group Psychotherapy*, *24*(1):25–31.

Petersen, M. L., 1975. Educational programs for team delivery. *Journal of Medical Education*, *50*:111–117.

Popper, K. R., 1957. *The Poverty of Historicism*. Boston: Beacon.

Popper, K. R., 1959. *Logic of Scientific Discovery*. New York: Harper & Row.

Popper, K. R., 1962. *Conjectures and Refutations*. New York: Basic. p. 67.

Popper, K. R., 1972. *Objective Knowledge*. London: Oxford Univ. Press.

Poynter-Berg, D., 1979. Field report summary of social work with groups in maternal and child health. *Social Work with Groups in Maternal and Child Health*. New York: Columbia University and Roosevelt Hospital.

Poynter-Berg, D. & Weiner, H., 1979. Workshop summaries. *Social Work with Groups in Maternal and Child Health*. New York: Columbia Univer-sity and Roosevelt Hospital.

Pratt, J. H., 1963. The tuberculosis class: An experiment in home treat-ment. In Rosenbaum & Berger (Eds.), *Group Psychotherapy and Group Function*. New York: Basic.

Quinn, J. & Powe, E., 1976. Memo, Department of Social Work. New York: St. Vincent's Hospital and Medical Center.

Rabiner, Wells, & Yager, 1973. A model for brief hospital treatment of the disadvantaged psychiatrically ill. *Journal of Orthopsychiatry*, *43*:774–782.

Reding, G. R. & Maguire, B., 1973. Non-segregated acute psychiatric admissions to general hospitals—continuity of care within the commu-nity hospital. *New England Journal of Medicine*, *289*(4):185–189.

Resnick, R. B., Schuyten, E., Cooper, E., & Schwartz, L., 1974. Narcotic antagonists: A point of view concerning treatment approaches. Paper presented at National Institute on Drug Abuse, Narcotic Antagonist Clinical Research Review Conference.

Resnick, R. B., Cooper, E., Schuyten, E., & Freedman, A., 1975. Opiate abuse: Differential diagnosis and treatments. Abstract submitted to APA Annual Meeting.

Rogers, C., 1951. *Client Centered Therapy.* Boston: Houghton Mifflin.

Sands, H. & Radin, J., 1978. *The Mentally Disabled Rehabilitant: Post Employment Services.* New York: Postgraduate Center for Mental Health.

Scheidlinger, S., 1980. Freud's group psychology. In S. Scheidlinger (Ed.), *Psychoanalytic Group Dynamics.* New York: International Univ. Press.

Schniewind, H. E., Jr. & Needle, A. P., 1978. Group psychotherapy: A component of primary health care. American Psychiatric Assoc. Annual Conference. BIAC, Beth Israel Hospital, Boston, Mass.

Schutz, W., 1966. *The Interpersonal Underworld*(FIRO). Palo Alto, Calif.: Science and Behavior.

Schoenberg, B. & Senescu, R., 1966. Group psychotherapy for patients with chronic multiple somatic complaints. *Journal of Chronic Disease, 19*:649–657.

Schwartz, W.B., 1981. The regulation strategy for controlling hospital costs. *New England Journal of Medicine*, 305(21):1249–1255.

Sclare, A. B. & Crocket, J. A., 1957. Group psychotherapy in bronchial asthma. *Journal of Psychosomatic Research, 2*:157–17.

Seligman, R., 1972. Emotional responses of burned children in a pediatric intensive-care unit. *Psychiatry in Medicine, 3*:59–65.

Sherman, E., 1979. Social work with groups in a hospital setting. *Social Work with Groups in Maternal and Child Health.* New York: Columbia Univ. and Roosevelt Hospital.

Shepard, M., 1980. The relation of psychiatric illness to the use of health services. In Robins, Clayton, & Wing (Eds.), *The Social Consequences of Psychiatric Illness.* New York: Brunner/Mazel.

Short, M. J. & Wilson, W. P., 1969. Roles of denial in chronic hemodialysis. *Archives of General Psychiatry, 20*:433–437.

Shulman, L., 1979. *The Skills in Helping Individuals and Groups.* Ataska, Ill.: F. E. Peacock.

Sorenson, E. T., 1972. Group therapy in a community hospital dialysis unit. *JAMA, 221*:899–901.

Stein, A., 1971. Group therapy with psychosomatically ill patients. In Kaplan & Sadock (Eds.), *Comprehensive Group Psychotherapy.* Baltimore: Williams & Wilkins.

Stein, A. & Weiner, S., 1978. Group therapy with medically ill patients.

Psychotherapeutic Approaches in Medicine. New York: Grune & Stratton.

Stern, M. J., Pascale, L., & McLoone, A., 1976. Psychosocial adaptation following acute myocardial infarction. *Journal of Chronic Disease, 29*:513–526.

Stolorow, R. D., 1975. Toward a functional definition of narcissism. *The International Journal of Psycho-Analysis, 56*(2):179–185.

Stolorow, R. D. & Lachmann, F. M., 1980. *Psychoanalysis of Developmental Arrests.* New York: International Univ. Press.

Strain, J. J. & Grossman, S., 1975. *Psychological Care of the Medically Ill.* New York: Appleton Century Crofts.

Tanaka, H., 1962. Group living on a psychiatric ward. *Social Work, 7*:51–58.

Tannenbaum, D. T., 1978. Group counseling for families with genetic disorders. *C.F. Social Work Highlights, 1*(4):7–11.

Tavris, C., 1976. The end of the IQ slump. *Psychology Today,* April pp. 69–74.

Tiger, L., 1979. *Biology of Hope.* New York: Simon & Schuster.

Titchener, J. L., Sheldon, M. B., & Ross, W. D., 1959. Changes in blood pressure of hypertensive patients with and without group psychotherapy. *Journal of Psychosomatic Research, 4*:10–12.

Trachtenberg, J., 1973. Team involvement and the problems incurred. New York: Memorial Hospital for Cancer and Allied Disease. RM0058 and Rehabilitation Grant RD-2311-M.

Truax, C. B. & Wargo, D. G., 1966. Psychotherapeutic encounters that change behavior: For better or for worse. *American Journal of Psychotherapy, 20*:499–520.

Usdin, G., (Ed.), 1977. *Psychiatric Medicine.* New York: Brunner/Mazel.

Valliant, G., 1977. *Adaptation to Life.* Boston: Little, Brown.

Valliant, G., 1979. Natural history of male psychologic health. *New England Journal of Medicine, 301*(23):1249–1254.

Visotsky, J. M., Hamburg, D. A., Goss, M. E., & Lebovitz, G. Z., 1961. Coping behavior under extreme stress. *Archives of General Psychiatry, 5*:423–448.

Viviano, M., 1969. Methodology of group psychotherapy in schizophrenia. *Group Analysis, 1*:133–135.

Weiner, H. J., 1958. Group work and the interdisciplinary team. *Social Work, 3*(3):76–82.

Weiner, H. J., 1959. The hospital, the ward, and the patient as clients: Use of the group method. *Social Work, 4*(4):57–65.

Weisman, A. D., 1972. *On Dying and Denying*. New York: Behavioral Publications.

Weisman, A. D. & Worden, J. W., 1977. *Coping and Vulnerability in Cancer Patients*. Boston: Massachusetts General Hospital.

Weisman, A. D. & Worden, J. W. The existential plight in cancer: Significance of the first 100 days. *International Journal of Psychiatry in Medicine, 7*(1):1–15.

Weisman, C. B., 1963. Social structure as a determinant of the group worker's role. *Social Work, 8*(3):87–94.

Wesley, L. E., 1978. Process recording, Department of Social Work. New York: St. Vincent's Hospital and Medical Center.

Williams, M., 1966. Limitations, fantasies, and security operations of beginning group therapists. *International Journal of Group Psychotherapy, 16*(2):150–162.

Winder, A. & Medalie, M., 1973. Support for growth in cystic fibrosis teenagers. In Patterson, Denning, & Kutscher (Eds.), *Psychosocial Aspects of Cystic Fibrosis*. New York: Columbia Univ. Press.

Wolberg, A., 1977. Group therapy and the dynamics of projective identification. In Wolberg & Aronson (Eds.), *Group Therapy: 1977*. New York: Stratton Intercontinental.

Wollersheim, J. P., 1970. Effectiveness of group therapy based upon learning principles in the treatment of overweight women. *Journal of Abnormal Psychology, 76*:462–474.

Wise, H., 1972. The primary care health team. *Archives of Internal Medicine, 130*:438–444.

Wise, H., Beckhard, R., & Kyte, I. A., 1974. *Making Health Teams Work*. Massachusetts: Ballinger.

Yalom, I. D., 1970. *Theory and Practice of Group Psychotherapy*. New York: Basic.

Yalom, I., 1980. *Existential Psychotherapy*. New York: Basic.

Yalom, I. D. & Greaves, C., 1977. Group therapy with the terminally ill. *American Journal of Psychiatry, 34*:396–400.

Youcha, I., 1976. Short-term in-patient group: Formation and beginnings. In Rabin & Rosenbaum (Eds.), *How to Begin a Psychotherapy Group*. New York: Gordon & Breach.

Youcha, I., 1976. Workshop presentation, Eastern Group Psychotherapy Society Annual Conference.

Youcha, I., et al., unpublished research. New York: Albert Einstein (personal communication).

Index